Advanced Floral Design

Advanced Floral Design

BY
REDBOOK FLORIST SERVICES
EDUCATIONAL ADVISORY COMMITTEE

Paragould, Arkansas

Advanced Floral Design

© 1992 by
Redbook Florist Services
Paragould, Arkansas

All Rights Reserved.

No portion of this book may be
reproduced without the written
consent of the publisher.

The brand names listed in this manual were selected by the Redbook Florist Services Educational Advisory Committee as examples which are suitable for the uses described. However, it is recognized that there are other brands of similar products available which may be equal to or better than the brand names included in the text, depending upon the designer's specific manner of use and personal preference.

Library of Congress Catalog Card Number: 92-80132

Printed by:
Printers and Publishers, Inc.
Leachville, Arkansas

Acknowledgments

Redbook Florist Services gives special thanks to each committee member who participated in the creation and development of this comprehensive floral training manual.

Frances Porterfield, RMC	Topeka, KS
Terry Lanker, M.Ed., RMC	Wooster, OH
Christy Holstead-Klink, M.S.	Nazareth, PA
Nancy Kitchen, AIFD, RMC	Rahway, NJ
Holly Money-Collins, AIFD, RMC	San Francisco, CA
Dianne Noland, M.S., RMC	Urbana, IL
Frankie Shelton, AAF, AIFD, PFCI, RMC	Houston, TX
Fay Weinstein, AIFD, RMC	Hillsdale, NJ
Gary Wells, AIFD, RMC	Kentwood, MI

Contents

Acknowledgments	v
Preface	xi
List of Illustrations	xv
List of Tables	xxvii
Introduction	1
Chapter 1 – History of Floral Design	5
Early Eras	6
Italian Renaissance	9
Japanese Influence	12
European Baroque and Dutch Flemish Styles	14
The French Period	18
English Influence	21
American Floral Design History	28
Chapter 2 – Terminology and Techniques for Advanced Design	37
Chapter 3 – Expanding the Principles and Elements of Design	63
Principles of Design	63
Elements of Design	71
Chapter 4 – Purchasing and Handling Fresh Flowers and Foliages	77
Purchasing	77
Care and Handling	93

Advanced Floral Design

Chapter 5 - Mechanics and Specialty Techniques — 137

- Floral Foams — 137
- Kenzan — 144
- Kubari — 145
- Glass Container Mechanics — 146
- Candles — 147
- Wall Hangings — 148
- Suspended Designs — 148
- Topiary Trees — 149
- Special Finishes/Container Coverings — 151

Chapter 6 - Advanced Design Styles — 157

- Mass Designs — 158
- Linear Designs — 166
- Line Mass Designs — 174
- Natural Design Styles — 179
- Miscellaneous Designs — 184

Chapter 7 - Sympathy Design — 195

- Casket Designs — 195
- Wreath Designs — 204
- Easel Designs — 208
- Arrangements — 213
- Creating a Setting — 214

Chapter 8 - Wedding Design — 219

- Bouquets — 220
- Flowers to Wear — 230
- Ceremony — 243
- Reception — 254

Chapter 9 - Uniqueness in Design — 265

- Developing Creativity — 265
- Recognizing Trends — 269
- Innovation — 270
- Styles Influences — 271
- Experimentation — 272
- Alternate Media — 273

Contents

Glossary 281

Bibliography 285

Index 289

Preface

Advanced Floral Design has been prepared for the person who seeks knowledge and professionalism as a floral designer.

A wide variety of unusual flowers and foliage are available year round from growers throughout the world. New products are continually being developed to assist florists in creating unique designs in less time. Likewise, the general public is becoming more informed about flower types, design styles, and flower availability. In order to remain competitive in the marketplace, many floral shops are expanding their "design menus" to include contemporary styles. For this reason, it is imperative that professional floral designers be skilled in all areas of design, from basic, traditional styles to modern, contemporary floral art.

Advanced Floral Design is intended to provide retail florists with a comprehensive pool of information regarding advanced floral design. A condensed summary of the history of floral design is provided to demonstrate the evolution of modern design styles. The essential tasks of conditioning specialty flowers and preparing mechanics for unique situations are discussed in detail. The fundamental principles and elements of floral design are expanded upon to demonstrate their application to advanced design styles. Important techniques and terminology are carefully explained and defined. Step-by-step instructions are given for the construction of advanced design styles, including wedding and funeral decorations. Additional suggestions are provided to assist individual floral designers in developing uniqueness in daily design work.

Many of the methods and ideas suggested in this book were drawn from the combined experiences of a select group of successful retail florists and floral industry professionals. The text is clear and concise and full of practical solutions to everyday problems. Illustrations provide reinforcement of the design techniques described. This book will enable the advanced florist

Preface

to master contemporary design styles. With practice, the floral designer will be able to create these designs with precision, speed, confidence, and creativity.

Advanced Floral Design was written for use as a reference and training manual for retail florists. It was written based on the assumption that the reader has mastered the principles, elements, mechanics, and design techniques required for basic floral arrangements. (The *Basic Floral Design* book from the Redbook series provides complete information on these subjects.) Despite the advanced level of much of the content, the information in this book is adaptable to floral shops of any size and to florists at all levels beyond basic design. For this reason, it is also highly useful to advanced floral design students.

List of Illustrations

Figure		Page
1.1	Ordered Symmetry of Egyptian Design	6
1.2	Greco-Roman Wreath	8
1.3	Italian Renaissance Flower Arrangements	10
1.4	Rikka Arrangement	12
1.5	Nageire Style of Ikebana	12
1.6	Shoka Arrangement	12
1.7	Traditional Three Main Placements for an Upright Moribana Arrangement	13
1.8	Baroque and Dutch Flemish Style Arrangement	16
1.9	French Rococo Style Design	19
1.10	Rococo Ornamentation of Vases	
	1.10a	20
	1.10b	20
1.11	Eighteenth Century English Arrangement	22
1.12	Typical English Tradition Containers	
	1.12a Wall Pocket	23
	1.12b Silver Stem Cup with Handles	23
1.13	Victorian Design	27
1.14	Victorian Design in an Epergne	28
1.15	Early Colonial Design	28
1.16	Typical Colonial Design	28
1.17	Five-finger Vase	31
1.18	Delft Brick	31
2.1	Abstract Design	
	2.1a	38
	2.1b	38
	2.1c	38
	2.1d	38

List of Illustrations

2.2	Basing	
	2.2a	40
	2.2b	40
2.3	Binding Points	
	2.3a Parallel	40
	2.3b Radiating	40
	2.3c Radiating	41
2.4	Clustering	
	2.4a	41
	2.4b	41
2.5	Detailing	42
2.6	Fibonnaci Principle of Proportion	43
2.7	Framing	45
2.8	Free-form	
	2.8a	45
	2.8b	45
2.9	Grouping	
	2.9a	46
	2.9b	46
2.10	Hana-mai	46
2.11	Ikebana	
	2.11a	47
	2.11b	47
2.12	Layering	48
2.13	Linear Arrangement	49
2.14	Lines of Confusion	50
2.15	Lines of Parallelism	50
2.16	Negative Space	52
2.17	New Convention Arrangement	52
2.18	New Wave	52
2.19	Parallel Systems Arrangement	53
2.20	Pavé	53
2.21	Pillowing	54
2.22	Sculpturing	
	2.22a	55
	2.22b	55
2.23	Sectioning	55
2.24	Sheltering	
	2.24a	56
	2.24b	56
2.25	Stacking	56
2.26	Tension	57
2.27	Terracing	57
2.28	Waterfall Style	58
2.29	Zoning	59

List of Illustrations

3.1	Advanced Design with both Radiating and Parallel Stems	64
3.2	Repetition within a Biedermeier Arrangement	65
3.3	Repetition of Foliage	65
3.4	Repetition of Foliage on Container (Leafwork) to Create Texture and Form	65
3.5	Symmetrical Balance	
	3.5a	66
	3.5b	66
3.6	The Golden Mean	69
3.7	The Golden Mean Applied to a Bridal Bouquet	69
4.1	Tight Bud Stage	
	4.1a Carnation	100
	4.1b Rose	100
4.2	Tenting Buds	101
4.3	Alstroemeria	107
4.4	Bouvardia	108
4.5	Calla	109
4.6	Calla Opening Technique	
	4.6a	110
	4.6b	110
	4.6c	110
	4.6d	110
4.7	Field-grown or Garden-type Flowers	
	4.7a Marigold	111
	4.7b Dahlia	111
	4.7c Zinnia	111
4.8	Gardenia	111
4.9	Gerbera	112
4.10	Iris	112
4.11	Lily	113
4.12	Cattleya Orchid	114
4.13	Spray Orchid (Dendrobium)	114
4.14	Rose	115
4.15	Stephanotis	117
4.16	Tropicals	
	4.16a Ginger	118
	4.16b Heliconia	118
	4.16c Bird of Paradise	118
4.17	Tulip	120
4.18	Tree Fern	122
4.19	Sprengeri	122
4.20	Plumosa	122
4.21	Ming Fern	122

List of Illustrations

4.22	Boston Fern	123
4.23	Ivy	123
4.24	Galax	123
4.25	European Extender	
	4.25a	125
	4.25b	125
4.26	Bamboo Extender	125
4.27	Water Well for Spring Flowers	
	4.27a	127
	4.27b	127
	4.27c	127
4.28	Re-shaping Allium	127
4.29	Bird of Paradise Opening	
	4.29a	128
	4.29b	128
4.30	Sealing Dahlia Petals	128
4.31	Splinting a Gerbera	129
4.32	Hyacinth Stake	129
4.33	Iris Opening	
	4.33a	129
	4.33b	129
5.1	Pre-caged Floral Foam	
	5.1a Corso™ Holder	138
	5.1b Corso™ Holder in a Topiary Arrangement	138
	5.1c IGLU® Holder	138
	5.1d IGLU® Holder in a Topiary Arrangement	138
	5.1e IGLU® Grande Holder	139
5.2	Individual Wreath Ring	139
5.3	Inserting Foam in a Container	140
5.4	Contouring	140
5.5	Lasso Taping Method	
	5.5a	141
	5.5b	142
	5.5c	142
	5.5d	142
5.6	Making Mass Extensions	
	5.6a Step 1	142
	5.6b Step 2	142
	5.6c Step 3	143
5.7	Making a Columnar Design Frame	
	5.7a Step 2	143
	5.7b Step 3	143
	5.7c Step 5	144

List of Illustrations

xix

5.8	Cutting Material for Kenzan Insertion		
	5.8a		144
	5.8b		144
	5.8c		144
	5.8d		144
	5.8e		144
	5.8f		144
	5.8g		144
	5.8h		144
	5.8i		144
5.9	Inserting Material into Kenzan		
	5.9a	Step 1	145
	5.9b	Step 2	145
	5.9c	Step 3	145
	5.9d	Step 3	145
	5.9e	Step 3	145
5.10	Kubari Partioning		
	5.10a		146
	5.10b		146
5.11	Kubari Wedging		
	5.11a		146
	5.11b		146
5.12	Designing Arrangements in Glass Containers		
	5.12a		146
	5.12b		147
	5.12c		147
5.13	Constructing a Permanent Wall Collage		148
5.14	Constructing Suspended Designs		
	5.14a		149
	5.14b		149
5.15	Constructing a Permenent Topiary Prop		
	5.15a		150
	5.15b		150
	5.15c		150
	5.15d		151
	5.15e		151
5.16	Photographic Finish		152
5.17	Leafwork Finish		152
6.1	Flemish Arrangement		
	6.1a	Step 2	160
	6.1b	Step 3	160
	6.1c	Step 4	160
	6.1d	Step 5	161
	6.1e	Step 7	161

List of Illustrations

6.2	Biedermeier Bouquet		
	6.2a	Step 1	162
	6.2b	Step 3	162
	6.2c	Step 5	162
	6.2d	Step 7	162
6.3	English Country Design Style		166
6.4	French Country Design Style		166
6.5	American Country Design Style		166
6.6	Proper Angles for Shin, Soe, and Hikae		168
6.7	180° Radius for Tip Placement		168
6.8	Upright Moribana Arrangement		
	6.8a	Step 1	168
	6.8b	Step 2	169
	6.8c	Step 3	169
	6.8d	Step 4	169
	6.8e	Step 5	170
6.9	Slanting Nageire Arrangement		
	6.9a	Step 1	170
	6.9b	Step 2	170
	6.9c	Step 3	171
	6.9d	Step 4	171
6.10	Parallel Design		171
6.11	New Convention Arrangement		
	6.11a	Step 2	172
	6.11b	Step 3	172
	6.11c	Step 4	173
	6.11d	Step 6	173
	6.11e	Step 7	173
	6.11f	Step 7	173
	6.11g	Step 9	174
6.12	Hogarth Curve		
	6.12a	Step 2	175
	6.12b	Step 3	175
	6.12c	Step 4	175
6.13	Crescent Arrangement		
	6.13a	Step 4	177
	6.13b	Steps 5 & 6	178
	6.13c	Step 7	178
	6.13d	Step 8	178
6.14	Phoenix Arrangement		
	6.14a	Step 1	179
	6.14b	Step 2	179
	6.14c	Step 3	179

List of Illustrations

xxi

6.15	Vegetative Arrangement		
	6.15a	Step 1	181
	6.15b	Step 2	181
	6.15c	Step 3	182
	6.15d	Step 4	182
	6.15e	Step 5	182
6.16	Waterfall Design		
	6.16a	Step 3	183
	6.16b	Step 4	184
	6.16c	Step 5	184
6.17	Free-form Arrangement		184
6.18	Hand-tied Bouquet		
	6.18a	Step 2	186
	6.18b	Step 3	186
	6.18c	Step 4	186
	6.18d	Step 5	186
6.19	Leafwork Table		
	6.19a	Step 1	187
	6.19b	Step 1	187
	6.19c	Step 2	187
6.20	Topiary		
	6.20a	Step 1	189
	6.20b	Step 5	189
7.1	Casket Saddle Mechanics		
	7.1a		196
	7.1b		196
	7.1c		196
7.2	Designing a Vegetative Casket Cover		
	7.2a	Step 1	197
	7.2b	Steps 2 & 3	197
	7.2c	Step 5	197
7.3	Designing a New Convention Casket Cover		
	7.3a	Step 1	198
	7.3b	Step 5	198
7.4	Designing a Waterfall Casket		
	7.4a	Step 2	198
	7.4b	Step 4	198
	7.4c	Step 5	199
7.5	Designing a Landscape Casket Cover		
	7.5a	Step 1	199
	7.5b	Steps 4-6	199
7.6	Designing an Abstract Casket Cover		
	7.6a	Step 2	199
	7.6b	Step 5	200

List of Illustrations

7.7	Designing a Foliage Casket Blanket		
	7.7a	Step 2	200
	7.7b	Step 3	200
	7.7c	Step 4	200
	7.7d	Step 5	201
	7.7e	Step 8	201
	7.7f	Step 9	201
7.8	Designing a Casket Scarf		
	7.8a	Step 1	201
	7.8b	Step 5	201
	7.8c	Steps 6 & 8	202
7.9	Designing a Children's Casket Cover		
	7.9a	Step 1	202
	7.9b	Steps 2 & 4	202
	7.9c	Step 7	202
	7.9d	Step 10	203
	7.9e	Step 15	203
7.10	Designing a European Funeral Wreath		
	7.10a	Step 1	203
	7.10b	Step 2	203
	7.10c	Step 3	204
	7.10d	Step 4	204
7.11	Designing a Triple-ring Foliage Wreath		
	7.11a	Step 1	204
	7.11b	Step 1	204
	7.11c	Step 2	205
	7.11d	Step 7	205
7.12	Designing a Solid Wreath Ring		
	7.12a	Step 1	205
	7.12b	Step 2	205
	7.12c	Step 4	205
7.13	Designing a Composite Grapevine Wreath		
	7.13a	Step 1	206
	7.13b	Step 2	206
	7.13c	Step 2	206
	7.13d	Step 3	206
	7.13e	Step 6	207
7.14	Designing a Modified Styrofoam Wreath		
	7.14a	Step 1	207
	7.14b	Step 4	207
	7.14c	Step 8	207
7.15	Designing a Braided Ribbon Wreath		
	7.15a		208
	7.15b		208
	7.15c		208

List of Illustrations

7.16	Designing an Easel Spray	208
7.17	Designing a Composite Easel Spray	
7.17a	Step 2	209
7.17b	Step 3	209
7.17c	Step 6	209
7.18	Designing a Contemporary Funeral Pillow	
7.18a	Step 3	210
7.18b	Step 4	210
7.18c	Step 6	210
7.19	Designing a Horsetail Cross	
7.19a	Step 1	210
7.19b	Step 2	210
7.19c	Step 3	211
7.19d	Step 4	211
7.19e	Step 6	211
7.20	Designing a Moss-covered Easel	211
7.21	Designing a Branch-covered Easel	212
7.22	Designing a Fabric-covered Easel	212
7.23	Designing a Bent Easel	
7.23a	Step 1	212
7.23b	Steps 2 & 3	212
7.24	Designing a Bamboo or Wood Tripod	
7.24a	Step 2	213
7.24b	Step 4	213
7.25	Abstract Vase Arrangement	213
7.26	Landscape Vase Arrangement	213
7.27	Curvilinear Vase Arrangement	214
7.28	Designing with Papier-maché Containers	
7.28a		214
7.28b		214
7.28c		214
7.29	Designing with Baskets	214
7.30	Creating a Proper Funeral Environment	215
7.31	Graveside Decorations	215
8.1	Glamellia	
8.1a	Step 1	221
8.1b	Step 2	221
8.1c	Step 5	221
8.1d	Step 8	222
8.1e	Step 10	222
8.1f	Step 10	222
8.1g	Step 14	222

List of Illustrations

8.2	Glamellia Bouquet	223
8.3	Hand-tied Bouquet	227
8.4	European Contemporary Bouquet	228
8.5	Glamellia Corsage	230
8.6	Horsehair Hat with Flowers	239
8.7	Floral Skull Cap	
	8.7a Step 2	241
	8.7b Step 3	241
	8.7c Step 4	241
	8.7d Step 5	241
	8.7e Step 8	241
	8.7f Step 11	242
8.8	Decorated Church Altar	244
8.9	Decorated Pedestals	244
8.10	Tree-like Altar Arrangements	245
8.11	Basic Chuppah	246
8.12	PVC Chuppah	
	8.12a Step 1	248
	8.12b Step 3	248
	8.12c Step 4	248
	8.12d Step 16	249
8.13	Choir Stall	250
8.14	Hand-tied Garland	250
8.15	Topiary	
	8.15a Step 2	252
	8.15b Step 5	252
	8.15c Step 6	253
8.16	Aisle Decorations	253
8.17	Taffeta Pew Bows	
	8.17a Step 1	253
	8.17b Step 2	254
	8.17c Step 4	254
	8.17d Step 5	254
8.18	Entrance Decorations	256
8.19	Cake Decorations	
	8.19a	257
	8.19b	258
8.20	Head Table Decoration	258
8.21	Auto Decorations	
	8.22a	259
	8.22b	259

List of Tables

Table		Page
1.	Basic Flower Needs	95
2.	Causes of Early Flower Deterioration	96
3.	Flowers Commonly Used Individually	105
4.	Comparisons of Differences and Qualities of Bouquet Styles	166

Introduction

Advanced floral designs are arrangements which require special mechanics, techniques, or skills. Many advanced designs are contemporary. This means they are either new or popular during a specific period of time. Some historical design styles enjoy revivals occasionally; therefore, they become contemporary again.

Sometimes a design is considered advanced or contemporary because its appearance is nontraditional. Compared to traditional Western arrangements, an ikebana design has an unusual appearance. Instead of a mass of flowers, ikebana employs as few as a single flower enhanced by foliage or branches to create a design with symbolism. Although a design of this kind might look simple, specific rules and techniques are used to create it. The same is true for many other advanced design styles. While some designers might be able to copy a picture of an advanced style, creating an original requires greater understanding.

Floral designers are often drawn to contemporary design styles because they provide both a challenge and an opportunity to be creative, artistic, and expressive. Many nationally and internationally-known designers are famous for their particular signature styles of design. Some designers specialize in a specific contemporary style. Others strive to create new styles, which often begin trends that are seen frequently at competitions and design shows.

The image of a floral shop is greatly influenced by the types of arrangements offered within. Flower freshness and design precision also contribute to this image, along with quality service. The florist who chooses to incorporate contemporary design styles into his business must strive for excellence in each of these areas without sacrificing profit. When all of these elements are

Introduction

successfully combined, the incorporation of advanced design styles into a shop's daily business will not only elevate the motivation of designers, it will also increase consumer awareness and improve the shop's image.

History of Floral Design

Chapter 1

*F*loral design is rich in its heritage and historical traditions. Knowing and appreciating the history of floral design is essential for professional floral designers. A study of the past eras of floral design not only reveals the development and relationship of past styles to present styles, but also provides an understanding of the plant materials that were available and how they were chosen and combined in designs during those periods. Studying historical floral designs provides inspiration and a wealth of ideas for contemporary designers.

No one knows when humans first enjoyed and used flowers in a decorative way, but many historians agree that floral decoration is as old as civilization itself. From the dawn of recorded history, when humans began to till the soil, flowers have been used to beautify the surroundings, to express feelings, and to adorn important ceremonies. (Teleflora Spirit, 27) Neolithic cave drawings show that even during the Stone Age, flowers were contemplated, perhaps even revered. (Erickson, 32)

Ancient Egyptians used bowls of lotus blossoms at banquets and offered vases of flowers as tributes during ceremonies. Flowers were also significant during Greek and Roman times. They were woven into garlands and wreaths and then worn. The influence of flowers has been felt throughout history by many people and cultures.

Each historical period of floral design influenced and contributed to contemporary floral design. This chapter will highlight some of the major eras of floral design history, from early Egyptian, Greek, and Roman designs to the influence of China and Japan. The Italian Renaissance, European Baroque, and Dutch Flemish styles are presented, as well as the French, English, and Victorian eras. The floral design history of North America will conclude this chapter on the history of floral design.

Early Eras

The early eras of floral design record the significant use of flowers in religious ceremonies, festivals, and for personal enjoyment. The early use and enjoyment of flowers during the Egyptian, Greek, and Roman periods are quite similar and will be discussed in this section.

Egyptian Influence (2800 - 28 B.C.)

The Egyptians were the first people recorded who decorated by placing cut flowers in vases for festivals and ceremonies. Garlands and wreaths adorned banquet rooms and people alike. Characteristic of this period was simplicity and highly stylized repetition. The use of wreaths and garlands in contemporary culture resulted from the Egyptian era influence.

From well preserved tomb pictures and Egyptian art, history records that the ancient Egyptians loved flowers and often used them for personal adornment and gifts and during festivals, burial processions, and ceremonies. The lotus flower is found as early as 2500 B.C. in Egyptian art. (Mitchell, 7) Vases and bowls of fragrant flowers and baskets or bowls of fruits and vegetables were offered as tributes or temple offerings during ceremonies or used to decorate banquet tables.

Flowers, foliage, and fruits were often woven or tied together, sometimes sewn into place, on collars, wreaths, and garlands. Chaplets, which were garlands or wreaths worn on a person's head, were also popular. Garlands and wreaths were given as gifts, worn for personal adornment, and used as offerings in festivals and ceremonies.

The Egyptians valued repetition; flowers and/or fruits were carefully alternated in rows in repeating patterns. A typical Egyptian floral design would be grouped in the orderly sequence of waterlily/leaf/bud/leaf/waterlily/leaf/bud, etc., set around the rim of a wide-mouthed basin or bowl. Flowers in garlands and wreaths were arranged in orderly sequences of colors and shapes. *(See Figure 1.1.)*

The plant materials used by the Egyptians were the water-loving ones that flourished in the fertile Nile Valley. Examples include acacia, anemone, bachelor's button, bittersweet, celosia, chamomile, fig, gladiolus, grapes, iris, ivy, jasmine, lily, the sacred lotus, lupine, marsh grass, narcissus, oleander, palm, papyrus, pomegranate, poppy, rose, and water lily. (Marcus, 23)

Figure 1.1 Ordered Symmetry of Egyptian Design

History of Floral Design

Notes

The preferred colors were bright, strong, vivid colors of medium value, such as midnight blue, green, red, burgundy red, yellow, gold, rose, purple, and black, as opposed to tints or tones, such as blue turquoise. The only exception was the lotus which was a delicate pink and blue. Flowers and fruit were arranged in a sequence of alternating colors.

For containers, a simple wide-mouthed basin or bowl was the favorite choice, although artifacts include vases, jars, and bowls in alabaster, dark green diorite, faience, slate, bronze, silver, and pottery. Metal loops or frogs were often attached to the bottom of the basin to hold flowers in place. (Marcus, 24)

Contemporary florists who wish to accessorize Egyptian-style designs might select potted palms, slender columns, or small tomb artifact reproductions with backgrounds of gauze drapes, wallpaper, or prints with simple repetitive patterns of appropriate colors or with hieroglyphics on them. (Erickson, 37) A backdrop suggesting stone relief or a carved stone typical of Egyptian art would be appropriate.

Egyptian Floral Design at a Glance

Design Styles		Containers
Flowers placed in a bowl in repeating order		Bowls, basins
Flowers placed in spouted vases		Spouted vases
Garlands, wreaths, flower collars, chaplets		

Flowers	Foliage	Colors
Acacia	Ivy	Vivid colors of medium value
Anemone	Palm	
Bachelor's button	Papyrus	Blue
Bittersweet		Green
Celosia, cockscomb		Red burgundy, rose
Chamomile		Yellow, gold
Gladiolus		Purple
Iris		Black
Ivy		
Jasmine		
Lily	Fruits	Accessories/Backgrounds
Lotus, Waterlily		
Lupine	Figs	Potted palms
Marsh grass	Grapes	Slender columns
Narcissus	Pomegranates	Gauze drapes
Oleander		Small tomb artifacts
Poppy		Prints with small patterns
Rose		Prints with hieroglyphics

Greek and Roman Era (600 - 146 B.C., 28 - 325 A.D.)

Greatly influenced by the Egyptians, the Greeks and then the conquering Romans, who adopted Greek culture as their own, used flowers in similar ways. All three cultures, Egyptian, Greek, and Roman, used flowers primarily for honoring the gods and heroes in religious and civic festivals, as well as for personal enjoyment. (Erickson, 37) Garlands and wreaths, including chaplets were the main floral designs of the period. **(See Figure 1.2.)** Loose petals and flowers were also strewn about at banquets and festivals. Unlike the Egyptians, Greeks and Romans did not place loose flowers in vases.

Flowers were valued for their fragrance and symbolism first, and color was second in importance. Vibrant colors, such as violet, rose, pale blue, sky blue, terra cotta, red, deep maroon, ivory, and white, were preferred. Muted and gray tones were not favored during the Greco-Roman period. Appropriate flowers and plant materials for this period include acanthus, anemone, apple blossoms, crocus, cypress, daisies, grains, grapes, honeysuckle, hyacinth, iris, laurel or sweet bay, lilies, myrtle, narcissus, poppies, quince, roses, violets, fragrant herbs, cones and acorns, ivy, olive branches, oak leaves, and pomegranate. (Marcus, 32)

Since flowers and foliage were most often fashioned into wreaths and garlands, vase arrangements were not common. The classic urns of the Greco-Roman period were used for religious or domestic purposes, not for flowers. Loose flowers or flower garlands were often positioned in baskets, cornucopias, or on trays for delivery as offerings or gifts. Romans gathered and often carried ceremonial flowers in scarves held across the body with both hands. The use of strewn rose buds, flowers, and petals during feasts and banquets was lavish. Both Nero and Cleopatra enjoyed having roses strewn about for ceremonies and entertaining.

Contemporary florists might choose to accessorize Greco-Roman period designs with props, such as columns; stone garden benches; large, flat baskets for offerings; urns; and marble. An interpretation of this period would be to use an urn as a floral vase, although in the Greco-Roman times, urns were used for religious or domestic purposes only. Displaying the period design in a niche or recess framed by columns would appropriately suggest the architecture of the day. Lengths of creamy white cloth, such as wool, cotton, or linen, make a suitable background for Greco-Roman designs.

Figure 1.2 Greco-Roman Wreath

History of Floral Design

Notes

Greco-Roman Period at a Glance

Design Styles | Containers

Garlands | None commonly used
Wreaths
Loose flowers for strewing

Flowers	Foliages	Colors
Acanthus	Cypress	Second in importance to
Anemone	Laurel, sweet bay	1. Fragrance
Apple blossoms	Myrtle	2. Symbolism
Crocus	Ivy	
Daisy	Olive branches	Vibrant colors
Grains	Oak leaves	Violet
Honeysuckle		Rose
Hyacinth		Blue
Iris		Red
Lily		Terra cotta
Narcissus		Deep maroon
Poppy		Ivory, white
Quince		
Rose	Fruits	Accessories/Backgrounds
Violet		
Fragrant herbs	Grapes	Columns
	Cones, acorns	Stone garden benches
	Pomegranates	Large, flat baskets
		Marble
		Creamy white cloth

Italian Renaissance (1400 - 1600)

The Renaissance ushered in the reawakening of intellectual pursuits and the revival of the arts. Gardening and floral designing became a part of this rebirth. The Italian Renaissance is regarded as the beginning of floral design as practiced in contemporary society. Flowers were cut from flower gardens, taken into homes, and arranged for everyday occasions, not just for church and state occasions. During this period, flowers were appreciated for their beauty, as well as their symbolic value. Specific flowers were chosen to portray emotions and ideals, such as the rose for sacred love, the violet and daisy for humility, and the white lily for chastity. (Marcus, 81) During the Renaissance, the white <u>Lilium candidum</u> appeared in so many paintings of the Annunciation (the angel Gabriel's announcement to Mary that she was to give birth to Jesus) that this lily became known as the Madonna Lily. (Mitchell, 7)

The Renaissance era produced large, overflowing arrangements, characterized by a pyramidal shape, bilateral symmetry, and bright masses of colorful flowers. *(See Figure 1.3.)* Smaller, casual arrangements of short-stemmed flowers were arranged in tight clusters or as airy bouquets. Characteristic of the Renaissance period were colorful arrangements of fruits (including tropical), vegetables, and flowers casually placed on trays and in baskets. Garlands, chaplets, and loose petals for strewing, reminiscent of the Greco-Roman period, were widely favored for pageants and festivals. The garlands of Luca della Robbia have been studied and copied for Christmas decorations.

Floral design during the Renaissance period was a study in nature. Taller flowers were placed above lower-growing ones, and the flowers were arranged so that each flower could be fully viewed with no stems showing. The most important flower was placed at the top of the arrangement; garlands were positioned to cascade from the vase to the table top. Common arrangement outlines included a circle, an oval or cone, or an equilateral triangle. Arrangement height was approximately one to two times the container height.

The plant materials used for Italian Renaissance designs were generally the smaller-sized flowers familiar to contemporary florists, such as anemones, bellflowers, carnations, columbines, daisies, forget-me-nots, irises, jasmine, lilies, lily of the valley, lupines, marigolds, monkshood, narcissuses, pansies, periwinkle, poppies, primroses, roses, stock, and violets. There were no cultivars or hybrids available, such as tea roses or long-spurred columbine. Other materials favored were wheat; foliage (laurel and boxwood); olive branches; and fruit, including apples, figs, grapes, oranges, peaches, pomegranates, and strawberries. The plant collectors of the sixteenth century introduced the lilac, canna, peony, crown imperial, and tulip, although these plants were rarely seen in Renaissance paintings, which serve as a reference of the floral design style of that period. The Renaissance floral artists chose flowers in bright, mixed colors and often arranged them all together in one vase with no apparent color scheme.

Urns made of bronze, marble, pottery, or Venetian glass were often featured. Fifteenth century Venetian glass was commonly textured with gadrooning, a beading or fluting process, and with raised dots to simulate appliqués of precious stones. Later craftsmen fashioned blown glass into tall vases with handles, small jugs, beakers, and tall-stemmed goblets. Simple bowls, vases, and jars made of stone, glass, pottery, and metal were commonly used. Terra cotta pottery was used widely by all

Figure 1.3 Italian Renaissance Flower Arrangements

History of Floral Design

Notes

classes, while silver trays and vessels were often depicted as being used at feasts. (Erickson, 38)

In contemporary display, backgrounds appropriate for Renaissance designs are marble, wood paneling, matte finishes, or velvet or moiré silk drapes in the rich colors of dark green, red, rose, or violet. These designs can be displayed on a low, wooden bench; a stone garden seat; a richly colored damask cloth; or patterned velvet cloth with petals and fruit randomly placed near the vase.

Italian Renaissance at a Glance

Design Styles

Mass arrangements of bilateral symmetry
   (circle, oval, cone, triangle)
   (one to two times container height)
Smaller casual arrangements of
   short-stemmed flowers
Colorful fruit, vegetable, and flower
   arrangements
Garlands, chaplets
Loose petals for strewing
Luca della Robbia garlands

Containers

Urns of bronze, marble,
   pottery, Venetian
   glass
Gadrooned Venetian glass
Blown glass vases, jugs,
   beakers, goblets
Bowls, vases, jars of stone,
   glass, pottery, metal
Terra cotta pottery
Silver vessels and trays

Flowers

Garden flowers
   (No cultivars)
Anemone
Bellflower
Carnation
Columbine
Daisies
Forget-me-not
Grapes
Iris
Jasmine
Lily (Madonna lily)
Lily of the valley
Lupine
Marigold
Monkshood
Narcissus
Pansy
Periwinkle
Poppy
Primrose
Rose
Stock
Violet

Foliages

Laurel
Boxwood
Olive branches

Fruits

Apples
Figs
Grapes
Oranges
Peaches
Pomegranates
Strawberries

Colors

All colors
No apparent color scheme

Backgrounds

Wood paneling
Velvet or moiré silk drapes
   in green, red, rose,
   and violet
Marble
Matte finishes

Accessories

Low wooden bench
Stone garden seat
Richly colored damask
   cloth
Patterned velvet cloth
Petals and fruit

Japanese Influence (1470 to present day)

Although the traditional Japanese arrangements are rarely designed by commercial florists, the Japanese ikebana style offers several ideas for the naturalistic use of plant materials and the use of rhythm and space in floral design. The Japanese influence has greatly contributed to the development of contemporary line and line mass arrangements.

In the seventh century, the introduction of Buddhism to Japan from China and Korea greatly influenced Japanese floral design. Ikebana, or Japanese flower arranging, however, has been practiced as a studied art form since 1470. Ikebana began when Ono-no-Imoko, a Buddhist priest, visited China in 621 and was impressed with Chinese painting and landscape arts. (Wright, 25) He took the idea of presenting floral offerings or sacrificial flowers at Buddhist altars back to Japan.

During the fifteenth century, around 1470, a sensation was created when the first arrangement in the rikka style was designed. (Sato, 21) The early rikka arrangements, which were designed for display in the temple, were often very large and elaborate and symbolized the entire universe. **(See Figure 1.4.)** The rikka, or standing arrangement, was influenced strongly by Chinese art, especially tall Chinese landscape paintings.

In the sixteenth century, Sen-no-Rikyu, the greatest tea master of all, created a design for the tea ceremony that was austere and simple and the complete antithesis of the rikka style. (Sato, 24, 25) The design was known as chabana, or tea flowers, and belonged to the nageire style, which means thrown-in flowers. The simple nageire style emphasized the natural beauty of flowers arranged as in nature and was more suitable for the home. Nageire designs were often arranged in tall containers as upright, slanting, or hanging forms. **(See Figure 1.5.)**

An intermediate style between the formal rikka and the informal nageire styles appeared in the seventeenth century; it was known as shoka or seika. The seika, or shoka, style is recognized by the three distinct points of the triangle or crescent shape; it has remained relatively unchanged since its origination. **(See Figure 1.6.)**

By the late nineteenth century, a fourth major ikebana style emerged, due partly to the Western influence in Japan. This style was called moribana, which means piled-up flowers. The arrangements were designed in a kenzan, or needlepoint holder, in low, shallow bowls or containers. Moribana arrangements often resembled miniature scenes from nature and were designed as upright, slanting, or hanging forms.

Figure 1.4 Rikka Arrangement

Figure 1.5 Nageire Style of Ikebana

Figure 1.6 Shoka Arrangement

History of Floral Design

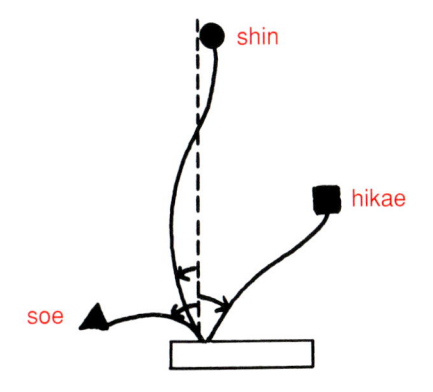

Figure 1.7 Traditional Three Main Placements for an Upright Moribana Arrangement

Basically, ikebana can be divided into three groups:

1. Classical or formal style, including rikka and shoka

2. Naturalistic or informal style, including nageire and moribana

3. Abstract or free style

The placement of three main parts, either flowers or branches, is characteristic of the ikebana styles of shoka, nageire, and moribana. **(See Figure 1.7.)** The three main placements have traditional and symbolic names: shin, representing heaven; soe, representing man; and hikae, or tai, representing earth. Shin, which means heaven or spiritual truth, is the tallest and most important placement. Its height is equal to or two or three times the width plus the depth of the container, depending upon the overall arrangement size. Soe is traditionally considered to symbolize man situated between heaven and earth and can also mean support, help, human creativity, and harmonizer. (Mitchell, 17) Soe is second in importance and is approximately two thirds to three quarters the length of shin. Hikae, or tai, meaning earth, body, or material substance, is the shortest material in the design and is approximately one third to one-half the length of shin.

A wide range of plant material is used in ikebana designs. Foliage, such as aspidistra, cedar, hemlock, holly, juniper, and pine, are used. Cherry, plum, peach, and quince branches in blossom and in leaf are favorites, along with willow, wisteria, bamboo, and hosta. The aster, azalea, camellia, chrysanthemum, clematis, day lily, hydrangea, iris, lily, magnolia, narcissus, orchid, peony, and rose are typical flower choices for Japanese floral design. More emphasis is placed on the form and flowers used than on the colors. Muted, subtle characteristic colors are green, blue, violet, and shell pink. Other preferences include delicate colors for spring; stronger, more varied hues for summer; the warm red, orange, and yellow scheme for fall; and green for winter. (Marcus, 118)

In contemporary display, Japanese containers are usually placed on bases, such as mats, panels, polished wood burls, or wood stands with legs, claw feet, or brackets. The background can be a plain or lightly-colored fabric, screen, or wall or wood panels that have been polished or stained. A background suggesting the tokonoma, the recessed area in Japanese homes where paintings, flowers, and art are placed, would be especially appropriate. The tokonoma is raised above floor level and can be framed by wood panels. Accessories from nature, such as shells, stones, and wood, can be used, along with Japanese wall hangings or artwork.

Japanese Influence at a Glance

Design Styles | **Containers**

For rikka and shoka (seika) — Tall bronze vases (usubata and ogencho) and low, rectangular containers (sunabachi or hiroguchi)

For shoka (seika) and nageire — Bamboo, tubular vases with one or more openings, hanging or standing boats, irregular root shapes

For nageire — Round bowl of pottery or bronze, low, oval or round dish, and tall, narrow-necked vases

For moribana — Low container in dark colors or sometimes in light blue and white

Flowers
- Aster
- Azalea
- Camellia
- Chrysanthemum
- Clematis
- Day lily
- Hydrangea
- Iris
- Lily
- Magnolia
- Narcissus
- Orchid
- Peony
- Rose

Foliages
- Aspidistra
- Cedar
- Hemlock
- Holly
- Juniper
- Pine
- Branches in leaf and flower
- Willow
- Wisteria
- Bamboo
- Hosta

Colors
- Secondary to form and flowers
- Muted, subtle colors of
  - Green
  - Blue
  - Violet
  - Shell pink
- Seasonal emphasis

Backgrounds
- Plain or lightly colored fabric, screen, or wall
- Wood panels
- Suggestive of tokonoma
- Japanese wall hangings or artwork

Accessories
- Shells, stones
- Wood

Bases
- Mats, panels
- Wood stands
- Wood burls

Notes

European Baroque and Dutch Flemish Styles (1600 - 1800)

Following the Renaissance and the revival of gardening and the appreciation of beauty in flowers, a new bold style of floral design emerged in the seventeenth century. The European

History of Floral Design

Notes

baroque (meaning a peral of irregular shape) style originated in Italy, spread north to the rest of Europe, and reached its full expression in the floral masterpieces of Dutch and Flemish painters, such as Jan Breughel, William van Aelst, Justus van Huysum, Jan van Huysum, and many others. The painters of that era painted beautiful floral masterpieces of many kinds of flowers. The artwork was not painted with a floral design model; it was painted with the artist's imagination and the resources of accurate botanical drawings the artist had drawn and kept in catalogs or files. The study of these paintings and still lifes in museums throughout the world is highly recommended as inspiration for contemporary floral designers.

These paintings were possible because of the prosperous economic conditions of the times. Many of the newly-prosperous business and government personnel were interested in having themselves and their newly-acquired art objects and possessions, as well as beauty in the form of floral artwork, painted for posterity. (Berrall, 26) The prosperity created a middle class who had more money to spend and created a widespread popularity of flowers for home and entertainment use.

The Dutch Flemish period was the age of discovery in horticulture. Merchant marines from Holland and England sailed and traded in the far corners of the earth. These voyages resulted in the introduction of many new plant materials, including chrysanthemums, cacti, nasturtiums, and giant sunflowers. The tulip had already been discovered in Persia and was so popular that a craze known as tulipmania swept Holland. These new flowers, along with the old standards, were numerous and provided the plant materials needed to create the elaborate mixed floral designs of this era.

The floral designs, as depicted in Dutch Flemish paintings, can be characterized into three main periods. The early style of the Dutch Flemish period shows paintings featuring the container. The container was the most important element while the flowers appeared flat. The emphasis was on the possession of wealth owned by the prosperous businessmen making the vase more significant than the flowers. During the intermediate period, the painters featured glass containers with the flowers. The artists liked the reflections of the stems in the glass containers. In the third and last period of Dutch

Flemish artistic interpretation, the painting featured the total connection between the flowers and the containers. Unlike the opulence of the containers in the early Dutch Flemish style, containers of common materials were shown in the paintings.

The Dutch Flemish period influenced contemporary styles of Western floral design more than any other period. The floral designs were massive, lush, and abundant symmetrical or asymmetrical designs with the largest most important flowers at the top and with voids or spaces along the composition edge. **(See Figure 1.8)** Asymmetrical movement from right to left or left to right and a sweeping *S* curve, later in the period, were characteristic of the baroque/Dutch Flemish style. The English painter, William Hogarth, created the *S* curve, calling it a "line of beauty" in his eighteenth century book, *The Analysis of Beauty*. Flowers were placed at all angles, showing front, sides, and the back; each blossom was featured and vital to the arrangement. The use of the striped, streaked, and fringed parrot tulips was common in Dutch Flemish designs. The flamboyant style included accents and accessories of fruit, nests, and additional flowers placed at the base of the container. Arrangement height varied from two to three times the container height.

As the artwork and literature of the period suggest, flowers were important and frequently contributed to the feeling of luxury and baroque indulgence at banquets and in homes. Banquet tables were decorated with baskets of flowers and garlands draping the fronts of tables and walls. Large, sweeping vase arrangements appeared as part of garden designs in urns placed in the gardens, in pavilions, or against clipped hedges. Inside the home in formal rooms, vase compositions stood in arched recesses or niches, on ledges, or on heavy marble tables placed against walls. (Marcus, 127) In bedrooms and sitting rooms, small casual bouquets were found.

Bold foliage, such as hosta, castor bean, canna, and coleus, were selected; large dramatic flowers which were spotted, flecked, striped, fringed, or streaked were favored during this period. Paintings of the period showed flowers of many different seasons placed together in one floral composition because the painter composed a mental picture of the arrangement and sketched it from those visualizations, not from actual designs. The

Figure 1.8 Baroque and Dutch Flemish Style Arrangement

History of Floral Design

Notes

flower selections pictured in the Dutch Flemish portraits are more feasible for contemporary designers because of year-around cut flower production than they were for floral designers of the seventeenth century. A partial list of flowers for the baroque/Dutch Flemish style includes double anemones, carnations, coral bells, crown imperials, cyclamens, foxgloves, hellebores, day lilies, hollyhocks, hyacinths, irises, larkspurs, lilacs, lilies, lupines, monkshood, narcissuses, nasturtiums, nerine lilies, double peonies, pinks, the flower and seedpods of poppies, roses, sunflowers, tulips, and old-fashioned snowball viburnums. Flowering branches and fruit were also incorporated into the designs.

Color schemes for this period were not subtle, but were characterized as bold masses and mixtures of colors with emphasis on medium to dark values with some lighter highlights. Some favored colors were dark red, blue, and purple. Many historians state that the art of color presentation in floral design was founded during the Dutch Flemish period. (Mitchell, 9)

The Dutch Flemish period was known for its variety of containers and vases. The most popular container for the profuse bouquets of the day was the classic urn, available in stone, metal, and glass, either highly decorated or plain. The metal urns were made with pierced rims so that the flower stems could be securely placed in the holes. Other containers included flasks, goblets, jugs, wide pedestal vases, and tall vases, as well as low bowls, baskets, and plates for fruit arrangements. As the seventeenth century progressed, beautiful glass vases manufactured in Germany and Venice were used. Also popular was the blue and white porcelain from China. Dutch craftsmen capitalized on this popular style and developed a more economical container known as delft.

Contemporary Dutch Flemish designs can be effectively displayed in a large area, in formal arched niches, or in a garden scene. Tapestry draping, flowered brocade, and dark silk or velvet drapes complete with tassels are appropriate backgrounds, as well as carved wood panels. Numerous accessories are used, including bird's nests with eggs, fruit, a loaf of bread with a knife, shells, jewels, watches, ornate rugs and draping fabrics, figurines, drinking cups, bowls, insects, ribbons and bows, uprooted plants, and velvet cushions. (Erickson, 42, 43)

Advanced Floral Design

Dutch Flemish at a Glance

Design Styles

Massive, lush designs (both symmetrical and asymmetrical)
Hogarth or *S* curve
Casual bouquets

Containers

Classic urns
Glass vases
Flasks, goblets, jugs
Low bowls, baskets, plates
Delft vases

Flowers (partial list)

Spotted, flecked, striped, fringed, streaked
- Double anemone
- Carnation
- Coral bell
- Crown imperial
- Cyclamen
- Foxglove
- Hellebore
- Day lily
- Hollyhock
- Hyacinth
- Iris
- Larkspur
- Lilac
- Lily
- Lupine
- Monkshood
- Narcissus
- Nasturtium
- Nerine Lily
- Double peony
- Pinks
- Poppy
- Rose
- Sunflower
- Tulip
- Snowball viburnum
- Flowering branches

Foliage

Bold foliage
Hosta
Castor bean
Canna
Coleus

Colors

Emphasis on medium to dark values with light highlights
Dark red
Blue

Backgrounds

Tapestry drapings
Flowered brocade drapes
Dark silk or velvet drapes complete with tassels

Accessories

Bird's nests with eggs
Fruit
Loaf of bread
Shells
Jewels
Watches
Figurines
Ornate rugs
Drinking cups
Bowls
Insects
Velvet cushions
Uprooted plants

The French Period (1643 - 1774)

At the beginning of the French period, Louis XIV and the court dominated every aspect of cultural life. The Louis XIV

History of Floral Design

era was a time of luxury and baroque magnificence. Louis XIV was the first of the French to have fresh flowers and potted plants brought into the palace. His reign set a precedence that the use of flowers was important. All of the decorative arts, such as the designing of tapestries and Sevres porcelain, flourished under royal patronage at the time of Louis XIV. Jean Baptiste Monnoyer was commissioned to paint flowers for tapestry designs and painted beautiful floral decorations for private residences, as well as designing beautiful floral engravings, for which he became well known. The French interpretation of the baroque style showed not only an accurate horticultural depiction of the flowers but also an artistic, graceful, and light touch in the display of flowers. These bouquets gave the effect of mass arrangements in the style of the Dutch Flemish period, yet they were not as massive. The floral designs of the Louis XIV reign were large in scale to appropriately embellish the opulent rooms of Versailles.

At the beginning of the eighteenth century, French artists and their patrons were ready for a fresh, lighter approach as opposed to the massive baroque style. In 1715, France was experiencing peacetime under the youthful King Louis XV and was ready for a change. This French period, also known as the French rococo (from the French *rocaille*, which refers to the delicate rock-and-shell ornamentation typical of that day), was an adaptation and a softening and lightening of the massive baroque and Dutch Flemish Styles.

During the Louis XV French period, fashion shifted to small, intimate, and elegant rooms and homes, lighter colors, and daintier furniture and decor items. The art forms of the day, including floral design, reflected a large degree of femininity during this period. The emphasis in the arts was on refinement and elegance, not overpowering massiveness.

The new style of floral designing included both tall and willowy designs, up to two times the container height, and small arrangements, which were often equal to and shorter than the container height. **(See Figure 1.9.)** Typical shapes of French rococo designs are a rounded shape, a relaxed fan shape, and a playful *C* curve replacing the *S* curve and displaying lightly bending arcs and short double curves of flowers and stems. Large flowers were chosen in smaller quantities and, along with smaller flowers and foliage, were positioned with openness and space around them for individual viewing. Flower stems were

Figure 1.9 French Rococo Style Design

often visible in designs from the French period. Because flowers were not massed and were used in smaller amounts, voids and spaces occurred within designs and their outlines. During this period, fashionable ladies carried bouquets or wore them tucked into bodices with tiny "bosom bottles" to keep them fresh. (Marcus 146) Entertaining at banquets, parties, and dinners was greatly enjoyed during this period of gaiety and fun. Floral settings were important for such occasions. Popular were designs in towering epergnes with candelabras or in low bowls or baskets displayed with arrangements of fruit, especially the favored pineapple.

The choice of French period plant material was large, such as acacia, anemone, amaryllis, aster, bachelor's button, balloon flower, buttercup, canterbury bells, carnation, crown imperial, daisy, hellebores, hyacinth, jasmine, double larkspur, lilac, lily, lily of the valley, marigold, narcissus, nicotiana, pansy, poppy, primrose, rose, variegated tulip, and viola, as well as flowering branches and ferns. The snapdragon and gladiolus were introduced during this period. Rococo color schemes combined light, pastel colors in subtle, analogous color harmonies, such as red, pink, and purple or yellow, soft green, and blue green. Accents of the dark colors of red, blue, violet, and black were used for contrast only.

During the French period, many containers were designed for flower use. Generally, the containers of this period were lighter in color and weight than those of the baroque period. The choice of containers ranged from bowls, baskets, shell and leaf-shaped dishes, and low shallow pedestal bowls (tazza), to epergnes, flasks, urns, Chinese cachepots or flower pots, and vases. Containers were available in glass, porcelain, pottery, and metals. The rococo ornamentation was very evident with fluted, curved vases displaying floral paintings and shell-shaped borders. **(See Figures 1.10a and 1.10b.)**

In contemporary floral display, typical backdrops for French rococo designs are both contrasting and complementing, such as patterned silk or velvet fabrics, tapestries, light-colored wallpaper with floral patterns, oak or walnut panels, Persian rugs, and richly upholstered pillows. Appropriate accessories include lace fans, porcelain figurines, leatherbound books, embroidery frames, tatting materials, or sheets of music reminiscent of the favored instrument of the day, the clavichord.

Figure 1.10a Rococo Ornamentation of Vases

Figure 1.10b Rococo Ornamentation of Vases

History of Floral Design

Notes

French Rococo at a Glance

Design Styles

Tall, willowy designs (two times the container height)
Smaller casual bouquet arrangements (equal to or shorter than the container)
Round and fan shapes
C curve

Containers

Highly ornamental
Vases, flasks
Urns, epergnes
Shell and leaf-shaped dishes
Baskets, bowls
Chinese cachepots or flower pots

Flowers

Lilac, rose (favorites)
Snapdragon, gladiolus (new)
Acacia
Anemone
Amaryllis
Aster
Bachelor's button
Balloon flower
Buttercup
Canterbury bells
Carnation
Crown Imperial
Daisy
Hellebores
Hyacinth
Jasmine
Double larkspur
Lily
Lily of the Valley
Marigold
Narcissus
Nicotiana
Pansy
Poppy
Primrose
Variegated tulip
Flowering branches

Foliage

Ferns

Colors

Light, pastel colors
Analogous color schemes
Red, pink, purple
Yellow, green, blue green
Accents of dark colors for contrast only

Backgrounds

Silk or velvet fabric, tapestry
Floral wallpaper
Oak or walnut panel
Persian rug

Accessories

Lace fans
Porcelain figurines
Pillows
Leather-bound books
Embroidery frames
Tatting materials
Sheet music

English Influence

Throughout history, the English have always loved gardening and flowers. Dating back to the Middle Ages, English homeowners tended small kitchen gardens to use the plants and flowers in cosmetics, homemade remedies, and for seasonings. Since flowers have always been important to the English culture, the early English floral tradition and the Victorian era will be discussed in this section.

Early English Tradition

The English first embraced the idea of using flowers as decoration under the influence of the conquering Romans who fashioned symmetrical garlands and wreaths. As early as the fifteenth and sixteenth centuries, the English people brought casual bouquets into their homes. (Teleflora Spirit, 29) Fragrance was an important prerequisite for flower selection, because the people thought the perfume would rid the air of pestilence. The English also created fragrant nosegays to carry, not for decoration, but for the fragrance of the fresh flowers.

The English tradition also embraced formality and symmetrical design, which was expressed in the formal gardens of many English homes. The reign of William and Mary from 1689 to 1702 marked the peak of formality in gardens. (Dutton, 6) As the formal garden became popular, the topiary form was developed as a shape in garden plants and in floral design.

During the Georgian period in the eighteenth century, the love and demand for fresh flowers was enormous. Flower girls peddled bouquets on the street; flower markets attracted a large clientele. The English loved fresh flowers and also appreciated dried arrangements for winter use. Everlastings, such as globe amaranth and strawflowers, were arranged in vases filled with sand and sold for enjoyment during the winter. During this period, beautiful swags of fruit and flowers were placed above fireplaces and doors and on staircase walls. The English also designed large fan-shaped bouquets of bellflowers, monkshood, or leaves to adorn the unused fireplace in summer and fall.

The eighteenth century English were eager plant collectors and patrons of artists skilled in botanical illustration. Some of the floral artists of that day were Georg Dionysius Ehret; Peter Casteels, who was Flemish; and Jacob van Huysum, a Dutchman and son of the baroque floral artist Justus van Huysum. The floral arrangements pictured in their works were beautiful compositions of mixed flowers, done on a smaller scale than during the baroque period. These English designs were filled with a tremendous variety of flowers from every part of the world, greater than the flower variety at any other time in history.

Floral designs during the Georgian period varied from small mixed bouquets in glass or brass bud vases to large mixed flower displays in urns, baskets, and vases. The height of the designs was generally one and a half times the container height, on a smaller scale than that used with the Dutch Flemish style. **(See Figure 1.11.)**

Figure 1.11 Eighteenth Century English Arrangement

History of Floral Design

Figure 1.12a Typical English Tradition Containers - Wall Pocket

Figure 1.12b Typical English Tradition Containers - Silver Stem Cup with Handles

The plant materials that were chosen for English arrangements are numerous and include all of the flowers previously mentioned in the other sections, as well as the following additions: catkin, clover, cyclamen, daphne, datura, geranium, hibiscus, passion flower, penstemon, phlox, plum and pomegranate blossoms, saxifrage, scabiosa, snowdrop, sorrel, spurge, trumpet vine, and veronica. Early in the English tradition, dark, rich colors were preferred, such as purple, blue, scarlet, and gold with occasional accents of lighter colors. The French rococo style added delicate colors to the favored color scheme, such as white and light blue with rose and silver. The English interpretation of French rococo was an arrangement with light-colored flowers that were chosen with texture in mind, such as roses, lilies, stock, and tuberose, to emphasize the weight and sturdiness of the English versus the French style.

Flowers were arranged in a wide array of container styles, such as urns of all sizes and shapes, silver or pewter stem cups with handles, wall pockets, jars, jugs, bowls, bottles, baskets, chalices, goblets, vases, and five-fingered posy-holders. **(See Figures 1.12a and 1.12b.)** Ceramics, including Wedgwood, metals, and glass, were the favored materials for English containers.

The English were well travelled and had eclectic tastes ranging from Chinese arts to Italian and French influences. Therefore, contemporary English designs can be effectively displayed with Chinese art, screens, or wallpaper showing landscape scenes, birds, or trees. Plain, glossy, or patterned fabrics in gold, rose, blue, or antique green can be used as backdrops. Wood-panelled backgrounds or the suggestion of a mantel or hearth would also make appropriate backgrounds. Ceramic objects, including figurines, rose jars, or ornamental vases, are characteristic accessories for English designs.

The Victorian Era (1830 - 1890)

Both arranging flowers and growing plants were very popular during the nineteenth century. The Victorian era was very important in the history of floral design. During this time, design and techniques were formulated and floral design was taught and recognized as a professional art.

The Victorian era, also called the Romantic Age, was a period of tremendous use and enthusiasm for flowers and plants. This period of floral designing, probably more than any other period, significantly contributed to establishing floral design rules and the everyday use of flowers and plants. Floral designing began to be considered an art form. Many people received formal schooling

Advanced Floral Design

Eighteenth Century England at a Glance

Design Styles

Small mixed bouquets
Large mixed flower arrangements
 (One and one-half times the
 container height)
Everlasting arrangements
Swags of fruit and flowers
Fan-shaped fireplace bouquets

Containers

Favored materials - Wedgwood,
 metals, glass
Glass or brass bud vases
Urns, vases, goblets
Baskets, bowls
Silver or pewter stem cups
 with handles
Wall pockets
Jars, jugs, bottles, chalices
Five-fingered posy-holders

Flowers

Additions to those previously listed
 listed in Dutch and French
 sections
Catkin
Clover
Cyclamen
Daphne
Datura
Geraniums
Hibiscus
Passion flower
Penstemon
Phlox
Plum and pomegranate blossoms
Saxifrage
Scabiosa
Snowdrop
Sorrel
Spurge
Trumpet vine
Veronica

Colors

Early-dark colors favored
 Purple
 Blue
 Scarlet
 Golden
After French Rococo
 influence additions of
 White
 Light blue
 Rose
 Silver
 Texture important

Accessories/Backgrounds

Chinese art
Screens/wallpaper of landscape
 scenes
Fabrics, plain, glossy, patterned in
 gold, rose, blue, or antique
 green
Wood panels
Suggestion of mantel or hearth
Ceramic objects, figurines, jars,
 vases

Notes

and seriously studied the techniques and styles of floral design. *Godey's Lady's Book* was a monthly guide that offered articles on many aspects of the home, including flower arranging, and a very important publication which helped establish rules, techniques, and guidelines for all floral designing of that day. Mechanics were discussed, as well as the care of fresh flowers, in the *Godey's Lady's Book*.

History of Floral Design

Notes

As quoted from the *St. Nicolas Magazine* during the 1870s, the following rules were listed to assist and encourage floral designers of the day:

"1st. The *color* of the vase to be used is of importance. Gaudy reds and blues should never be chosen, for they conflict with the delicate hues of the flowers. Bronze or black vases, dark green, pure white, or silver, always produce a good effect, and so does a straw basket, while clear glass, which shows the graceful clasping of the stems, is perhaps prettiest of all.

"2nd. The shape of the vase is also to be thought of. For the middle of a dinner-table, a round bowl is always appropriate, or a tall vase with a saucer-shaped base. Or, if the center of the table is otherwise occupied, a large conch shell, or shell-shaped dish, may be swung from the chandelier above, and with plenty of vines and feathering green, made to look very pretty. Delicate flowers, such as lilies of the valley and sweet peas, should be placed by themselves in slender tapering glasses; violets should nestle their fragrant purple in some tiny cup, and pansies be set in groups, with no gayer flowers to contradict their soft velvet hues; and - this is a hint for summer - few things are prettier than balsam blossoms, or double variegated hollyhocks, massed on a flat plate, with a fringe of green to hide the edge. No leaves should be interspersed with these; the plate will look like a solid mosaic of splendid color.

"3rd. *Stiffness* and crowding are the two things to be specially avoided in arranging flowers. What can be uglier than the great tasteless bunches into which the ordinary florist ties his wares, or what more extravagant. A skillful person will untie one of these, and, adding green leaves, make the same flowers into half a dozen bouquets, each more effective than the original. Flowers should be grouped as they grow, with a cloud of light foliage in and about them to set off their forms and colors. Don't forget this.

"4th. It is better, as a general rule, not to put more than one or two sorts of flowers into the same vase. A great bush with roses, and camellias, and carnations, and feverfew, and geraniums growing on it all at once would be a frightful thing to behold; just so a monstrous bouquet made up of all these flowers is meaningless and ugly. Certain flowers, such as heliotrope, mignonette, and myrtle, mix well with everything; but usually it is better to group flowers with their kind - roses in one glass, geraniums in another, and not try to make them agree in companies.

"5th. When you do mix flowers, be careful not to put colors which clash side by side. Scarlets and pinks spoil each other; so do blues and purples, and yellows and mauves. If your vase or dish is a very large one, to hold a great number of flowers, it is a good plan to divide it into thirds or quarters, making each division perfectly harmonious within itself, and then blend the whole with lines of green and white, and soft neutral tint. Every group of mixed flowers requires one little touch of yellow to make it vivid; but this must be skillfully applied. It is good practice to experiment with this effect. For instance, arrange a group of maroon, scarlet, and white geraniums with green leaves, and add a single blossom of gold-colored calceolaria, and you will see at once that the whole bouquet seems to flash out and become more brilliant.

"Lastly. Love your flowers. By some subtle sense the dear things always detect their friends, and for them they will live longer and bloom more freely than they ever will for a stranger. And I can tell you, girls, the sympathy of a flower is worth winning, as you will find out when you grow older, and realize that there are such things as dull days which need cheering and comforting."

The language of flowers was also carefully studied and applied during the Victorian era. During this time, flowers had symbolic meanings, and their placement and presentation in a nosegay or arrangement conveyed sentiment and emotion. Following are examples of Victorian meanings attached to certain flowers:

Chamomile - patience, humility

Foxglove - sincerity, adulation

Heliotrope - eternal love

Larkspur - fickleness

Marigold - grief, cruelty in love

Rosemary - remembrance

Thyme - activity, bravery

Violets, blue - loyalty

Violets, white - innocence

The color of the rose determined its meaning. For example, red is love, white is silence, and yellow is infidelity. A common practice was to send messages and to communicate with others, particularly in courtship, through the sending and receiving of nosegays.

Notes

History of Floral Design

Figure 1.13 Victorian Design

Victorian ladies delighted in other related floral design skills, such as preserving flowers, skeletonizing leaves, and patiently fashioning artificial flowers that resembled dahlias, passion flowers, or camellias from shells, wax, beads, and fabric.

The Victorian era has been called the battle of styles because many styles were adapted and imitated. The period was influenced by baroque, classic, and rococo styles. The Victorians liked two kinds of compositions more than others: large compact masses or light, open, and informal arrangements.

The compact mass bouquet was generally round or oval, and its outline was softened by arching or curving elements or foliage. Within Victorian designs, neither spaces nor a center of interest was obvious. *(See Figure 1.13.)* The proportions were never dramatic because the arrangement height varied from being half (or less) to equal the height of the container. A distinct Victorian quality in floral designs was the use of weeping or trailing plant materials, such as fuchsias and bleeding hearts, to lend a romantic or wistful quality to the design. Brilliant flowers that were streaked, marbled, or bicolored greatly pleased Victorian tastes. Victorians loved to include foliage for the symbolic meaning, texture, and contrast.

The Victorian era of floral designing is responsible for the custom of sending women flowers to wear or carry for social events. Every Victorian lady appeared at social gatherings with a nosegay of fresh fragrant flowers to sniff if overcome by faintness or fumes. These nosegays of flowers and herbs were arranged around a central group of fragrant flowers, such as roses, and framed in lace paper or placed in specialized metal or porcelain holders. Some holders even had a folding tripod stand for holding the bouquets upright on the table between dances or while taking tea. (Erickson, 90)

The love of the unusual and uncommon characterized the Victorian taste in flowers. Plant materials with bizarre markings, such as streaked carnations and tulips, spotted calceolarias, lilies, and pinks, boldly striped salpiglossis and morning glories, anemones, pansies, and primroses with conspicuous eyes, and the unique patterned foxglove, passion flower, and fuchsia were popular. Other favorites were baby's breath, cineraria, dahlias (honeycombed types especially), ferns, freesias, gardenias, plumed grasses, honesty, fully-opened roses, salvia, stephanotis, sweet peas, sweet Williams, and verbenas.

Masses and mixtures of colors delighted the Victorians. Although the Victorian designers had definite rules about not mixing colors that clashed, they did employ contrast in color use. Complementary or contrasting colors were considered more pleasing than color harmonies. The favored colors were rose, lavender, dark purple, magenta shades, red, orange, mustard, and cinnamon-yellow. This range of colors is excellent for backgrounds, along with dark green, brown, and dark red. Therefore, contemporary florists should use tablecloths and drapes in these colors, dark wood panels, marble tabletops, and ornamental stands when displaying Victorian designs.

A myriad of containers was used to create Victorian floral designs. Glass was the favored material, and ceramics, metal, and porcelain were also available. The urn and epergne were often used. The favorite Victorian epergne had a bowl or basket-shaped base for low, cascading flowers or for fruit with a trumpet rising out of the base for taller flowers. **(See Figure 1.14.)** Other containers included tuzzie muzzie holders, bottles, cornucopias, wall pockets, and all shapes of vases.

Contemporary Victorian designs can be accessorized with figurines, fans, shells and shell-covered boxes, period oil lamps, whatnot shelves loaded with knick-knacks, ornately bound albums, portrait photos of the period, Victorian greeting cards, Valentine's Day cards or postcards, and glass paperweights. An overstuffed and often cluttered look, as well as a cozy and comfortable feeling, are often associated with the Victorian era.

Figure 1.14 Victorian Design in an Epergne

American Floral Design History (1620 - 1830)

Early American floral design styles were influenced by European styles, yet they remained uniquely American because of the native plant materials used and the simpler design style. In seventeenth century America, luxury items, such as vases and pottery, were scarce. Simple designs of a casual naturalistic style were influenced by the Italian Renaissance and della Robbia style, as well as the Shakers. **(See Figure 1.15.)**

In the eighteenth century, during the late colonial period or colonial Williamsburg period, flowers and arrangements were seen more frequently in colonial interiors. Interiors were lighter; furniture had more graceful and elegant lines. Flower arrangements in the late colonial period were fan-shaped or triangular and were influenced by a sequence of styles from the baroque and Dutch Flemish styles to the French rococo style and William and Mary period of England. Queen Mary loved to show off as many flowers as possible and artfully packed both fresh and dried flowers into her trademark five-fingered vases. American interpretations of these styles were always simpler and more modest than the European counterpart. **(See Figure 1.16.)** Colonial ladies often arranged bowls of flowers of only one type, such as lilacs, roses, hyacinths, or snapdragons, and added a

Figure 1.15 Early Colonial Design

Figure 1.16 Typical Colonial Design

History of Floral Design

Notes

Victorian Era at a Glance

Design Styles

Compact masses often softened by foliage at the edges
Open, informal arrangements
Two-tier arrangements - flowers in the top, fruits or vegetables in the lower section of an epergne
Nosegays

Containers

Glass favored
Also ceramic, metal, porcelain
  Urns, epergnes
  Vases, bottles
  Tuzzie muzzie holders
  Wall pockets
  Cornucopias
  Baskets

Flowers

Unusual and uncommon favored
Streaked carnations or tulips
Spotted calceolaria, lily, pinks
Striped salpiglossis, morning glory
Anemones, pansy, primrose with "eyes"
Foxglove
Passion flower
Fuchsia
Fully-opened rose
Cineraria
Dahlia (honeycombed especially)
Double aster
Freesia
Gardenia
Salvia
Stephanotis
Sweet pea
Sweet William
Verbena

Other

Ferns
Plumed grasses
Honesty

Colors

Mixture of colors
Contrasts and complements with a touch of yellow
Rose
Lavender
Dark purple
Magenta shades
Red
Orange
Mustard
Cinnamon - yellow

Backgrounds

Tablecloths and drapes in Victorian colors (see above); also dark green, brown, dark red
Dark wood panels
Marble table tops
Ornamental stands

Accessories

Figurines
Fans
Glass paperweights
Shells, shell-covered boxes
Period oil lamps
Whatnot shelf and knick-knacks
Ornate albums
Victorian greeting cards, Valentine's Day cards, postcards

Late Colonial Period (American Style) at a Glance

Design Styles

Symmetrical arrangements
Casual bouquets arranged in a bowl
Bouquets combining fresh and dried flowers
Designs of all one type of flower with a filler added

Containers

Bowls, baskets
Delft brick
Five-finger vases
Epergnes
Stem cups
Jars, jugs, pots
Wall pockets
Urns

Flowers

Rose
Geranium
Hyacinth
Daffodil
Lilac
Lily
Tulip
Snapdragon
Stock
Baby's breath
Wildflowers
Violet, bluet
Solomon's seal
Daisies
Black-eyed Susan
Dried flowers

Other

Ferns
Grasses
Seed pods

Colors

Monochromatic schemes
Colorful mixtures
Favored colors
    Yellow
    Green
    Blue green
    Blue
    Rose
    Pale gold and white
    Pale blue, accents of blue or green

Backgrounds

Fireplace
Period Chippendale table or chest beneath a mirror
On twin tables beside a sofa
Plain wood walls
Walls painted pale yellow, soft green or peach
Near a window draped with long brocade curtains

Accessories

Figurines
Vases
Candles, candlesticks
Book or Bible
Period portrait
Lacquer or porcelain box

Notes

History of Floral Design

Figure 1.17 Five-finger Vase

Figure 1.18 Delft Brick

filler, such as pearly everlasting or baby's breath. The arrangement height was equal to the container height. Flowers bloomed abundantly in America and offered tremendous variety for arrangements. Dried materials were arranged in combination with fresh flowers.

Colonial designs were often colorful mixtures, although monochromatic schemes were enjoyed in that day. Yellow, green, blue green, blue, and rose were favorite colors in floral designs. The French influence inspired subtle combinations of pale gold and white, as well as pale blue with accents of blue or green.

Eighteenth century colonial vases varied from wide bowls of pottery, porcelain, pewter, silver or Delft brick to a five finger vase, epergne, or stem cups with two handles, also known as a loving cup. **(See Figures 1.17 and 1.18.)** Baskets, jars, jugs, pots, wall pockets, and urns held many colonial designs.

Accessories for colonial designs were simple figurines or vases, candles and candlesticks, leather-bound books or Bibles, period portraits, and lacquer or porcelain boxes. Contemporary colonial designs can be effectively displayed near a fireplace, on a period Chippendale table or chest beneath a mirror, on twin tables beside a sofa, or near a window draped with long, brocade curtains. Plain wood walls painted white or walls painted pale yellow, soft green, or peach colors would also be appropriate. (Marcus, 220)

With the influence of the William and Mary period of England, the American colonial period incorporated fresh and dried materials together in floral designs. The use of native grasses and wildflowers were a common trait of colonial arrangements. This period is important because it introduces a beautiful, rich, and simple style of arranging with grasses, fruits of the harvest, and fresh or dried flowers that is uniquely eighteenth century America with a touch of England.

Flowers and floral design have played important roles for personal enjoyment and religious decoration for many people and cultures throughout the centuries. A study of floral design history reveals the relationship of past floral designing practices and customs to contemporary styles of design. How fascinating to learn that thousands of years before Christ, Egyptians were fashioning wreaths to adorn their surroundings. The Romans strewed fragrant flowers in tremendous quantities at banquets. The English initiated the tradition of sending flowers to ladies for social events. Many fascinating customs and origins of floral design techniques and traditions can be revealed by the study of floral design history.

All floral designers should be encouraged to study the history of floral design. Studying the diverse and fascinating styles of the past can help contemporary designers become more creative and professional. Paintings from the respective periods provide an excellent reference of the design styles of specific eras discussed in this chapter. For examples of these paintings and other art forms, consult the following reference books.

Berrall, Julia S. 1953. <u>A History of Flower Arrangement</u>. London and New York: The Studio Publications, Inc., in association with Thomas Y. Crowell Company.

Marcus, Margaret Fairbanks. 1952. <u>Period Flower Arrangement</u>. New York: M. Barrows & Company, Inc.

<u>Notes</u>

History of Floral Design

Notes, Photographs, Sketches, etc.

Advanced Floral Design

Notes, Photographs, Sketches, etc.

History of Floral Design

Notes, Photographs, Sketches, etc.

Terminology and Techniques

Chapter 2

Advanced floral design involves specialized techniques, as well as technical terminology which is used to explain or describe arrangements. It is important for floral designers to understand these terms in order to be successful at creating advanced designs. This chapter defines the key terms and techniques used in advanced design. Definitions include design styles, theories, and principles, some of which are modified from their use in traditional design. Illustrations help to demonstrate word meaning. Knowledge of the terminology and techniques that follow will enable floral designers to communicate as professionals in a common language.

Abstract (Design Style) - A nonclassical form with crossed stems; the focus is on color, shape, or texture of materials. Signaled by nontraditional focal areas or multiple focal areas. Free-formed, yet balanced. Unaltered materials used in unusual ways, often no central radiation point. Extreme contrasts are often used, such as round forms and straight lines. *(See Figures 2.1a through 2.1d on page 38.)*

Abstract Experimental Floral Design (Design Style) - A departure from traditional design which uses decorative materials combined with natural products. The shape of the flowers is at times unrecognizable through the use of special techniques, such as bundling and stacking. Elementary forms, such as globes, cubes, and pyramids, are often the basis of abstract and experimental compositions. Geometric forms, rhythm, structure, texture, and tension are other ingredients for an abstract arrangement. This is the opposite of realistic floral design.

Accent (Term) - An additional element that enhances or adds emphasis to the primary structure of a composition.

Advanced Floral Design

Achromatic (Color Theory) - Without color: black, white, or a combination of both.

Airbrush (Technique) - The coloring of materials with floral spray paints.

Altering a Flower's Appearance (Technique):

- Composite Flower or Foliage - Construction of a large flower or foliage rosette from the petals or leaves of many smaller flowers, such as a glamellia constructed with gladiolus petals that have been glued or wired together to resemble a camellia or gardenia.

- Detaching - Removing a flower's petals to give the flower a new shape. This often causes the flower to resemble a bud or a completely different variety. Works well on roses, gerberas, and calla lilies.

- Massaging or Bending - An ikebana technique used to bend branches or flowers. This technique is done by applying gentle pressure with the thumbs, fingers, and body heat of both hands. Pussy willows, oak branches, and Scotch broom respond quickly to this technique.

- Reflexing - Folding back the petals of a flower, such as a rose, cymbidium orchid, tulip, or torch ginger.

- Tailoring - Stapling or gluing leaves, lace, or other material to a gardenia collar or gardenia shield. Used behind a camellia, rose, chrysanthemum, or gardenia. Tailoring supports and protects the flower while enhancing the flower's appearance.

- Tinting - Using a commercial floral paint or spray paint to change or enhance the color of a flower or foliage.

Analogous Color Harmony (Color Theory) - Colors that are next to each other on the color wheel. (A color wheel is provided in the back of the book for reference.)

Asymmetrical *(Modern)* Arrangement (Design Style) - The weight on either side of the center of gravity of an

Figure 2.1a Abstract Design

Figure 2.1b Abstract Design

Figure 2.1c Abstract Design

Figure 2.1d Abstract Design

Terminology and Techniques

Notes

asymmetrical arrangement is not equal. Outer points may appear to create a triangle when visually connected. An informal design style heavily dependent on the form and impact of the materials used.

Axis (Term) - The central line of any symmetrical or nearly symmetrical arrangement. In a design, the axis is placed in the center and can be a principle structure about which flowers and foliage are arranged.

Balance, Physical and Visual (Design Principle) - Two types of balance in floral design. Physical balance is constructed equilibrium or stability within a design. It enables the design to stand on its own without falling over. Visual balance is achieved by constructing a design that is harmoniously arranged so that it is pleasing to the eye. Following are types of visual balance.

- Asymmetrical Balance - Acheived when there is unequal visual balance between two halves of a composition divided by a central vertical line. Results in a design or display with a natural appearance.

- Open Balance - Occurs when specific principles of symmetrical, asymmetrical, and radiating balance do not apply. Instead, integration of these principles occurs, promoting balance from within the structure of the design.

- Radial Balance - Identified by stems emerging from a central point. When constructing a design using radial focus, the various lines should not bisect the axis.

- Symmetrical Balance - Achieved when both sides of a composition share the same visual weight. This balance tends to be formal and have a man-made appearance.

Banding (Technique) - The process of taping or joining materials together in a floral design.

Base Line (Term) - A horizontal line just above the lip of the container which tends to establish the length or width of the composition. Visualizing this line helps maintain balance in an arrangement and determine where materials can be placed.

Basing (Technique) - When the horizontal plane or ground surface of a composition is arranged with intricate textural detail to provide a decorative foundation from which the major composition rises. Design techniques, such as clustering, layering, pillowing, terracing, and the pavé method are often used to achieve different effects. This creates a focal interest at the base of the composition. When the basing technique is used properly, there should be space between the "base layer" and the upper materials in a composition. Basing works well with parallel systems design. **(See Figures 2.2a and 2.2b.)**

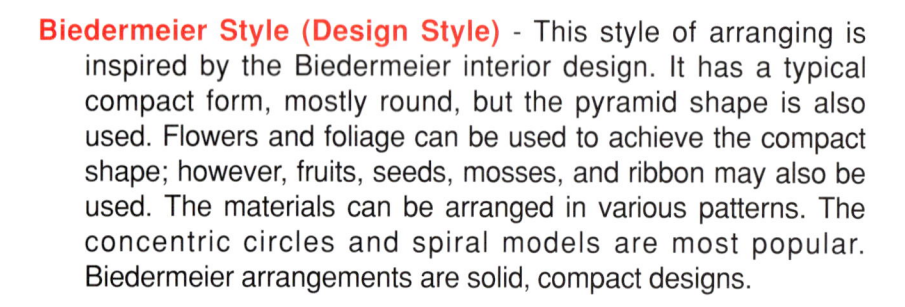

Biedermeier Style (Design Style) - This style of arranging is inspired by the Biedermeier interior design. It has a typical compact form, mostly round, but the pyramid shape is also used. Flowers and foliage can be used to achieve the compact shape; however, fruits, seeds, mosses, and ribbon may also be used. The materials can be arranged in various patterns. The concentric circles and spiral models are most popular. Biedermeier arrangements are solid, compact designs.

Binding (Technique) - Tying or uniting similar materials into units or bunches.

Binding Point (Term) - Imaginary or physical point where lines in an arrangement unite with the base line. Binding points are most often radiating or parallel. **(See Figures 2.3a through 2.3c on pages 40 and 41.)**

Botanical (Design Style) - Considered a new American design style which features at least five plant parts of a main flower used in the design. These five plant parts are stems, blossoms, foliage, buds, bulbs and/or roots and they illustrate the life cycle of the main flower. Other flowers can be used in this design style but should be subordinate to the main flower.

Bouquet (Design Style) - Flowers and foliage designed in a manner that allow them to be held or carried in the hand. Often wired and taped, loose or tied. Frequently, tied bouquets are designed with a spiral stem placement. Mistakenly synonymous with floral arrangement.

Bunching (Technique) - A labor-efficient method of working with small-stemmed dried flowers, such as star flowers. A bunch is gathered together and wrapped with floral wire. It is then

Figure 2.2a Basing

Figure 2.2b Basing

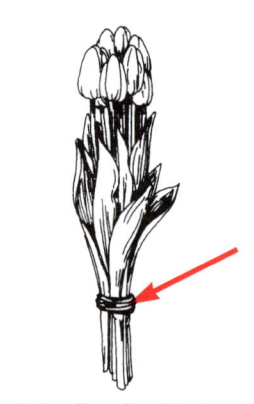

Figure 2.3a Parallel Binding Point

Figure 2.3b Radiating Binding Point

Terminology and Techniques

41

Figure 2.3c Radiating Binding Point

Figure 2.4a Clustering

Figure 2.4b Clustering

inserted into the design with a wire hairpin, eliminating the need for picking.

Bundling (Technique) - Quantities of material are bound together in one unit and worked into an arrangement. For example, three amaryllis are bound together with raffia to create the effect of one flower. Shocks of corn, sheaves of wheat, and a thatched roof are examples of how the bundling technique is used in non-floral situations. New and experimental floral designers are using this technique to develop increasingly elaborate designs.

Chroma (Color Theory) - Purity of a color, or of its freedom from white or gray. Also, the intensity of a distinctive hue or saturation of a color.

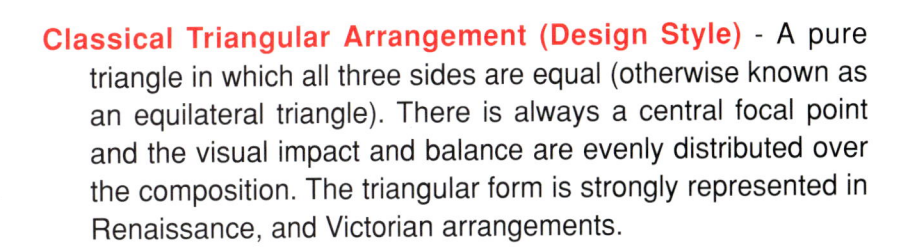

Classical Triangular Arrangement (Design Style) - A pure triangle in which all three sides are equal (otherwise known as an equilateral triangle). There is always a central focal point and the visual impact and balance are evenly distributed over the composition. The triangular form is strongly represented in Renaissance, and Victorian arrangements.

Closed Form (Term) - A material, such as a carnation, whose form stops the eye in a design. Other examples are a pompon or an open iris. Mass flowers are often closed forms. This is in opposition to an open form which facilitates continued eye movement.

Clustering (Technique) - The technique of placing materials close together with little or no space in between. This technique maximizes the materials' colors, textures, or shapes and achieves a mass emphasis. *(See Figures 2.4a and 2.4b.)*

Commercial Floral Design (Term) - The creative organization of plant materials and accessories with an appreciation for profitability, durability, saleability, suitability, and originality.

Composition (Design Principle) - The organization or grouping of different principles and elements to achieve a unified design.

Advanced Floral Design

Concinnity (Term) - A skillful, harmonious arrangement of parts. Elegance, especially of style. In floral design, skillfulness is selecting the right flowers, foliage, and container and presenting them with emphasis on harmony and design elegance. The total look is more than the sum of the parts.

Conditioning (Term) - The overall process of preparing flowers properly after they arrive at a business. This generally includes re-cutting stems, removing lower foliage, placing them in preservative-treated water, and allowing them to stand at room temperature.

Contemporary Design (Term) - A generic name for a current trend, on the leading edge.

Crescent Arrangement (Design Style) - The shape of the arrangement resembles a half moon or part of a circle. The focal point of a crescent-shaped design is usually near or below the center. Pliable materials, such as Scotch broom, are useful in creating a crescent line.

Depth (Design Principle) - To achieve depth, flowers of different stem lengths are used. Some flowers are tucked in deep, while others are left long and flowing. Using varied textures and colors can also help achieve depth in an arrangement. Generally, the more depth, the better the design.

Design (Term) - To plan and fashion plant materials artistically or skillfully using the principles and elements of design, primarily rhythm, focal point, balance, form, and texture.

Design Style (Term) - A floral design with a distinctive or characteristic mode of presentation, construction, or execution.

Design Techniques (Term) - The manners and means which make it possible for horticultural and decorative materials to be transformed into floral art. Examples are layering, basing, and terracing.

Detailing (Technique) - Unexpected nuances that bring a superior creative flair to a design. To develop detailing skills, an artist must train his mind to explore possibilities for unexpected creativity. *(See Figure 2.5.)*

Figure 2.5 Detailing

Terminology and Techniques

Earth Line (Term) - The line where the earth meets the horizon. In an arrangement, the imaginary line where plant materials grow from the container.

Elements of Design (Term) - Line, form, color, and texture. Tangible ingredients which all objects possess. Building blocks from which all flower arrangements are constructed.

Equilateral *(Classic)* Triangle Arrangement (Design Style) - A floral design in which all sides of the triangle are equal.

Feathering, *or Frenching* (Technique) - The process of taking flowers apart, particularly mass flowers, such as carnations or chrysanthemums, to make smaller units of those flowers.

Fibonnaci Principle (Type of Proportion) - A sequential number system developed by a mathematician known as Leonardo of Pisa (or Leonardo do Fibonnaci). The number system may be used to determine proportion based on mathematics. The system works as follows: 1 + 1 = 2, 2 + 1 = 3, 3 + 2 = 5, 5 + 3 = 8, 8 + 5 = 13, 13 + 8 = 21, etc. Thinking in terms of a floral design, if the main line of an arrangement is 21 inches tall, an attractive second placement would be 13 inches tall and a third placement 8 inches tall. This principle is only a guide to finding proportion. **(See Figure 2.6.)**

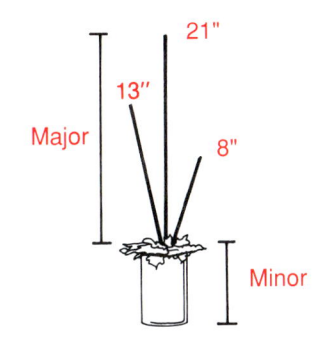

Figure 2.6 Fibonnaci Principle of Proportion

Flemish (Design Style) - Opulent designs reminiscent of bouquets found in fifteenth century Dutch/Flemish paintings. While they were composites and never existed in history, these designs are possible for contemporary florists to create, due to the wide assortment of flower and plant materials available. An important aspect of this style is a total disregard for compatibility; therefore, bulb flowers are combined with tropicals, fruits, and other accessories. Seemingly endless varieties of flowers and foliage are found in this symmetrical, crowded, massed, oval design with flowers facing outward, in profile, or showing the backs. Large flowers, such as lilies, tulips, and crown imperials, are placed at the top. Rich, varied colors and textures and many accessories, such as insects, birds nests, and shells, are used in these still-life groupings.

Flobs, *or Floral Objects* (Design Style) - *See Abstract Experimental Flower Design.*

Flower and Foliage Classifications (Design Element):

- Filler Flowers and Foliage - Multifaceted, used to fill in between and or to emphasize other flowers and foliage. Examples include statice, gysophila, and sprengeri fern.

- Form Flowers and Foliage - Materials with distinctive shape requiring prominent placement in the arrangement. Examples include orchids, papyrus, and birds of paradise. Often used as a focal point.

- Free-form Line - Line material with unpredictable movement. Examples include curly willow and kiwi vine.

- Line Flowers and Foliage - Materials with vertical stem structures, such as gladiolus, liatris, and lycopodium. They are used to add strength and create lines in floral arrangements.

- Mass Flowers and Foliage - Materials with clusters of petals or leaves at the end of a stem which form a round structure. Examples include carnation, rose, and pittosporum.

Focal Area (Design Principle) - The point of interest in a floral arrangement. All other parts are secondary to the focal area. In a radial arrangement, the place where all the stems appear to join. The focal area can also be a large flower, a ribbon, or other important commanding elements.

Forcing (Technique) - Deliberately exposing flowers or branches to elements that will cause them to open quickly, such as warm temperatures and light.

Form (Design Principle) - A shape that has a third dimension. Following are various types of forms.

- Circle - A closed, plane curve consisting of points which are equally distant from a point, called the center, within it.

- Crescent - A form which is less than a complete circle and has end points which are narrowly defined.

Notes

Terminology and Techniques

45

Figure 2.7 Framing

Figure 2.8a Free-form

Figure 2.8b Free-form

- Equilateral - Achieved when all sides are equal.

- Hogarth Curve - A lazy *S*, serpentine, or backward *S* line.

- Isosceles Triangle - A triangular form in which two sides are equal length and the third side is a different length.

- Open - A freely-shaped form, without defined space.

- Oval - An expansion of a round shape, similar to an egg.

- Rectangular - A parallelogram, the angles of which are all right angles.

- Right Angle - Characterized by two lines connecting at a ninety-degree angle.

- Scalene Triangle - Characterized by an asymmetrical triangle which has different degrees of length, sides, and angles.

- Square - A four-sided plane figure, the sides of which are all equal and all angles right angles.

Framing (Technique) - The use of branches or flowers to enhance or contain other materials. Framing isolates and calls attention to the focal area of a composition. It is also used to enclose an entire design and pull the visual impact into the design. *(See Figure 2.7.)*

Free-form (Design Style) - Non-geometric; embodies flowing lines and outlines. May include crossed stems. Often used to describe a design which has no distinct shape. *(See Figures 2.8a and 2.8b.)*

Gluing (Technique) - One of four basic methods of attaching materials when constructing a floral design. (The three other methods are picking, sewing, and tying.) Gluing utilizes liquid glues, aerosol glues, glue guns, and hot melt glue (glue pan).

Advanced Floral Design

Golden Mean (Type of Proportion) - Developed by Euclid, a Greek mathematician, it is the process of dividing a line by 1.6 to equal a ratio of 1 to 1.6. It is used to find the height or length of the materials in a design. The golden mean proportion is almost identical to the numbers in the Fibonnachi principle. The length or height of a design may be divided by 1.6; the proportion will reveal the major and minor section of most designs.

Graded Plane (Technique) - Placement of flowers or foliage in a sequence which begins with the largest and decreases to the smallest. A form of sequencing.

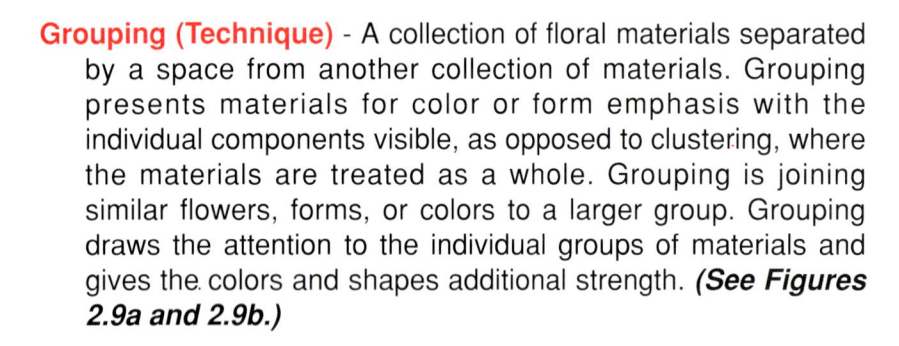

Grouping (Technique) - A collection of floral materials separated by a space from another collection of materials. Grouping presents materials for color or form emphasis with the individual components visible, as opposed to clustering, where the materials are treated as a whole. Grouping is joining similar flowers, forms, or colors to a larger group. Grouping draws the attention to the individual groups of materials and gives the colors and shapes additional strength. **(See Figures 2.9a and 2.9b.)**

Hana-mai (Design Style) - A style of the Ohara school of ikebana which uses crossed stems. Also known as dancing flowers. **(See Figure 2.10.)**

Hand-tied Bouquet (Design Style) - A bouquet that is held in the hand and constructed by adding material with the other hand and tying around the point of connection.

Harmony (Design Principle) - To be in harmony, all parts of a floral arrangement should blend well together. This can apply to color, texture, and types of materials used.

Hue (Color Theory) - A true color. Examples include red, blue, and yellow. The name of a color. (Refer to the color wheel provided in the back of the book.)

Ikebana *(Ee-kay-bah-nah)* (Term) - General term given to all schools of oriental style design. Means "giving life to flowers." Some ikebana designs feature three main lines called shin, soe, and tai (heaven, man, and earth). In traditional ikebana, flowers and plant materials are used as they would appear in nature, with respect for seasons, growth habits, and color

Figure 2.9a Grouping

Figure 2.9b Grouping

Figure 2.10 Hana-mai

Terminology and Techniques

Figure 2.11a Ikebana

Figure 2.11b Ikebana

harmonies. Compared to Western style floral design, the container assumes more importance in ikebana design. Various types of historical design include rikka, shoka, nageire, moribana, free style, and abstract. In contemporary society, there are over 3000 separate schools of ikebana. Each has its own principles and headmaster. **(See Figures 2.11a and 2.11b.)** Following are major schools of ikebana and major design styles taught within each.

- Ikenobo - Founded by Ono-no-Imoko in approximately 621 A.D. It is the oldest school of floral design. Major design styles are rikka, shoka, moribana, nageire, and free style.

- Ohara - Founded by Unchin Ohara around the end of the 1900s. It became very popular with common people. Major design styles are moribana, nageire, hana mai, and free style.

- Sogetsu - Founded by Sofu Teshigahara after World War II. Considered a very modern approach to floral design. Teshigahara became the first post World War II millionaire in Japan. Major design styles are moribana, nageire, and free style.

Interpretive Design (Term) - A composition that expresses the designer's feelings and ideas.

Juxtapose (Term) - To place a material side by side or close together.

Lacing (Technique) - Interweaving plant material to form a mechanic that will support a design. Used for clear glass vase arrangements and some hand-tied bouquets.

Landscape Arrangement (Design Style) - Initially, landscape arrangements seem quite similar to the vegetative arrangements. Upon close observation, the influence and discipline of the landscape architect is seen. The assembly of the materials and the techniques, such as terracing and layering, are essential. Often, taller flowers are placed in the back and shorter flowers in the front. In landscape designs, there is little staggering of stem lengths within the same cluster. Instead, staggered heights occur between the flower groups. Differences in height prevent rigidity in this type of arrangement. The most appropriate flowers to feature in landscape designs are those that would actually be planted in a garden. Using only seasonal flowers together in an arrangement provides a more authentic look. Stones, mosses, and gravel can be used as part of the foundation of the arrangement. This design style often contains a man-made structure, such as a fence or bridge.

Layering (Technique) - Placing materials/products on top of one another with little or no space in between. *(See Figure 2.12.)*

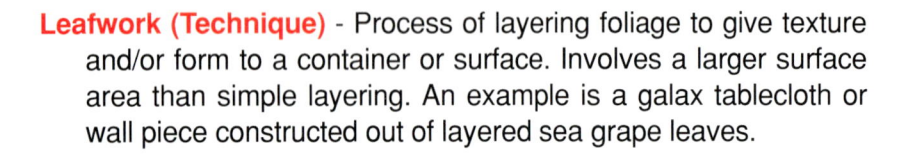

Leafwork (Technique) - Process of layering foliage to give texture and/or form to a container or surface. Involves a larger surface area than simple layering. An example is a galax tablecloth or wall piece constructed out of layered sea grape leaves.

Line (Design Principle) - The path the eye automatically follows in an arrangement is the primary line of the design. All other lines must be secondary.

- Broken Line - When the natural foliage, bracts, or branches on a stem are removed or partially removed to increase the separation between parts. This increases the speed with which the eye might move along the stem.

- Continuous Line - When the natural foliage, bracts, or branches on a stem are left in their original state.

- Contour Line - The outline or silhouette of the materials used.

- Curvilinear Line - Consisting of, or bounded by, curved lines. Forming or moving in a curved line, or a line that is characterized by curved lines.

- Diagonal Line - A slanted line which creates a feeling of mobility, instability, or dynamic tension.

- Floating Line - A line which seems to have no weight.

- Hanging Line - Cascading lines which appear to be support-seeking or weighted. An apple on a branch is an example.

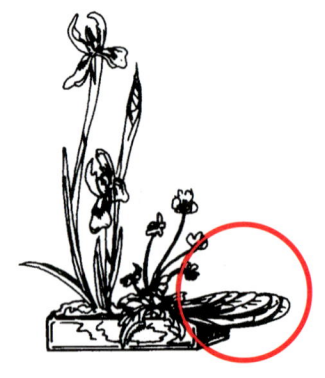

Figure 2.12 Layering

Terminology and Techniques

49

- Hogarth Line - An elongated *S*-shaped line, also known as "the line of beauty."

- Horizontal Line - A flat line parallel to the surface of the earth. The horizontal line may balance an arrangement.

- Implied Line - An imaginary or invisible line created in the mind's eye by extension from actual, existing lines.

- Intermediate Line - A secondary line that bends away from the primary line.

- Primary Line - Usually the first placement in a composition. It establishes the spine or central vertical axis of the design.

- Radiating Line - Any of a group of lines that spread outward from a central point.

- Support-seeking Line - Line that need support to be maintained. A cable line on a suspension bridge is an example.

- Vertical Line - A line with a ninety-degree angle to the horizon. This line emphasizes strength.

Linear Arrangement (Design Style) - Linear means "of or in lines." There is a clear distinction between two types of linear arrangements. *(See Figure 2.13.)*

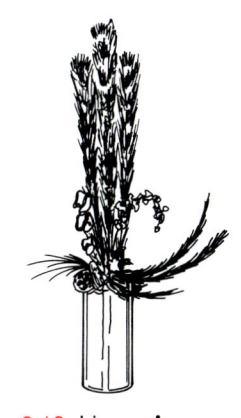

- Formal Linear Arrangements - Created with a few taut lines, which may be vertical, as well as horizontal and diagonal, to give a feeling of movement and shape. The play of lines can be curved, straight, or in parallel forms. Through the use of a minimum amount of material, the beauty of the flower and stem is optimally highlighted. Restraint is of the utmost importance in this form of arrangement. "Less is more."

- Interpretive Linear Arrangement (Western Line Arrangement) - The principal use of taut lines and forms which may be curved, flowing, or at right angles to one another. The open space between the flowers should not be filled or the accent of the line will be lost.

Figure 2.13 Linear Arrangement

Where possible, the line of the arrangement must be accentuated. Linear arranging is extremely functional; nothing is allowed that is not distinctly structural. The innate quality of the material must be completely and correctly emphasized. In an interpretive linear arrangement, there may be more than one focal point. Form, rhythm, and proportion are the essential elements in this type of linear design.

Lines of Confusion (Technique) - While crossed stems are seldom used in commercial floral design, a few Japanese ikebana schools arrange flower stems or branches in a very controlled but crisscrossed manner. These are called lines of confusion. *(See Figure 2.14.)*

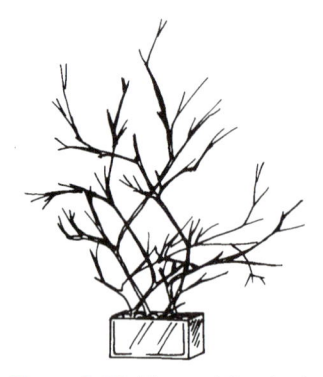

Figure 2.14 Lines of Confusion

Lines of Parallelism (Design Style) - Lines that have the same direction or course are called parallel. The term parallel is derived from the Greek word parallelos, meaning beside one another. The flower stems are placed parallel to each other horizontally, vertically, diagonally, or in any direction. Differences in height prevent rigidity in parallel arrangements. Choose flower species with straight, rising stems to establish the rising lines in an arrangement. Multi-branched material is not usually suitable for this style. *(See Figure 2.15.)*

Figure 2.15 Lines of Parallelism

Mechanics (Term) - Method of constructing supports within which a composition may be designed. Includes any element used to support or secure a design. Examples are wet floral foam for constructing an arrangement, wire and tape for constructing a corsage, caged floral foam, and waterproof tape.

Mille de Fleurs Arrangement (Design Style) - Mille de Fleurs literally means one thousand flowers and suggests that many flowers and many varieties of flowers are used. Mille de Fleurs are designed principally in circular shapes; however, in contrast to the Biedermeier, the flowers are not rigid and tight, but loosely and delicately arranged. A variant of Mille de Fleurs is Mille de Couleurs which translates into one thousand colors; therefore, an exuberance of colors is used in the arrangement. The Mille de Fleurs and the Mille de Couleurs, like the Biedermeier, are space-occupying arrangements.

Minimalism (Term) - The use of few materials. Some forms of ikebana could be considered minimalistic.

Terminology and Techniques

Notes

Mirroring (Term) - Repetition of the same material at different heights and depths, especially when one piece is in front of and lower than the other.

Moribana (Design Style) - An ikebana design that is arranged in a low, flat dish. Moribana styles include upright, slanting, cascade, heavenly, and contrasting. There are many variations on each of these styles and each school takes a different approach and often a different name for each style.

Motion (Term) - A visual quality of design reflecting the way eye movement is controlled by the placement of materials. It is a means by which balance can be achieved.

- Continuous Motion - Created by a circle or a triad with the eye continually moving around the circle or from point to point of a triangle.

- Free and Variable Motion - Achieved by material moving in opposite directions, as well as those that repeat the same movement. The utilization of circular, vertical, diagonal, horizontal, and implied lines in the same composition would create free and variable motion. Balance is achieved through motion.

- Kinetic Motion - Actual movement as opposed to the appearance of movement. Though plant materials have no perceptible motion unless acted upon by an outside agent, kinetic motion can still be part of a design, as when a candle flickers or when pendulous materials in a bridal bouquet move while the bouquet is being carried down the aisle.

- Mechanical Motion - Actual movement in an arrangement by a powered source, such as electricity or a battery.

- Repetitious Motion - Lines moving in the same direction.

- Static Motion - The effect of masses or forces in an arrangement that are in equilibrium (motionless).

Mound Arrangement (Design Style) - Arrangement shape that resembles half of a globe.

Advanced Floral Design

Nageire (Design Style) - An ikebana style which means thrown-in flowers. It is distinguished by flowers arranged in a tall vase. Styles include upright, slanting, cascading, heavenly, and contrasting. Names and design principles vary within each school.

Natural Framework (Technique) - Cross placement (interweaving) of the stems of both flowers and foliage inside the container, not intended to be seen. Used in the lacing technique.

Naturalistic Design (Design Style) - Emphasizes the beauty of flowers without contrivance or manipulation. The container is in harmony with the design.

Negative Space (Design Principle) - Totally empty space within the materials used in a composition; open space within a composition. This absence of material allows the viewer to stop and visually catch his breath; it is similar to a rest in music. Negative space is often enclosed by positive space, such as in a wreath. *(See Figure 2.16.)*

Figure 2.16 Negative Space

New Convention Arrangement (Design Style) - The new convention and parallel systems arrangements are often confused with one another; however, there are clear differences. Both styles of arranging utilize the parallel technique. However, in the new convention style there are not only vertical but horizontal groups. It is desirable that these horizontal groups are juxtaposed to the left and right and the front and back of the arrangement. The horizontal groups are always placed at right angles (90 degrees), and they should be a reflection of the vertical groups in the arrangement. It should be possible to draw an imaginary rectangle or square around a new convention arrangement. Techniques, such as terracing, layering, and strong grouping, are important to this style. A way of making a new convention arrangement more interesting is the use of framing, which may not only be angular, but of a contrasting circular form. *(See Figure 2.17.)*

Figure 2.17 New Convention Arrangement

New Wave (Design Style) - This style features discordant blends of colors and geometric shapes; unusual presentation of products in unexpected ways characterized by the alteration (painting, etc.) of materials. A sculptured-looking design; flowers are not used for their natural shape, color, or stems. Contemporary containers are necessary. *(See Figure 2.18.)*

Figure 2.18 New Wave

Terminology and Techniques

Novelty Arrangement (Design Style) - An arrangement that incorporates some type of non-floral element. An example would be a turkey shape made of chrysanthemums.

Parallel Placement (Technique) - The use of a few flowers in parallel positioning within a style of design. Parallel lines may be placed in traditional types of arrangements, as well as abstract and new wave designs. This is an advanced technique and requires skill when incorporating into traditional styles.

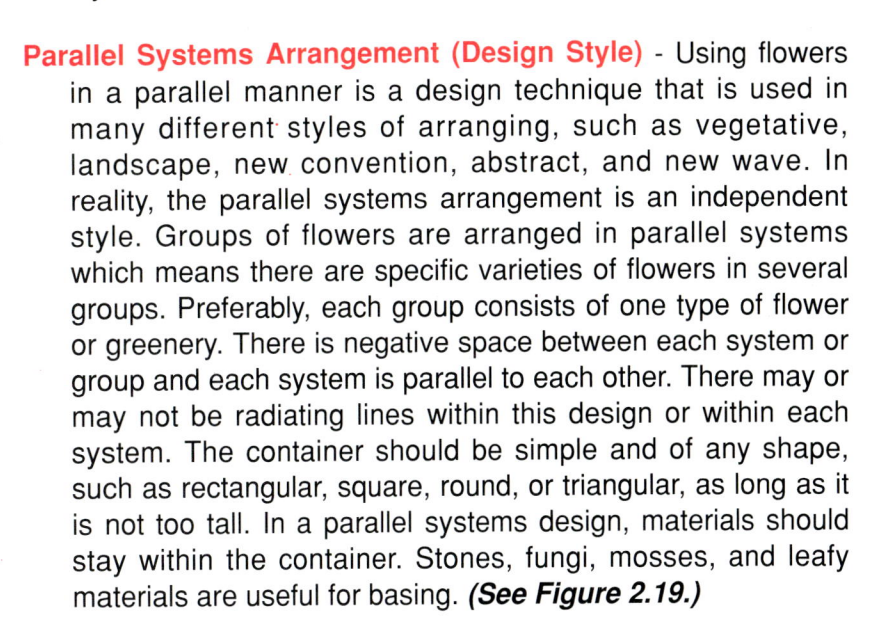

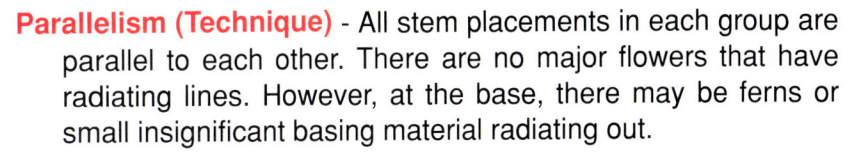

Parallel Systems Arrangement (Design Style) - Using flowers in a parallel manner is a design technique that is used in many different styles of arranging, such as vegetative, landscape, new convention, abstract, and new wave. In reality, the parallel systems arrangement is an independent style. Groups of flowers are arranged in parallel systems which means there are specific varieties of flowers in several groups. Preferably, each group consists of one type of flower or greenery. There is negative space between each system or group and each system is parallel to each other. There may or may not be radiating lines within this design or within each system. The container should be simple and of any shape, such as rectangular, square, round, or triangular, as long as it is not too tall. In a parallel systems design, materials should stay within the container. Stones, fungi, mosses, and leafy materials are useful for basing. *(See Figure 2.19.)*

Figure 2.19 Parallel Systems Arrangement

Parallelism (Technique) - All stem placements in each group are parallel to each other. There are no major flowers that have radiating lines. However, at the base, there may be ferns or small insignificant basing material radiating out.

Pavé (Technique and Design Style) - Most commonly used in jewelry, pavé describes gems laid close together to cover the base metal. In floral design, the base or mechanics are covered with many small jewel-like elements, such as carnations, roses, and cranberries. Sometimes this technique is expanded to actually be a complete design. *(See Figure 2.20.)*

Phoenix (Design Style) - A round form that has a burst of material rising out of it, giving the impression of another design.

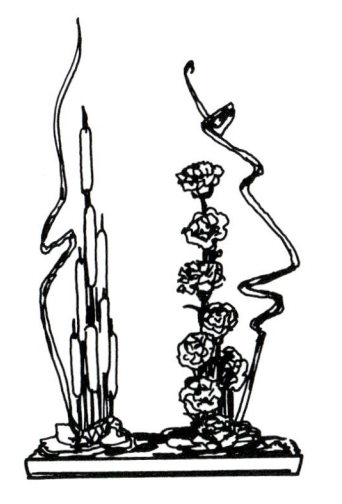

Figure 2.20 Pavé

Advanced Floral Design

Picking (Mechanic) - One of four basic ways of attaching materials to a floral design. The five kinds of picking include wood, metal, wire, water tube, and natural picking. Natural picking refers to a piece of the original stem or branch used to secure a flower or pod.

Pillowing (Technique) - The use of dome or mounded materials as a surface. The result is a base or cushion, which at regular intervals, is depressed and looks similar to rolling hills, clouds, or pillows. Pillowing literally means "growing in bunches;" therefore, bunches of short flowers are joined together to form rolling hills. *(See Figure 2.21.)*

Figure 2.21 Pillowing

Plating or Braiding (Technique) - To weave, interlace, or entwine together as in three or more strands: ribbon, raffia, bear grass, or flower stems (rose, carnation, gerbera, freesia). This technique can also be seen with the braided stems of the Ficas benjamina plant.

Point to Point Connection (Term) - When one grouping is connected to another grouping visually or physically. An example is the connecting lines or cables on a bridge.

Polarity (Design Principle) - The principle by which a design gains strength through opposition of textures, forms, colors, or spaces.

Positive Space (Design Principle) - The space occupied by flowers or foliage. The section of a floral design where flowers are actually placed.

Principles of Design (Term) - The main components of every floral design: rhythm, proportion, unity, focal point, harmony, repetition, and balance.

Proportion (Design Principle) - The comparative size relationship between ingredients within a design. For example, small flowers and small foliage used together are in harmony; medium flowers should be used with medium-sized foliage; large flowers should be used with large-sized foliage. Also, the size of the container should be in proportion to the size of the materials and size of the design.

Pruning (Technique) - Selectively removing branches, foliage, florets, or petals to create desired voids and produce materials

Terminology and Techniques

which appear to be more sculpture like. Pruning makes the material lighter and may reveal a more interesting shape, thus giving it a more important appearance.

Realistic Floral Design (Term) - In realistic floral design, the horticultural material is clearly recognizable. Materials are not altered from their natural state. The arrangement is not only created in the traditional forms, such as triangular, they can also contain new convention and parallel systems arrangements. This is opposite of abstract experimental floral design.

Rhythm (Design Principle) - To create rhythm in an arrangement, repetitious lines, forms, shapes, or colors must be used. This repetition allows the eye to flow through the design.

Right Triangle Arrangement (Design Style) - A type of asymmetrical arrangement where the vertical line is perpendicular to the horizontal line. A ninety-degree angle is formed.

Salt and Pepper (Technique) - The mixing of floral materials throughout a design. Opposite of grouping or clustering.

Scale (Design Principle) - The size relationship of a design and all its parts - flowers, foliage, container, and accessories- should be in proportion to the setting in which it is placed.

Sculpturing (Technique) - Placing materials in distinct zones and bringing them to the center of the design. Allowing the material or the design to adapt a carved or molded form. *(See Figures 2.22a and 2.22b.)*

Secondary Colors (Color Theory) - Colors formed by mixing two primary colors (red, blue, and/or yellow) in equal amounts to form violet, green, or orange. (A color wheel is provided in the back of the book for reference.)

Sectioning (Technique) - Segregating types of materials within a group. *(See Figure 2.23.)*

Sequencing (Technique) - The materials in a composition move in a progressing pattern of change. It is often used to create distinctive contemporary arrangements. Sequencing is most forceful when there is a gradual transition in color, form, and

Figure 2.22a Sculpturing

Figure 2.22b Sculpturing

Figure 2.23 Sectioning

texture. It is not necessary, however, that all three change for the sequencing technique to be properly expressed. In a composition, for example, the color, form, and size of the flowers all move in the proper sequence. Size moves from small to large, color moves from dark to light, and texture moves from smooth to coarse.

Sewing (Technique) - One of the four basic ways of attaching materials to a design. Used in the construction of horse and casket blankets and novelty wedding bouquets, such as parasols, muffs, and leis. It includes the use of needle and thread, stapling, straight pins, and hairpins made of wire.

Shadowing (Technique) - A technique used to give a composition a three-dimensional appearance by the close placement of one material immediately behind or in front of a primary material. The material is placed lower than the primary and appears as its shadow.

Sheltering (Design Style or Technique) - Material that is protected or contained and is viewed by peering inside. It may also be a design that is constructed below the container line and protected by the walls of the container. **(See Figures 2.24 a and 2.24b.)**

Space (Design Element) - Three-dimensional area in and around a design.

Stacking (Technique) - Placing materials side by side and on top of each other as if stacking something. **(See Figure 2.25.)**

Style (Term) - A recognizable form of design or school of thought. Style is the end result.

Surrealistic Design (Term) - A design that aims to create a fantasy or dream-like quality based on a mental image from the subconscious workings of the mind. Salvador Dali and Giorgio de Chirico have contributed to this approach.

Symbolic Design (Term) - Designs with subjective thoughts or ideas expressed through the materials used. Symbolic designs often project ambiguous imagery to the viewer.

Symmetrical (Form) - While a symmetrical arrangement can take on many shapes, its weight is always balanced on either side

Figure 2.24a Sheltering

Figure 2.24b Sheltering

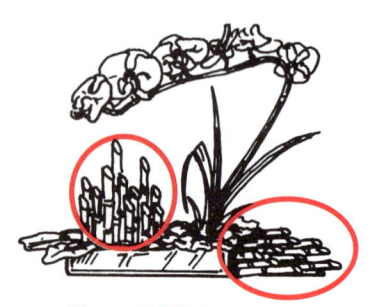

Figure 2.25 Stacking

Terminology and Techniques

of a central (imaginary) line that can be drawn through the center of the arrangement. (The central imaginary line in a design is the center of gravity.)

Synergy (Term) - The result when the total effect of a design is greater than the sum of its parts. All of the elements work together to create a unified and pleasing arrangement.

Tailoring (Technique) - Trimming materials to give them a sculpted or fitted look. Stapling leaves behind a gardenia is an example.

Technique (Term) - A means to an end. Not to be confused with style. Technique is an application.

Tension (Combination of Design Principles) - While difficult to explain, tension is one of the most essential elements in contemporary floral art. Tension is created through rhythm (the harmonious correlation of parts), texture, and structure. The placing or partitioning of the materials is extremely important. An important element of tension is the amount of open space between the materials. Instead of 1-2-3-4, more interesting compositions can be made, such as 2-2, 3-1, or 1-3. The "feeling" for what can or cannot be done is of the greatest importance. *(See Figure 2.26.)*

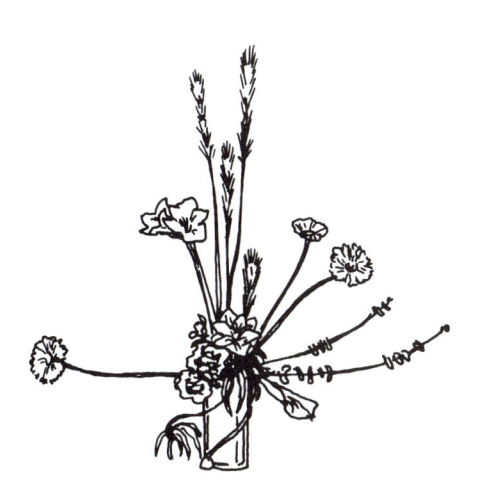

Figure 2.26 Tension

Terracing (Technique) - A technique of placing like materials in stair-step fashion to create levels with space in between. Any series of the same form rising above the other. Terracing achieves depth. *(See Figure 2.27.)*

Texture (Design Principle) - The tactile quality or feeling of materials used. It can apply to flowers, foliage, containers, or accessories. Examples of texture are rough, smooth, and nubby. Generally, materials of similar texture should be incorporated into an arrangement.

Figure 2.27 Terracing

Tufted Arrangement (Design Style) - A compact style of arranging using short flowers. A tufted arrangement is made more interesting through the use of nicely-formed branches or twigs or sprays of flowers which are allowed to "grow" from the base, thus creating a light and airy effect.

Tying (Technique) - One of four basic ways of attaching materials to a floral design. A hand-tied bouquet usually consists of a wide variety of floral materials featuring stems that are crossed or placed spirally. The bouquet is tied together with string, wire, or raffia. Hand-tied bouquets are never arranged in foam and are often placed in clear glass containers.

True Form (Design Style) - Following the principles and proportion of any given design style with absolutely no interpretive influence.

Unity (Design Principle) - The effect created by the cohesive use of materials.

Vegetative Arrangement (Design Style) - Vegetative derives from vegetation. Overgrowth (unstructured) is the best description of a vegetative arrangement. An arrangement that copies nature or that which one finds in nature. Grasses, mosses, stones, driftwood, and sand are ideal materials to use on the bases of such arrangements. Never use perfectly cultivated flowers. They will destroy the character of the arrangement.

Void (Design Principle) - A section within a design where there are no flowers. A void in a design may be good or bad. For example, a void can enhance a line or form by allowing it to be seen. In contrast, too many voids might make an arrangement appear incomplete.

Waterfall Style (Design Style) - A revival of the late 1800s romantic cascading design, the waterfall design can be a hand-tied bouquet placed in a vase or an arrangement constructed in floral foam. Long, trailing materials are needed, particularly to begin the flowing design. It is essential that the material literally looks as if it jumps from the center of the container and cascades to the desired length. Inside placement and depth are created by an overlay of materials. Typical of the waterfall style is the layering of one material over another to allow diversity. Generally, smaller varieties of flowers are combined with larger varieties to achieve the "untidy" appearance of a waterfall. Bear grass, flat fern, asparagus plumosus, conifer, vines, and twigs are used, as is the addition of ribbon, tulle, or copper wire as a decorative element. The first impression is that of little design style; however, it can be one of the most difficult styles of floral art to master. *(See Figure 2.28.)*

Figure 2.28 Waterfall Style

Terminology and Techniques

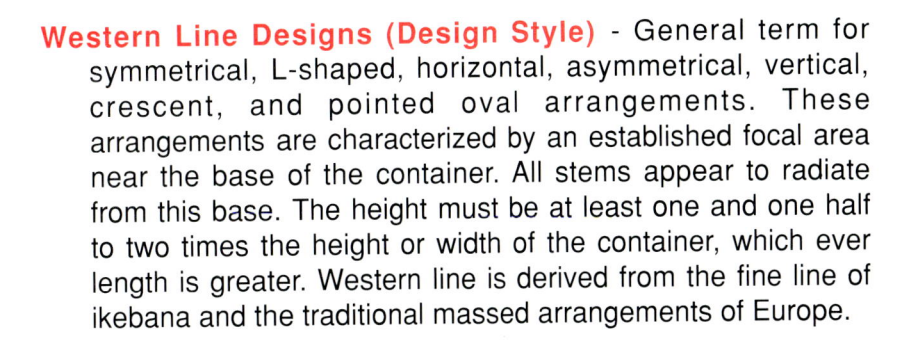

Western Line Designs (Design Style) - General term for symmetrical, L-shaped, horizontal, asymmetrical, vertical, crescent, and pointed oval arrangements. These arrangements are characterized by an established focal area near the base of the container. All stems appear to radiate from this base. The height must be at least one and one half to two times the height or width of the container, which ever length is greater. Western line is derived from the fine line of ikebana and the traditional massed arrangements of Europe.

Wrapping (Technique) - Binding individual or groups of floral items together with thread, metallic wire, fabric, ribbon, or yarn, to add color, texture, interest, and distinction to floral designs. This rediscovered technique originated many years ago. The inspiration could have come from many places: American Indian artifacts; aborigine artifacts; ikebana; or from contemporary artists who have wrapped trees, buildings, columns, and even islands with fabric and other materials.

Zoning (Technique) - Similar to grouping in that space must be evident between each piece of floral material. There must be ample space between each zone of materials so that the grouping stands out with clear independence. When expensive flowers, such as lilies and orchids, are featured (zoned) at the top of an arrangement, this gives them prominence in the design. *(See Figure 2.29.)*

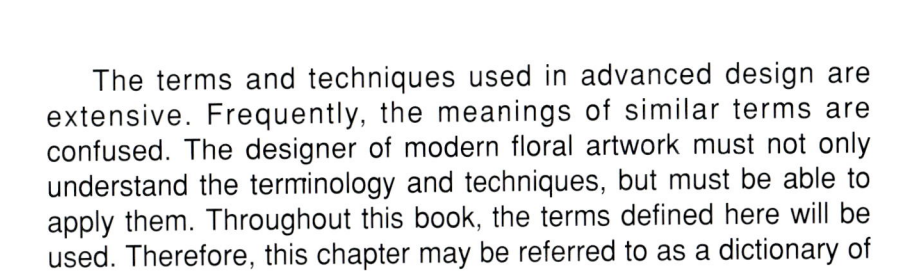

Figure 2.29 Zoning

The terms and techniques used in advanced design are extensive. Frequently, the meanings of similar terms are confused. The designer of modern floral artwork must not only understand the terminology and techniques, but must be able to apply them. Throughout this book, the terms defined here will be used. Therefore, this chapter may be referred to as a dictionary of floral terminology.

Advanced Floral Design

Notes, Photographs, Sketches, etc.

Terminology and Techniques

Notes, Photographs, Sketches, etc.

Expanding the Principles and Elements of Design

Chapter

3

A working knowledge of the principles and elements of design enable floral designers to select materials, visualize arrangements, and create them successfully. If a completed arrangement seems unsatisfactory, most likely one of the principles or elements of design has been applied incorrectly or ignored completely. Everything known to man is governed by dictates of elementary design principles. Whether found in the intrigue of a landscape, the geometric simplicity of a skyscraper, or the intricate detail of a floral arrangement, there are common ingredients in designs of any kind.

In examining the elements present in a single apple, one can identify color intensity, a waxy texture, a rounded form, and space in the form of the dimpled ends where the flower and stem grow. (Webb, 198) These elements contribute to the visual appeal of the apple. Likewise, these elements influence one's perceptions of floral arrangements.

This chapter discusses the principles and elements applied to the design of advanced floral arrangements and the expansion of these guidelines. Advanced designers might find it helpful to review basic principles and elements of design as outlined in Redbook Florist Services' textbook *Basic Floral Design*.

Principles of Design

The principles guiding design are a constant that allow floral composition to be pleasing and distinctive to the human eye. The principles are radiation, repetition, balance, depth, rhythm, focal area or center of interest, space, proportion, harmony, and unity.

An advanced designer intrinsically applies basic principles to floral art. Every designer has heard the saying, "Once you know the principles of floral design, you can break them." Must a designer break principles in order to create an advanced, unique

Advanced Floral Design

design? Most likely the answer is no. However, expanding, accentuating, and focusing on these universal guidelines should be considered. When incorporated into floral art, these principles provide insight that leads to infinite possibilities of creative expression.

Proportion

Proportion is a ratio of the comparative relationship between items or elements of a design as it pertains to size, shape, quantity, parts, or dimensions of that design.

In floral design, proportion usually refers to the height of the flowers in relation to the container. Traditional design often dictates that the placement of the first main flower in a design be at least one and one-half to two times the width or height of the container, whichever length is greater. One can often identify a beginner's design work by the shortness of the arrangement. However, proportion is more than a quick rule of thumb. Proportion refers to the size relationship within an entire design. This principle remains the same whether one is observing architecture of a building, a swimming pool, or a floral composition.

In advanced design, the proportion often exceeds the one and one-half measure, and it may be expanded to three and one-half, four, or even five times the height or width of the container. The height is balanced by tension, which in this instance is the placement of material, such as rock, pods, or moss, near the base.

To gain additional insight into the principle of proportion, refer to pages 69 through 71 in this chapter and study the Golden Mean and Fibonnaci principles.

Radiation

Radiation refers to dissemination from a central point. It may be expressed by plant material placed in a rhythmic sequence originating from a central point.

Beginning floral arrangements are often designed with stems radiating from a center. In contrast, an advanced design might have radiating stems and parallel stems all within the same design. *(See Figure 3.1.)* It is important in such a design to keep parallel and radiating lines separate and distinct. In this way, each placement adds a dimension to the composition.

Designers should remember that radiating lines emerge from a specific point; they may then spread outward. Parallel lines

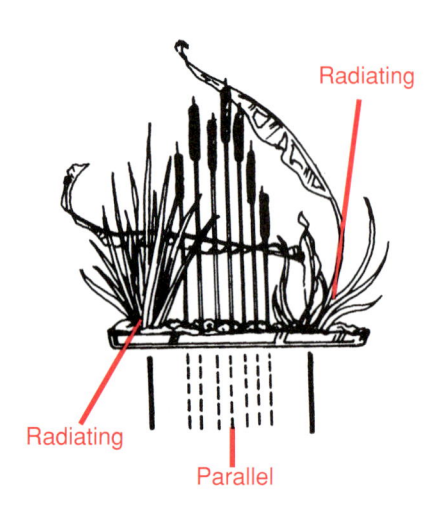

Figure 3.1 Advanced Design with both Radiating and Parallel Stems

Expanding the Principles and Elements of Design

Figure 3.2 Repetition within a Biedermeier Arrangement

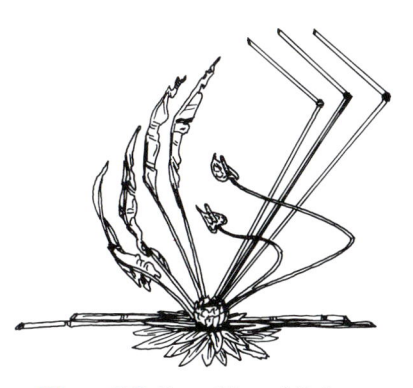

Figure 3.3 Repetition of Foliage

Figure 3.4 Repetition of Foliage on Container (Leafwork) to Create Texture and Form

have separate binding points emerging from the baseline of a container or an imaginary horizontal line just above the lip of the container, where the floral foam would most likely be placed.

There is also spiral radiation or lines that radiate outward in a spiralling motion, such as a nautilus shell. A floral example of spiral radiation is the repetitive placement of ti leaves, spiralling from a central origin to form a line within the design.

Repetition

Repetition is the process of repeating material within a design to give it emphasis and provide unity. It also serves to connect the design to another design or to an environment. This may be achieved through a variety of applications, such as repetition of line, forms, objects, textures, colors, and patterns.

Repetitious use of materials in advanced design may be seen in a Biedermeier arrangement. A Biedermeier is characterized by concentric rings of flowers and foliage. Each ring consisting of a specific flower is repeated. The repeated circular placement of specific flowers gives Biedermeier arrangements a unique appearance. *(See Figure 3.2.)*

Other examples of advanced repetition are the techniques of sequencing and shadowing. Sequencing is the process of placing like materials in a gradual or progressive pattern, often outlining an arrangement or dramatizing a form. In contrast, shadowing creates a three-dimensional effect by the lower placement of one material so that it emphasizes the primary material giving it depth. *(See Figure 3.3.)*

Another example of advanced repetition is layering, or more specifically, leafwork. Leafwork is a larger form of layering and is the process of repeating foliage by precisely layering one type on top of another, always covering the stem ends. As stated above, leafwork is used on a large scale to create large areas of texture, which will enhance an existing form *(see Figure 3.4)*.

Balance

Balance is the visual and physical stability of a floral design. If the observer's center of focus can move to the various components of a design without abrupt interruption, the design is most likely in balance. On the other hand, if a design is out of balance, it might appear to be leaning, top heavy, or lopsided. It might give the viewer an uncomfortable or uneasy feeling. For example, if carnations are placed only to one side of an arrangement and there is nothing but baby's breath on the other, the design will most likely appear to be leaning in the direction of the carnations.

There are four types of visual balance that advanced designers should consider when initiating a floral design: symmetrical, asymmetrical, radial, and open balance.

Symmetrical balance is achieved when both sides of a composition share the same visual weight. This balance tends to be formal and have a man-made appearance. **(See Figure 3.5a.)** Symmetry can be observed in nature by dividing a chrysanthemum in two sections. The designer will find that each half is a mirror image of the other. This symmetry, or mirror image, may be true of an arrangement if both halves are visually equal.

Asymmetrical balance can be noted when an arrangement is balanced without the two halves being equal. Asymmetry appears informal, yet active and vigorous, often giving the feeling of spontaneity. This balance often appears in unaltered nature. A running stream, grassy meadow, or grove of trees can seem asymmetrical. **(See Figures 3.5a and 3.5b.)**

In floral design, an asymmetrical triangular arrangement is characterized by the placement of a vertical line bisected by a diagonal line. If the designer draws a line from each point of these lines, the outline forms a scalene triangle. Understanding the scalene triangle may assist designers in combining plant material, such as branches, pods, and seeds, or in combining smaller arrangements to achieve an asymmetrical composite design.

Radial balance can be identified by noting whether all stems appear to radiate from a central point. Visualizing the opening of a fan illustrates the noticeable lack of balance that occurs when any one of the fan blades is dislodged and fails to meet at the expected point of connection.

Open balance occurs when specific principles of symmetrical, asymmetrical, and radiating balance do not apply. Instead, integration of these principles occurs, promoting balance from within the structure of the design. This concept can be illustrated by using parallel lines in a rectangular form and radiating lines originating from the same focus. **(See Figure 3.1 on page 64.)**

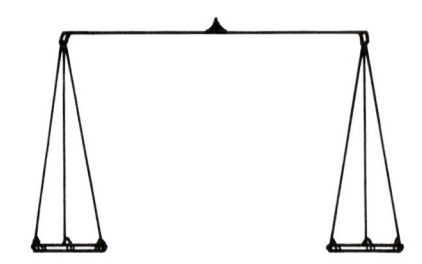

Figure 3.5 Symmetrical Balance

Figure 3.5b Symmetrical Balance

Depth

In the broad sense, depth is accomplished through placement of plant material on different levels. Skillful use of depth adds intensity to a floral design. Depth can be achieved by placing

Notes

materials on different levels in the foam. Depth can also be the sheltering of a flower underneath foliage; however, the flower should continue to be visible. Placement of materials on the inside and outside of the arrangement and in the front and back of the arrangement creates a multidimensional design. For example, creating depth in a vegetative arrangement might be accomplished by placing a larger grouping of plant material toward the back and a shorter, denser grouping in the foreground. The area in between could be left open so that the lines of both will be apparent.

Depth should be a component in every design. Intentional use of depth opens the view and enables the intricacy and uniqueness of a design to be fully appreciated. As with a three-dimensional movie, the design acquires qualities that make it look as if it is coming to life.

Rhythm

Rhythm allows the eye to move from one place to another within a floral composition. Such movement is facilitated by repeating textures, forms, colors, and lines. Repetition of curves and planes or sequenced spacing of flowers and foliage unite the design, coaxing the eye to move freely.

To visualize rhythm, the designer might study the movement of a piece of curly willow. The curving, twisted line, which begins at the thickest part of the stem and keeps the eye moving through the tip, is rhythm in motion. Any abrupt interruption to the rhythmic flow, such as severing the branch, would pull the focus to the severed section and interrupt the rhythmic flow.

Focal Area/Dominance/Center of Interest

The focal area or center of interest is the point to which the eye is first attracted. The focal area in a basic design is usually just over the tip of the container near the center of the design. In contrast, contemporary styles of design often feature several points of interest rather than a single focal area. For example, a vegetative design might have three or four areas of interest. Because there are several points for the eye to travel to, these areas are not as clearly defined as in basic design styles. Instead, the multiple centers of interest may be created by the placement of line grouping and a textured base. Color and form can be used to create attention.

Unity

Notes

Unity is created when components of an arrangement are tied together to produce harmonious continuity. Traditionally, it was thought that to achieve unity, plant material must be blended throughout a design. However, in European style arrangements, where flowers and foliage are grouped, clustered, pavéd, terraced, and layered, this concept is an expanded, advanced perspective of unity.

A beginning designer should observe a beautiful garden style arrangement. Unity is present if the garden arrangement appears complete and joined together. If there is a lack of unity, the arrangement might appear disjointed or separate. Upon closer examination, the advanced designer will see very distinct groups, such as groupings of irises or cattails. In addition, there might be three or four different groupings or clusterings of flowers and foliage.

Continuity might possibly be achieved by using mass or foliage-type ground cover to connect the various parts. As a result, balance will occur as groups on one side of the design are stabilized by groups on the other side. Identical material need not be repeated throughout the design, but equal distribution of form, line, and texture should enhance overall unity.

Space

Space is the three-dimensional area in which a design exists. For example, the vertical and horizontal line, together with the front and the back, comprise the outline of a symmetrical arrangement. Turning space into interesting patterns is a basic function of floral design. Empty portions of designs are termed as voids or negative space. Space where plant material is placed is termed positive space. The negative space is just as important as the positive, because these empty areas add interest and distinctiveness to designs. For example, for a wreath to have impact, it must have a voided area in the center. If one were to fill the voided area, the wreath could lose its form. Another example of space is the distance between the parts of design. In an advanced style design, the distance can be more dramatic, allowing the lines, forms, and textures to be more defined.

The space between flowers can either narrow the focus or expand the perspective of the design. For example, in a formal linear arrangement, tight, close placement in the focal area draws the eye inward, while broad spacing in the vertical area pulls the eye upward.

Expanding the Principles and Elements of Design

Major:
Height of Design = 1.6

Minor:
Vase = 1

The Golden Mean
a = 1
b = 1.6

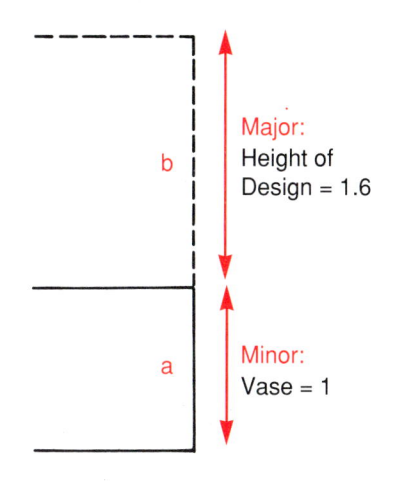

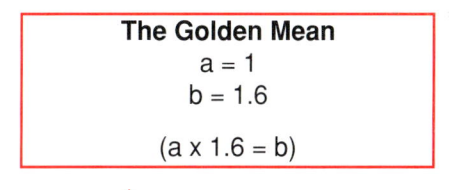

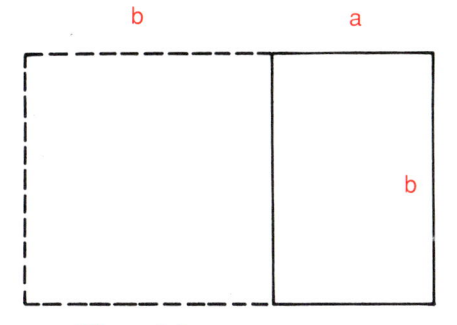

(a x 1.6 = b)

Figure 3.6 The Golden Mean

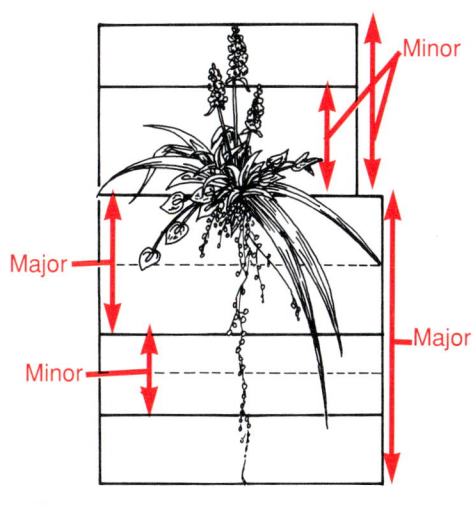

Figure 3.7 The Golden Mean Applied to a Bridal Bouquet

Harmony

A harmonious relationship between the components of a design can be achieved through the careful blending of textures, shapes, plant materials, and colors. This will promote a satisfying relationship between the materials and the purpose of the arrangement. While this is not to imply a limit on sizes, colors, textures, or materials, a pleasing, logical combination of parts and elements should be sought. For example, the use of long-lasting, tropical flowers with varying forms and differing, brilliant colors should be blended to clarify, not confuse, the design. An arrangement of pink heliconias, pink anthuriums, and pink protea combined with tropical foliage creates an exotic flavor. Pine cones would not blend effectively into the setting of a tropical mood. The accessories and container used should also be considered when constructing a design. In addition, combining flowers of short vase life with those known to have a long vase life will result in an imbalance shortly after the design is completed.

As in a song, harmony includes several differing parts. Sung separately, the lines may sound pleasant. However, if the parts are sung together, each line complements the other, which, in turn, maximizes the potential of the whole song.

The Golden Mean

The Golden Mean, often termed the golden cut or golden section, was formulated by a mathematician named Euclid, who lived in Alexandria around 300 B.C. As early philosophers did, Euclid sought to find a geometric law in art. Art and beauty were harmonious, and harmony came from proportions; therefore, the proportions must be fixed.

The formula for the gold section is to cut a finite line so that the shorter part is to the longer part what the longer part is to the whole. *(See Figure 3.6.)* The resulting proportion is about 1 to 1.6, which is roughly the ratio of 5 to 8, 8 to 13, or 21 to 34. Many plants grow according to this constructional principle of proportion. It seems to provide an economical use of space, one which artists recognized in nature long before its existence could be scientifically proven. (Webb, 198)

When constructing a wedding bouquet, one can find the major and minor proportions; the length of primary, secondary, and tertiary flower placement; and the focal area by using this principle. *(See Figure 3.7.)*

To further use this principle in floral design, consider the following problem.

If a branch is 36 inches tall, what size container would be proportionate to the branch?

Solution:

                Branch X Mean = Container
                36 inches ÷ 1.6 = 22.5
                  Major   Minor

Dividing 36 inches by 1.6 equals 22.5 inches, which will be the height of the container. The largest section after division is termed the major, and the smaller section is the minor.

One can also determine how tall a branch should be by changing the formula. For example:

            22.5 inches X 1.6 = 35 inches
      Container X Mean = Height of Primary Branch

Secondary and tertiary placements may also be found by continuing to divide the numbers by 1.6.

The Fibonnaci Principle, developed by Leonardo of Pisa (or Leornardo de Fibonnaci), is surprisingly similar in the number sequence for obtaining proportion. Fibonnaci, an Italian mathematician who lived during the Middle Ages, discovered that the principle to a beautiful, mathematical relationship could be obtained by adding 1 + 1 = 2, 2 + 1 = 3, 3 + 2 = 5, 5 + 3 = 8, 8 + 5 = 13, 13 + 8 = 21, etc. The proportion became apparent by taking the sequential sum of each. For example, if the designer has a branch that is 21 inches tall, a pleasing secondary placement might be 13 inches, and a third 8 inches. The designer should note how surprisingly similar to the golden section this is.

To expand these principles, designers should remember that delicate stems used in a design do not usually factor into the formula. Additional tension in the form of texture or weight added to the focal area or container needs to be balanced by extra height in the design, resulting in a ratio of 3 to 1, 4 to 1, and 5 to 1. Leaves, mosses, and stones are examples of materials which might be used to create tension.

To achieve a pleasing design, the Fibonnaci Principle may also be used as numbers of flowers incorporated into a design. For instance, combining three irises, five cattails, and eight carnations can give a design asymmetrical balance. Balance of this type can be very pleasing because the design looks balanced but not controlled. It should appear to be natural.

Notes

Expanding the Principles and Elements of Design

Notes

The Golden Mean and Fibonnaci Principle are tangible examples of naturally occurring proportion. Designers should remember these are only guidelines and not hard and fast rules.

Elements of Design

Color, form, line, and texture comprise the elements of design. They are the physical characteristics of materials used in floral compositions. A designer must study the properties of each element in order to successfully combine them with the principles of design. This combination is the foundation of floral design.

Color

Color and color harmonies have been thoroughly discussed in the Redbook Florist Services *Basic Floral Design* textbook. Designers should review this information to ensure that the basic color theory is completely understood before continuing here. A color wheel is provided in the back of this book for reference.

Certain concepts of color should be considered when creating advanced floral designs. For example, color is affected by lighting, backgrounds, textures, plant material forms, container shapes, and surrounding colors. It is important to begin with a basic plan or idea and decide what mood one wishes to create. Is the effect to be stimulating or peaceful, active or quite, bright or subdued, dramatic or unobtrusive?

Color can establish a particular mood. Monochromatic or analogous colors often express a quiet, restful effect when strong intensities are avoided. Conversely, colors, such as yellow and violet or yellow, blue, and red, are more dramatic and stimulating. (Sparnon, 14)

In basic design, colors of specific floral varieties are often positioned throughout an arrangement. Advanced design is often distinguished by grouping flowers or clustering similar plant materials or objects together. An analogous color combination, which features colors that are next to each other on the color wheel, is often considered an advanced combination. For this combination to be successful, one must have the right tints, tones, and shades of colors. For example, burgundy carnations, reddish purple grapes, and purple liatris work well together because they contain similar tones within the various colors. On the other hand, if each of those flowers had a yellow cast, the combination might not be as pleasing. Grouping colors can add a dramatic effect to a design. Flowers and colors tend to have more impact when grouped.

Although meaning and impact of color and color combinations are affected by an individual's preferences and experiences, it is generally accepted that there are common psychological reactions to colors. For example, red excites and green has a quieting effect. An understanding of the potential of color to create specific impressions increases a designer's ability to manipulate color to promote a desired effect.

Form

Form is the three-dimensional, external shape of an object, such as a leaf, flower, or entire composition. At all times, advanced designers should be aware of their surroundings, finding geometric shape in everything. This will promote a better understanding of form, which will enable them to incorporate form into design work. Every floral design can be classified as a specific geometric form as described in Chapter 2 in this book. Understanding these basic forms will allow advanced designers to combine them with each other to create interest and uniqueness in floral design.

Line

A line is the visual path the eye follows to produce motion. Line is produced by the use of linear materials, such as stems, branches, or line flowers, or it is developed by the placement of material in sequence, creating a sense of direction. Many advanced designs feature strong lines. Often, several different types of opposing lines are used within the same design to create tension and interest. Advanced designers should possess a full understanding of the characteristics of line as described in Chapter 2.

Texture

Texture is the tactile quality of a surface: rough, coarse, fine, nubby, shiny, dull, or smooth. The texture of materials incorporated into a floral design can either unify or divide the composition.

Texture used in advanced design is often more adventurous than that used in traditional arrangements. Regardless, a good guideline for texture is to either use a complete blend or a definite contrast. An example of a textural blend is a collage of skeletonized leaves, dried roses, and papery hydrangea blossoms. These materials are then interwoven around a curly

Notes

Expanding the Principles and Elements of Design

<u>Notes</u>

willow branch and mounted on layered rice paper. Conversely, contrasted textures might be a twisted, dry strelitzia leaf in a low, flat lalique crystal bowl. The leaf may be placed to one side of the bowl with two paired off anthuriums rising from a central point out of the strelitzia. Crested cockscomb and reindeer moss might be added at the base to unify the design.

Texture, pattern, and color can determine weight in an arrangement. For example, a rough, tomentose (hairy) leaf appears heavier than a larger skeletonized leaf. Maiden hair is finer than oak leaves and variegated rubber plant leaves have more dominance than soft, gray, sickle-shaped eucalyptus foliage. By carefully observing a material or object, designers will learn to appreciate and understand tactile values and qualities. Through the senses of touch and sight, designers learn the strength of pine boughs, the delicacy of gardenias, the smoothness of flax, and the silkiness of bamboo or willow. (Sparnon, 18) By experimentation, designers may find inspiration as combinations of various textures create distinctive floral compositions.

The principles and elements of design are terms that man has attached to explain the beauty of his environment. Labels, such as depth, line, form, space, and balance, are used to provide a common language as designers attempt to reorganize a tangible environment into a spiritual experience.

The principles and elements of design are the framework upon which floral design is founded. Careful attention to these details allows each designer, through experimentation, to develop a unique style.

Advanced Floral Design

Notes, Photographs, Sketches, etc.

Expanding the Principles and Elements of Design

Notes, Photographs, Sketches, etc.

Purchasing and Handling Specialty Flowers and Foliage

Chapter 4

Proper floral care at the retail level is absolutely essential if the florist wants to supply the long-lasting products customers demand. The care actually starts prior to arrival by the purchase of superior quality products that have previously received proper care and continues from the moment a flower or foliage product enters the shop until the moment it leaves. To be effective at floral purchasing and handling, the florist must first have an understanding of flower structure, classification, and naming. He must then build on this foundation with the knowledge of how to meet the flower needs of water, food, healthy environment, and hygiene. This information should then be incorporated as an integral part of the training of every shop employee. The designer of advanced arrangements, in particular, should master this information.

A good florist understands and utilizes the basics of flower care and handling, and a true floral professional goes beyond the basics to combine skills and to incorporate them into real-life situations that arise in the shop. The floral professional also realizes the unique peculiarities of each flower and foliage and adapts care and handling procedures to meet these specific needs.

Flower care and handling does not have to be overwhelming. If care is incorporated into an organized daily schedule so that all flowers used in designs are properly treated and potentially long-lasting, the florist can benefit from an outstanding reputation and repeat sales, and the customer can benefit from long-lasting maximum flower enjoyment.

Purchasing

The success of a floral shop hinges on the owner's ability to purchase the proper quantities of quality products at a fair price.

There is more involved in purchasing perishable products than many florists realize. The freshness, quality, and price should all be carefully considered before products are purchased.

Purchasing is a combination of skills. In this chapter, many areas of purchasing are discussed that will assist florists in becoming skilled buyers of specialty flowers and foliage. Understanding and using the terms used by growers and wholesalers will assist a retail florist in making intelligent purchases. This section includes a discussion of factors that affect the manner in which perishable products are purchased with specific emphasis on specialty cut flower crops.

Supplier Options

A florist may have several different companies from which he or she can purchase fresh products. They may not all operate in the same manner, but they should provide florists with quality products at a competitive price. Following is a discussion of the five types of suppliers most commonly found in the United States.

Wholesaler

The wholesaler buys in bulk quantities, breaks bulk, and sorts shipments into smaller lots to distribute to retailers. Some advantages are that the wholesaler has access to the global marketplace and can offer a wide variety of products. Some wholesalers sell both perishable products and hardgoods, while others specialize in one or the other. Some wholesalers are also retail growers, while others offer fresh flowers but have limited quantities of green and blooming plants. Other advantages are that purchases can be made in small minimum quantities and large freight costs are not involved, although there are usually delivery charges. Many wholesalers also offer a route truck service. Normally, suppliers operate out of a central location in large cities.

Market

Many large cities have a central location where wholesalers, growers, and distributors are located under one roof. In other cities, the three groups are located in the same centrally-located business district. This gives a florist a chance to do what could be called one-stop shopping. In a market situation, a florist has a better opportunity to compare quality, price, and freshness. Additionally, the florist can more easily search for unique,

Notes

Purchasing and Handling Specialty Flowers and Foliage

Notes

specialty flowers in this buying environment. Each company has its own business policy that florists should abide by. Some market wholesalers will have only their basic product selection on the market, while their varietal crops are sold at other locations.

Route Supplier

A route supplier is an independent business person who buys from an importer or grower. This supplier drives a refrigerated truck and carries a selection of products a florist can buy. Most route suppliers accept standing and special orders. Their credit policies may differ from those of wholesalers. A florist should not confuse a route supplier with the route truck service which is provided by wholesalers to customers in outlying areas.

Grower or Importer

Large volume flower shops often purchase fresh products directly from growers or importers. Some smaller shops also buy direct in order to obtain the specialty flowers they desire. This allows them to eliminate the middleman (wholesaler), thus reducing flower costs and increasing variety and freshness. In order to purchase directly, however, the florist is usually required to purchase a large volume (often full cases of each product) and must also pay significant freight charges.

One of the most popular direct purchasing practices is that of mainland florists buying tropical products directly from Hawaiian growers. The growers will send overnight air shipments anywhere. Assorted or mixed quarter boxes are very popular with retail florists. Before purchasing retail, florists should investigate the practices and policies of various suppliers so they can make intelligent and cost-effective purchases.

Selecting a Supplier

A florist should be selective about from whom he purchases products. Most florists are serviced by several wholesalers or other suppliers. This gives them the opportunity to select each supplier's best product. One may have better carnations and another may have better chrysanthemums. A supplier should be cooperative and should display a knowledge of his customer base. Suppliers should possess a knowledge of a wide variety of flowers and foliage, as well as of procedures for caring for them.

A florist may gain valuable information through a few conversations with the owner or manager of a wholesale company. A florist should interview these people as to where they buy the fresh products they sell and how they are pre-treated before reaching the retail level. The florist should examine the facility to see how flowers are processed and how they look in the coolers. An owner might also talk to other owners or buyers who deal with a prospective supplier that they are investigating. Other florists will often provide valuable insights into the services and fresh products provided by the supplier on a regular basis. Following is a discussion of various things florists should consider when selecting suppliers.

Supplier Quality

The quality of the products being sold should be the first and most important factor considered when selecting a supplier. A floral shop's success is dependent on the quality of the products and services sold. A shop's customers are more likely to remember how long a bouquet of flowers lasted than what type of flowers were sent. A florist should base his selection of suppliers on the same criteria. The quality of the supplier is affected by the three factors discussed below. These factors will assist owners in deciding from whom they will purchase.

Buying Habits

The buying habits of a supplier can be identified by the product quality of the flowers and foliage offered by that company. A supplier should have regular shipments of products scheduled to arrive on the same day of the week, every week. A supplier who can meet the supply and demand of his customers is usually ordering correctly. However, it is also possible for a supplier to order too much product on a regular basis to ensure that ample product is available.

The rotation policy of a supplier can greatly affect the quality of flowers and foliage that a florist receives. Stock flowers should be almost sold out on the afternoon before a fresh shipment arrives. Flowers that remain from the previous shipment should be the first ones used. When paying full price, a florist might request that only the freshest products be sent to his shop. Older products might be purchased at a discount.

A florist should possess an understanding of the stages of development when considering the quality of flowers. This will protect him from purchasing products that were cut when they were too green, products that are too old, or products that were too mature when cut. The supplier should be able to turn over the

Notes

Purchasing and Handling Specialty Flowers and Foliage

Notes

stock purchased within 2 or 3 days to guarantee freshness. A florist should be aware of the rotation of products within a supplier's operation. An observant florist should be able to recognize particular rotation schedules when looking in suppliers' coolers.

Care and Handling Methods

The methods used when handling and caring for flowers differs at the wholesale level. Wholesalers should use floral preservatives and other treatments to assist in increasing the vase life of flowers. Suppliers are not responsible for fully conditioning flowers for the retailer's use. They are only supplying the basic requirements needed by flowers and foliage. Following is a list of questions a florist should ask when selecting a supplier.

- Does the supplier use floral preservative on a regular basis?

- Does the supplier use other special treatments on crops that will benefit from them, such as STS or a hydrating solution?

- Does the supplier use coolers that are kept at the appropriate temperatures for the flowers being stored in them? For example, special coolers are often used for orchids and tropicals.

- Are the flowers properly maintained? Are buckets and coolers cleaned and sanitized regularly?

- Does the supplier use proper tools when processing flowers and foliage?

- Does the supplier package the products so that they are not damaged in delivery or shipping?

After some investigating, a florist should be able to select a wholesaler who sells only quality flowers and foliage. A florist should continually monitor the activities and business practices of the suppliers he deals with to ensure that the quality level is consistently maintained.

Up-to-date Product Knowledge

A supplier should familiarize himself with new varieties of flowers and foliage and should begin keeping them in stock as they become available from growers. They should also stay abreast of new products and techniques being used in post-harvest care. If the supplier carries hardgoods, they should stock the products that are needed for proper flower care at the retail level.

The best way to judge a wholesaler's product knowledge is to ask for product by its botanical or varietal name. The supplier should also know what special treatments a product has received at the grower level. A florist can also investigate the seasonal selection of flowers offered by a supplier over an extended period of time. This will help determine whether or not he is aware of the seasonal trends in flowers and foliage.

Product Availability

Most suppliers attempt to offer a wide variety of flowers and foliage for shops to purchase. These products are usually received from a variety of growers, located in different regions and countries. Occasionally, weather conditions interrupt the normal availability of fresh products. Certain flowers and types of foliage are only available during specific seasons of the year. Florists should be familiar with these seasonal flowers and other crops that are affected by weather. A good supplier will assist a florist in obtaining information concerning the availability of such fresh products.

Wholesalers are frequently forced to predict how busy their customers are going to be, because each florist has not accepted the responsibility of ordering early. A florist should expect a supplier to stock the basic flowers, such as carnations, roses and chrysanthemums. A florist should not expect to find an extremely wide variety of seasonal and specialty flowers if he does not carry them in his shop on a regular basis. Florists who purchase seasonal and unusual flowers on a regular basis will find that suppliers will also carry them on a regular basis.

It is up to the florist to order specialty flowers early enough for the supplier to obtain them. It is also the florist's responsibility to order flowers for weddings or parties at least 1 or 2 weeks before they are needed. In the same respect, a florist should have placed the bulk of his holiday order with the supplier 1 month to 6 weeks prior to the holiday. Many suppliers frequently manage to obtain

Notes

Purchasing and Handling Specialty Flowers and Foliage

Notes

products regardless of when a florist calls; however, a florist should not expect this type of rush service on a regular basis.

Services Offered

Most suppliers offer a variety of services to assist retailers in purchasing products. Daily delivery service is usually available to local florists for a minimal charge. Supplier-operated route trucks and shipping services are also frequently offered to shops that are located in outlying areas. A florist should try to select a group of wholesalers that can service his shop on a daily basis.

Credit policies are another consideration florists should investigate. Florists should thoroughly understand and abide by the policies offered by a wholesaler. It is the florist's responsibility to account for sales in his shop and to secure the funds needed to pay for products purchased on credit. Some suppliers also accept major credit cards.

Rebate or incentive programs may be offered by a quality supplier. These programs involve the awarding of points or credits based on the dollar value of a florist's purchases. These points or credits are often redeemable for a variety of benefits, such as free products, travel, and other bonuses.

Return policies on flowers of poor quality or that are poorly developed is something that florists often do not think about until the situation arises. A reputable supplier will most likely refund money, replace products, or credit a florist's account if inferior products are delivered. A florist should contact the supplier immediately when a problem arises. The florist should not wait until it is convenient to report the poor quality of a product. Suppliers want and need to be able to determine if there is a problem with an entire shipment or if the quality problem was isolated to only a few bunches.

Written information might also be of service to florists. Newsletters, care and handling pamphlets, and fresh product booklets that relate to the various facets of floriculture are of the utmost importance. Literature that a florist can take back to his shop can be used to augment a shop's in-house educational program.

Some suppliers offer educational programs throughout the year. These programs may be given to support product lines that the supplier sells or as an educational service. Educational care and handling seminars are very beneficial programs which should be offered by suppliers. Informative design programs will assist florists in using seasonal or unusual flowers and foliage in a proper manner.

Price

Product price is a concern to every florist. The competition within the floral industry makes the cost of an item a vitally important factor in determining the profitability of a business. Wholesalers normally use a fair percentage markup across the board. Higher quality products usually command a higher price, unless there is an oversupply of a particular product on the market. Oversupply usually brings the wholesale price down so that the products can be sold quickly.

Florists should be cautious of wholesalers with extremely low flower prices. Flowers that are old or of poor quality are frequently sold cheaply. These are of the grade and quality purchased by street vendors. Familiarity with the grading systems used by growers will help prevent a florist from purchasing products of a low grade.

Industry Knowledge

A well-rounded supplier should have an understanding of the entire floral industry, from grower to retailer, and he might subscribe to a variety of publications to gain an overview of the entire industry. Educational classes can also be beneficial to both retailers and suppliers. A supplier should visit the domestic growers that he deals with on a regular basis. The supplier might also attend conventions and classes that are geared toward the grower and wholesale portion of the industry. Most states have associations for growers and suppliers, which often prove beneficial to both groups. A series of informal conversations will assist a florist in determining how knowledgeable and interested a supplier is about the industry as a whole.

Factors to Consider when Purchasing Fresh Flowers and Foliage

There are several factors and terms that a florist should be aware of and understand. These factors affect the products that are available from wholesalers. Appropriate purchases can be made as long as the florist is aware of these outside considerations, such as where a product is grown and the seasonality of different crops. Following is a discussion of the important factors that can affect the purchasing of fresh flowers and foliage.

Notes

Purchasing and Handling Specialty Flowers and Foliage

Notes

Quality of the Product

Many factors can affect the quality of a product. Where a product is grown, how it is shipped and stored, and what stage of development it is harvested in are some of the main factors that should be investigated. The following factors are frequently associated with flower quality problems. Some terms that a florist should be familiar with are also discussed below.

Stage of Development

Every flower has a specific point during its development when it should be harvested for best performance. Flowers that are cut too early do not develop properly. Flowers that are cut too far into the development stage will have a shorter vase life. A florist should have an understanding of the stages of development as they apply to different flowers. Following are some of the terms that are used to describe the way a flower develops and eventually opens.

- Bullhead - This is a term that refers to a growth characteristic most commonly found in older varieties of roses. The blossom begins to open but does so in a fuller, flat fashion because the inner petals have not developed. This type of flower has overlapping petals in the center of the bloom. Normally, the outer petals will open to reveal this ball-shaped center of interlocked and overlapped petals.

- Bullet - A bullet is a rose that has been harvested too early in its development. It will remain in a tight ball instead of opening properly.

- Disbud - Disbudding is a process performed by the grower which involves removing all side bud shoots from each main stem. This allows the main bloom to receive the plant's concentrated energies. This normally results in single-flowered stems with one main large terminal. The remaining flower may be called a disbud. For example, disbud chrysanthemums, which usually refer to single-flowered stems with medium-sized flowers, are smaller than standard or football chrysanthemums (although the standards are also produced by disbudding).

- Cull - This is the name for the process of removing inferior or dying flowers during grading after harvest or during the daily maintenance of flower displays. A cull is a lesser quality flower, perhaps damaged, smaller, or deformed.

Previous Care and Handling

Some growers pre-treat flowers to extend their vase life. A grower may pre-treat flowers with an ethylene-reduction treatment, such as STS, to protect them from ethylene gas damage or with another chemical to prevent leaf yellowing, moisture loss, and other types of deterioration which frequently occur during shipping. These flowers are usually of better quality, and they arrive at the floral shop a short time after being harvested. A florist should be aware of any pre-treatment that a flower receives so that it will not be treated again. Some flowers may be held in cold storage for too long. These flowers may take up water and appear to be fresh; however, their vase life is a great deal shorter than may be expected. Sometimes, it is difficult to determine if this is the case until the flowers have been in the shop for 1 or 2 days.

Most wholesalers are not prepared to fully condition flowers that are shipped to their location. They should care for the flowers in a manner that will assist in promoting longer vase life. A florist should inspect the flowers for signs of aging before purchasing them. Yellow foliage and transparent or slimy foliage below the water line are indicators that flowers have been in storage for an extended period of time.

Where the Product is Grown

Flowers and foliage are grown and shipped all over the world. Each grower has different climates and growing procedures that he must deal with. Some regions and countries can only grow field crops from late spring to early fall. Meanwhile others can produce year round. Other areas grow the majority of their flowers in greenhouses. Advanced horticultural technology has assisted many flower-producing countries in producing quality flowers and foliage. Following are some points regarding production location which should be considered when buying fresh flowers and foliage.

Notes

Purchasing and Handling Specialty Flowers and Foliage

Notes

Domestically-grown Products

Products that are grown domestically are grown under controlled conditions in greenhouses or outside as field crops. Florists should realize that shipping time for domestically-grown fresh product can be shorter than the time needed to ship flowers from other countries. Florists should also understand domestic pricing systems because the free enterprise system is internationally used.

Internationally-grown Products

The United States imports a large amount of flowers from around the world. A florist should be aware of the different areas of the world that produce flowers. Crops that are grown internationally are also grown inside greenhouses and in fields. The factors that most affect imported fresh products are labor costs and currency exchange rates. Developing third world countries have very inexpensive labor forces. This allows them to produce products less expensively. On the other hand, the exchange rate between foreign currency and the United States dollar can cause the price of foreign fresh products to rise or fall. Both of these factors could create an inconsistency in price. Some countries also receive governmental subsidies, which allow them to sell their products for lower prices. In many countries, highly advanced production techniques are used, and this results in products of excellent quality.

Greenhouse-grown Crops

Crops grown within a controlled environment usually produce products of higher quality. All watering and fertilizing is strictly monitored to produce the best yield possible. Flowers need a specific amount of light to develop properly. Available sunlight hours is the only uncontrollable factor that the grower normally has to deal with; however, some growers have installed special lights to assist with this problem. Many seasonal flowers are available year round, because they are grown in greenhouses where atmospheric conditions are controlled to recreate specific seasonal climates. Crops native to certain geographical regions can also be grown in controlled greenhouses. This allows them to be produced outside their native area. The specialized care that greenhouse crops receive sometimes causes their price to be higher than that of crops grown in fields.

Field-grown Crops

Flowers grown in the field are normally available in great abundance during the warmer months of the year. Annual and perennial crops are grown in California, Mexico, and other regions of Central and South America. These areas can usually produce fresh products year round, while other producing countries can only grow field crops during part of the year.

Field flowers are at the mercy of the weather. The winter months can prove to be very hard on crops, such as baby's breath and statice. The most damaging weather conditions are frost, heavy rain, strong wind, or extreme drought.

Summer annuals are the most common field-grown crops available from California. These crops include marguerite daisies, marigolds, zinnias, asters, and other colorful flowers. The Central and South American countries produce a variety of flowers in their fields with some protection, such as pompons, roses, carnations, and alstroemeria. Countries in West Africa are becoming known for growing crops of ornamental pineapples, heliconia, ginger, and orchids, while other African countries are growing crops of protea, anthuriums, and amaryllis.

A florist can purchase flowers and foliage from a worldwide selection. Understanding where a flower or foliage crop is grown can assist one in making intelligent purchases. A florist can purchase quality products, regardless of where they are grown, by checking for their hallmarks of quality.

Price

There are many factors that affect the price a supplier charges for his product. Supply and demand set the climate of the marketplace for both domestic and international fresh products. The value of the dollar also has an effect on the price of all crops that are grown internationally. The following factors also affect the wholesale prices one pays for flowers.

Availability/Seasonality

All flowers have a time of year when they are in production and are available on the market. This is referred to as the availability period. Many flowers, however, are available on a year-round basis, but they still have a peak season or seasonality. Their price may be higher at the beginning and end of the season. During the peak cutting time, the price drops. In other words, most

Purchasing and Handling Specialty Flowers and Foliage

Notes

flowers have peak cutting periods and periods of low production that affect their prices.

Suppliers' Buying Habits

The manner in which suppliers purchase their bulk product shipments can affect the price retailers must pay for fresh product. Suppliers place standing orders for products that are staples in their region. This practice assures suppliers that certain amounts of fresh products will be available for sale year round. Placing standing orders with growers also assists suppliers in obtaining the extra fresh flowers needed to service retailers during holidays. Florists should support their fresh product suppliers to ensure that a steady supply of products will be available. A florist should realize that saving a few pennies occasionally by continually switching suppliers can cost a great deal of money in the long run or when they need products most. The retailer should investigate ways of assisting suppliers in assuring that quality products are available at a good price throughout the year.

Standing Orders

A florist should be able to project the needs of his shop. A standing order allows the florist to purchase the same quantity and type of flower for the same price on a regular basis for an extended period of time. For example, a florist might purchase a quarter pack of carnations twice a week year round. The pack would have the same color mix in every shipment. Prices for flowers purchased according to standing orders are typically lower than normal, because they are usually purchased consistently and in specific quantities, which reduces the sales risk factor, as well as the processing labor, for the supplier. A good supplier will work closely with a florist to establish a profitable standing order plan customized for a specific shop's needs.

Discounts

A florist can often negotiate the price he pays for a product that is bought in quantity. A purchasing schedule that is set up prior to the need can also provide one with a negotiating tool. Following are explanations of three types of discounts that are available from most wholesalers. A florist should find out what discount methods are practiced by the wholesalers with which he deals.

Quantity Discounts

Many times a supplier can discount the prices of flowers and foliage when they are purchased in bulk or large quantities. A florist who buys a case of sprengeri will normally pay less per bunch than someone who buys only a few bunches. A florist should investigate the quantity discounts offered by different suppliers.

Supplier-generated Discounts

A supplier may run sales on a product that has been overstocked. A grower may ask a supplier to take more of a product than he needs because there is an abundant supply available. In this case, the grower will reduce the price of the product to the supplier.

In either case, the supplier will probably sell the product to the retailer for a reduced price. A florist may also choose to pass the savings on to the consumer via a cash-and-carry special. Summer is the season when suppliers frequently hold sales.

Cash Discounts

Some suppliers may offer discounts to florists who pay cash when flowers are purchased. These discounts can range from 2 percent to 5 percent. Occasionally, these discounts are extended to florists who pay their bill in full on a weekly basis. Checks are usually accepted as cash payments. Cash discounts can provide a better cash flow situation for a supplier, as well as a better purchasing option for the florist.

Shop-related Factors to Consider when Purchasing Fresh Flowers and Foliage

A florist should be in business to make money. When too little or too much of a product is purchased, the profitability of the business is affected. The following considerations might assist a florist in becoming a more efficient buyer. For the most part, these are factors over which a florist has total control.

Notes

Purchasing and Handling Specialty Flowers and Foliage

Notes

Shop Budget

Every shop should have an overall budget that includes a separate budget for the purchase of fresh products for everyday use. A second budget should be developed that will allow a florist to determine the appropriate amount that should be spent for special events such as weddings and parties. Both of these budgets should include a percentage for shrinkage (flowers bought but not sold before perishing). Purchasing perishable products successfully hinges on the budget one is willing to operate under. The following information can assist one in purchasing wisely.

Everyday Budgeting

Projecting the daily needs of a flower shop can be difficult. A florist needs to carry enough products to meet his or her clients' needs. Accurate records of purchases and sales made everyday should be kept. An owner/manager can then refer to these records for a specific period from the past year. A comparison of the previous year's figures to those of the current year should give the owner/manager an idea of the amount of a product that should be purchased. The owner/manager should look at the trends the shop's customer base is following as well. This comparison and observation of trends should assist a florist in determining what percentage of the allotted budget can be spent for fresh flowers and foliage.

A florist should also look to see how much of a product is left from previous purchases. If a florist bought three bunches of alstroemeria on the previous day, but has not sold them yet, then he should not purchase any more until the others have been sold or are no longer useable.

Special Events Budgeting

A florist should calculate a budget for all special events, such as parties and weddings. First, the florist should calculate an event's wholesale budget by arriving at the percentage of cost of goods. For example, if a florist sells an $800.00 party and he uses a 25 percent divisional markup, his budget would be 25 percent of $800.00, or $200.00. The $200.00 figure must include all perishable products and hardgoods that will be used to complete the party. Proper planning for special orders will help ensure a smoother, more profitable outcome.

Inventory Control/Stock Rotation

A florist should set up a stock rotation plan to control the inventory of fresh flowers and foliage. A dating or coding system will help assure that flowers are used as they were purchased, rather than through indiscriminate selection. Flowers should be disposed of and replaced with fresh products when they have not sold in their allotted time period. The idea is to use the oldest flowers before using the freshest ones. A florist should totally rotate through purchased stock two or three times each week.

Storage Space Availability

Some shops have limited cooler space. It is best to limit the numbers of flowers that are purchased when this is the case, because most flowers should be refrigerated to achieve the longest vase life possible, especially roses, wilt-sensitive flowers, and short-lived flowers. If a great deal of extra product is needed to fill orders for holidays or special events, the florist might consider renting a refrigerated truck so that all of the products and arrangements can be stored under the proper conditions.

Customer-related Considerations

When purchasing flowers, a florist should buy the varieties that the customers want. A shop should introduce new products in small amounts so that a new market can be cultivated for the products. The quality of the flowers is also of the utmost importance. Research has shown that consumers prefer products that last 7 to 10 days. Many consumers judge the quality of the flowers they purchase solely on how long they last. The following factors should be considered when purchasing flowers and foliage. They actually work together instead of separately.

Target Market

A florist's target market is the segment of the population that the shop would like to serve. A florist needs to identify his target market and to gear his advertising, selling, and merchandising efforts to this segment. For example, the gray market, which is a mature market segment of people 55 years and older, tends to purchase traditional flowers and arrangements. The couples market tends to try new flower varieties and arrangements. A florist should purchase products to satisfy his customers' needs,

Notes

Purchasing and Handling Specialty Flowers and Foliage

Notes

as well as to educate them about new designs and flower varieties that are available.

Customers' Buying Habits

A florist should track the buying habits of his customers. The gathered information will prove whether or not a shop has targeted the right market. There are three sources of information that a florist should use to track consumers' buying habits: dump sheets, compiled sales and price point information, and suppliers' invoices. A shop's dump sheet informs the owner of what fresh products did not sell. The compiled sales and price point information, generated daily, identifies the fresh products that were sold. The suppliers' invoices remind the owner of the fresh products that were purchased. If an owner compares the information from these three sources during the same time period, he will be able to compile a list of products that are popular in his market.

This type of comparison should be made frequently, approximately twice a month. The results of each comparison should be recorded so that a pattern can be established. Information like this will not only assist a florist in making wiser purchases, it can also assist in improving a shop's profit margin, inventory practices, and stock rotation.

Over the course of time, an owner should reevaluate the buying habits of his shop's customer base. He or she may find that there has been a change in the customers. The florist could find that the original market has relocated or has been transformed into a totally different market. Knowing what customers want and educating them as to what is available will keep the business in line with its growth projections.

Care and Handling

Care and handling procedures involve the watchful attention and focused activities directed toward the perishability factor (limited life) of fresh flowers and foliage. Proper care and handling is necessary for the survival and success of any floral business. In selling advanced floral designs, florists must deal with a greater number of varieties of flowers and foliage that are being produced in an expanding global marketplace and shipped through an increasingly complex distribution system. Flowers must survive the shipping journey, and care and handling procedures are an essential part of this survival.

Advanced Floral Design

Proper care and handling may be referred to in some texts as Chain of Life procedures. This refers to a philosophy and program based on the concept of focusing on proper care for flowers through every link or step in the chain of distribution (grower-wholesaler-retailer). As a result, the maximum vase life of fresh products can be enjoyed by the consumers who purchase them. In actuality, care and handling is a way of thinking, in addition to life-prolonging actions. The true floral expert should develop a strong understanding of flower needs and should make this a part of his daily thinking. These thoughts should then be transferred into actions to meet the needs of the products. This section discusses basic care and handling procedures, as well as specific pointers for maximizing the life span of specialty flowers and foliages. For a more in-depth discussion of flower care and handling, refer to Redbook Florist Services' book *Purchasing and Handling Fresh Flowers and Foliage*.

Basic Needs for Fresh Cut Flowers and Foliage

A designer must always remember that he or she is working with living products, and just like humans, animals, and other living things, flowers have basic needs for healthy, long lives. Cut flowers and foliage have special requirements because they have been cut off from the mother plant and the ideal conditions found in the growing environment. Their needs must be filled in other ways for the flowers to continue living after being placed in bouquets, arrangements, and other designs. An understanding of these requirements is an important foundation for proper floral care. Table 1 on page 95 reviews the basic needs of flowers.

Flower Deterioration

Designers and customers are greatly frustrated when maximum flower life is not realized. It is particularly frustrating when a typically long-lasting flower, such as alstroemeria, lasts only a few days. The most common cause for early deterioration and short life is a failure to meet flower needs. Sometimes this failure occurs at several points along the distribution chain, and sometimes it happens at only one point, such as the retail flower shop. Floral designers must learn to recognize and prevent these problems. The causes of early flower deterioration are reviewed in Table 2 on page 96.

Notes

Purchasing and Handling Specialty Flowers and Foliage

Notes

TABLE 1

BASIC FLOWER NEEDS

Flower Needs	Explanation of Needs
Water	Flowers are composed of more than 90 percent water! Water is needed to carry dissolved nutrients through the network of tiny vessels, up the stem and leaves, to the flower. Water keeps the flower firm, fresh, and alive after it has been separated from its mother plant.
Food	Flowers need an energy source (food) to carry on life-giving processes. When cut from the mother plant, a flower loses its source of nourishment; therefore, food must be provided by the florist.
Healthy Environment	Flowers need air to support life-giving processes. Air must be clean and fresh because pollutants, including gases, such as ethylene, can inhibit life and cause damage. Temperatures also affect life-giving processes. Warm temperatures, such as those during the growth process, encourage growth and development. Cool temperatures, such as those in a cooler, slow down development and help flowers live longer. Excessively hot or cold temperatures will cause damage.
Hygiene (Sanitation)	Clean water, environment, and tools help prevent the growth of stem-clogging, disease-causing organisms that inhibit flower life.

Care and Handling Steps

The key to delaying deterioration and prolonging flower life is meeting flower needs. This involves a series of life-prolonging procedures which incorporate specific tools and techniques. Sometimes these life-prolonging procedures are called the Chain of Life, because each person in the flower distribution chain (grower-wholesaler-retailer-consumer) must follow these steps before maximum flower life can be realized. Retail florists are a very important link in this chain because they help the flowers recover from shipping and prepare them for the enjoyment of the consumer. Floral designers should maintain a positive attitude

Advanced Floral Design

TABLE 2

CAUSES OF EARLY FLOWER DETERIORATION

Reason for Early Deterioration and Short Life	Explanation	Remedy: Steps to Preventing Early Deterioration Problems
Inability of stems to absorb water	Stems are dirty and clogged with debris, soil particles, or bacteria; flower stems probably were not cut during processing; dirty or improper solutions may have been used.	Maximize water uptake by re-cutting stems; using warm water; lowering solution pH with preservative or other special treatment; using clean water; maintaining clean buckets; using proper conditioning techniques.
Excessive water loss	Flowers were not unpacked quickly enough, were stored dry too long, and/or were exposed to drafts, high temperatures, or low humidity.	Minimize water loss by unpacking shipments immediately; using proper refrigeration; using proper packaging; using finishing sprays and dips.
Not enough food	The improper type or amount of flower food (preservative) is used, or it is not used at all.	Ensure proper nutrition by using flower preservative in all handling and design situations; measuring preservative correctly by following manufacturer's directions.
Disease and microorganism development	Rigid pest and disease control is not used during the growing process and/or flowers are kept in unsanitary or improper conditions (wet and warm) during shipping or holding.	Prevent development by using proper steps and products to clean and sanitize; following a strict, frequent sanitation schedule.
Ethylene gas	Sensitive flowers are not treated properly or are not treated at all with an ethylene-reduction treatment, and/or they are exposed to high temperatures, poor ventilation, poor sanitation, or ethylene-producing machinery or crops.	Prevent ethylene damage by using strict sanitation; avoid the storage of fruit or any other food in the cooler; removing flowers from sleeves and boxes upon arrival; avoiding putting flowers in loading areas where they are exposed to engine exhaust; purchasing only ethylene-sensitive flowers that are pre-treated with an ethylene reduction treatment like STS or treating them in the shop.
Improper environmental conditions	Flowers are poorly packaged and/or are shipped, held, or displayed in improper conditions, such as warm temperatures, low humidity, and poor ventilation (which can be found in trucks and coolers that are not made for floral use and in many home situations).	Keep flowers in proper environmental conditions during storage and display by using a floral cooler built to maintain the floral-specific conditions of 34 to 36 degrees Fahrenheit and 85 percent or higher relative humidity; avoiding the exposure of chilling-sensitive flowers to temperatures below 50 degrees Fahrenheit; using proper storage conditions and time for the cooler or other storage area; using proper packaging.

Purchasing and Handling Specialty Flowers and Foliage

Notes

and never assume that cut flowers will last only a few days, regardless of the care given them. The life-prolonging techniques described here are absolutely essential for all cut flowers, even those that are in the shop for a short period of time (1 to 2 days). Working to ensure maximum flower life can result in success that is twofold: minimal shrinkage and waste, and maximum customer enjoyment of floral purchases. Flowers that are long lasting may provide valuable advertising.

An overview or flow chart of the entire care and handling process, from arrival in the shop to purchase by the customer, is provided here. The overview shows how proper care and handling include a series of important steps that work together to promote long flower life. The overview is ideal for placing in flower shop workrooms for use by everyone involved in processing, handling, or designing flowers.

Care and Handling: Sequence of Events Overview

A. Prepare for arrival of flower shipment:

1. Make room in coolers by discarding old flowers and combining buckets of remaining flowers.

2. Sanitize buckets and fill them with a clean, warm, preservative solution that has been properly mixed.

B. Unpack and inspect flowers immediately upon their arrival:

1. Remove wilt-sensitive flowers first.

2. Place other flowers in a cooler if processing cannot be completed for 1 to 2 hours.

C. Prepare and process:

1. Prepare flowers that will be dry-stored.

   a. Keep them in wrappers or other special boxes.

   b. Place boxes in cool storage until needed.

2. Process flowers that will be stored in solution or used for display or design.

   a. Remove lower leaves.

Advanced Floral Design

 b. Ensure that stem ends are even.

 c. Cut the stems.

D. Pre-treat and condition:

 1. Pre-treat flowers that require special treatment for leaf-yellowing, stem clogging, wilt sensitivity, ethylene sensitivity, or other special problems.

 2. Condition flowers in floral preservative solution.

 a. Keep flowers moist in solution for at least 2 hours.

 b. Exceptions: Flowers that open quickly, such as tulips, or those that are open or are going to be stored in solution for a few days can be put directly in the cooler.

E. Place flowers in a floral cooler:

 1. Flowers that are stored dry should be placed in a cooler immediately after preparation.

 2. Observe other flowers and place them in coolers based on their stage of development and the manner in which they will be used.

 3. Label all buckets with a code that specifies arrival date.

F. Use flowers properly in design, display, and sales:

 1. When designing, remove only those flowers from the cooler that will be needed within a short period of time. Do not remove entire buckets or boxes of flowers.

 a. Soak floral foam bricks and bouquet holders in floral preservative solution, and add pre-mixed solution to vases and other containers.

 b. Use special dips and sealers for shatter-sensitive flowers.

Notes

Purchasing and Handling Specialty Flowers and Foliage

Notes

      c. Apply finishing spray to designs, if desired.

      d. Place finished designs back in a cooler.

  2. For display, label all buckets with proper names.

      a. Do not place too many flowers in a bucket.

      b. All buckets can be kept in the cooler, or selected ones may be placed prominently to attract impulse shoppers, then rotated into the cooler for 6 to 12 hours.

  3. At the time of a sale, package flowers to protect them from weather and damage. Include care information and floral preservative packet(s), and use water tubes, especially for wilt-sensitive flowers if they will be out of water for 2 hours or more (1 hour or more in hot weather).

G. Follow a strict sanitation schedule:

  1. Sanitize buckets, tools, and coolers regularly.

  2. Keep fruits, vegetables, and other food out of the cooler.

  3. Remove dying, diseased, and broken flowers, leaves, and other debris from the cooler on a daily basis.

H. Maintain flower storage and display regularly:

  1. Check store and cooler displays daily.

      a. Add preservative solution to arrangements.

      b. Make sure all flowers are placed in buckets so that all stems are in the solution.

  2. Re-cut stems every 2 to 3 days.

  3. Reorganize cooler stock weekly to prepare for upcoming flower shipments.

Advanced Floral Design

Specialty Cut Flower Techniques

All cut flowers need to be processed, conditioned, and environmentally controlled to promote long life. Certain situations arise in the shop, however, that require a special focus or technique that involves a combination of skills. Some of these techniques are highlighted below, along with examples of applicable situations.

Bud Opening

Bud opening involves steps that promote the opening of tight flowers that might have been harvested too soon or that come from a grower who normally harvests in the tight bud stage. There are advantages to bud-cutting or cutting tight, as long as it is not so tight that the flowers will not open. Advantages include less bruising in transit and longer vase life compared to flowers that are cut at the normal stage. The proper follow-up technique must be executed on arrival, however, to ensure success with these crops. The bud-opening technique described here encourages opening more quickly than regular care and handling procedures. It is meant to crack open tight flowers to a stage where they will open under normal care and handling conditions. Flowers that commonly arrive in the tight bud stage are carnations, miniature carnations, chrysanthemums, roses, gladioli, and gypsophila. Pictures of some tight bud flowers are shown in **Figures 4.1a and 4.1b**.

Bud opening techniques could be utilized in the following situations. For example, a florist may review a shipment of roses that are tight on Thursday and need them for a wedding on Saturday. In another case, tight gladioli may arrive on a particular day that are needed for funeral or church pieces the next day. Likewise, a last-minute holiday fill-in shipment of carnations may arrive tight and be needed the next day for design work.

One of the primary things that must be considered when using the bud-opening technique is time. It can take from several hours to 2 days or more for buds to open, depending on the flowers and environmental conditions. While the florist cannot always control the planning, he should determine whenever possible if time is needed for bud opening. This decision should be based on conversations with the wholesaler regarding flower stage, as well as on past experience with specific growers' products. Another consideration is sufficient room. Since bud-opening requires warm temperatures, there must be enough space in the shop for keeping extra buckets out of the cooler. The keys to bud-opening

Figure 4.1a Tight Bud Stage - Carnation

Figure 4.1b Tight Bud Stage - Rose

Purchasing and Handling Specialty Flowers and Foliage

are warm temperature, high humidity, and optimum solution uptake. The steps are explained next.

1. Process flowers by removing lower leaves and re-cutting stems under warm water. Stems can then be dipped in a stem-sanitizing solution. This will help remove stem-clogging dirt and bacteria from stems which encourages solution uptake and promotes faster bud opening.

2. Put flowers in a bud opening solution that is made by mixing twice the recommended rate of preservative with warm (100 to 110 degrees Fahrenheit) water. This may be called a 2 percent solution. (Additional manufacturer's directions may be given on the label.)

3. Place the bucket with flowers and solution in a warm, but not hot, location (approximately 68 to 70 degrees Fahrenheit). To speed up the process, flowers can be covered with a sheet of plastic as shown in **Figure 4.2**. This helps maintain higher temperature and humidity under the tent. The plastic should be taken off once or twice a day to allow for ventilation. In hot areas, flowers should be closely observed to ensure the temperature does not get too high under the tent.

4. This process usually takes 12 to 14 hours and sometimes longer. When the flowers start to open, the plastic can be removed, the flowers transferred to a preservative solution mixed at the normal rate, and placed in the cooler.

5. Note that regular care and handling procedures which encourage hydration, such as rose hydration treatments, may be sufficient for bud opening if the flowers are kept in warm temperatures until opening is started.

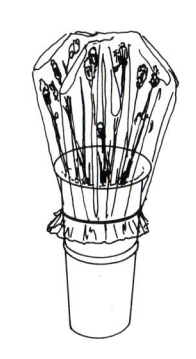

Figure 4.2 Tenting Buds

Holding at a Development Stage

Sometimes, the situation opposite to bud-opening arises: flowers have already opened to the stage needed so further opening is not desired. Regular care and handling is still important in order to encourage longevity, but additional steps are needed to delay further development. Flowers that commonly need to be retained at a certain stage are roses, tulips, daffodils, and anemones.

An example, of an applicable situation involves roses that arrive on Thursday and are not needed until Saturday for a wedding and are already at the right stage. In another case, tulips may arrive on Monday for use in Monday through Wednesday work and are already opening.

The florist can take a preliminary step in holding a flower at a particular stage of development if he or she knows that the flowers are arriving on a particular day and will not be used for 2 or 3 days, particularly in remote areas with less frequent deliveries. The step involves attempting to order a variety that is known to open slowly. There can be a tremendous difference in opening characteristics between cultivars of the same species. With roses, for example, the white cultivars Cascade and White Masterpiece and the red Samantha and Royalty take longer to open and maintain good form and color compared to some other varieties of the same colors. The same is true for tulip cultivars and other flowers. This step requires planning and interaction with the wholesaler but can be well worth the effort. In other cases, if flowers arrive and development-retention efforts are needed, the florist can follow the steps below. They key is cool temperatures.

1. Remove the flowers immediately from shipping boxes.

2. Process flowers immediately by removing lower leaves, re-cutting stems, and using stem dip (these life-prolonging steps are essential).

3. Place flowers in preservative solution. Preservative is still needed to prolong life. It may be helpful to mix this solution with cool or lukewarm water so that the heat of the water will not promote opening. Often, the flowers that are open the most have been kept in water, and they do not have the stem-clogging problems. However, if the flowers are dry and limp, warm water should be used.

4. Cool temperature is the key to delaying further opening. Unless the flowers are dry and limp (in which case they should remain out of the cooler 1 hour for uptake), they should be placed immediately into the cooler. Sleeves may be left on, particularly for tulips,

Notes

Purchasing and Handling Specialty Flowers and Foliage

Notes

but flowers need to be watched carefully so mold will not develop.

- This method does not apply to chill-sensitive flowers, that cannot be put into the cooler.

- If bulk products in boxes arrive in a fairly open stage and are not to be used for a few days, they may be stored dry in the cooler at 34 to 36 degrees Fahrenheit (unless they are wilt sensitive or have minimum storage ability). Boxes should first be opened and the products loosened to allow for air flow, then replaced and covered with a plastic liner and placed in the cooler.

Quick Revival

Quick revival can be likened to emergency steps that are used to revive humans. The flower "patient" needs stabilizing procedures and close observation, followed by techniques to promote continued recovery and a healthy, long life. Quick revival is a combination of previously discussed care and handling steps that help maximize water and food uptake and minimize water loss. It is different from typical conditioning, because it is a more intense application of procedures: processing is done more quickly, warmer temperatures are used, and all possible steps are taken to maximize water uptake (rather than one or two steps). Flowers that need to be revived quickly are those that arrive in a limp, wilted state or those that are observed in the shop in such a state. Wilt-sensitive flowers and/or flowers that have been dry shipped for long distances are likely candidates for these procedures.

The possibilities for using quick revival techniques range from one or two roses in a bucket that exhibit bent neck the day after arrival in the shop to flowers in a bucket where solution ran out or in a box that was dry stored for a prolonged period.

The key to quick revival is water - maximum uptake and minimum loss - along with the life-giving food source. The steps to take are listed below.

1. Remove stressed flowers from the shipping boxes, cooler, etc., immediately upon discovery.

2. Remove lower foliage. (Do not spend excessive time with this. For very leafy crops, such as roses, the remainder of the leaves can be removed after revival.)

3. Re-cut stems under water, using warm water.

4. For roses, place them in a warm, pH-lowering, hydrating solution of citric acid or a chemical with similar action for 30 to 60 minutes (this can also be used for chrysanthemums and other flowers according to label recommendations), and then transfer flowers to a preservative solution. For other flowers, dip stems in a stem-sanitizing solution; then, put them in warm preservative solution (plain water or water plus bleach will not be as beneficial). Even ethylene-sensitive flowers can be treated in this manner, with recovery being the key, and silver thiosulfate (STS) or other special treatment can be used after revitalization. For single stems of roses (such as those found with bent neck 1 or 2 days after arrival in the shop), the entire bloom, stem, and foliage can be submerged under water for approximately 20 minutes; then, the stems should be placed back into preservative solution.

5. Keep flowers in a warm (68 to 70 degrees Fahrenheit) and humid area. If the area is known to be dry, a sheet of plastic can be placed over the flowers. Flowers can be left here for 6 to 12 hours to encourage solution uptake and corresponding recovery. Roses may be placed in the cooler sooner if they show signs of recovery. (Conditioning roses in the cooler in the dark actually helps maximize uptake and reduce bent neck problems.)

6. After recovery, keep flowers in preservative solution and place them in the cooler.

Using Individual Flowers and Florets

Individual flowers or florets (part of a flower cluster) may be those that are cut from a blooming plant or from an individual cut flower inflorescence (cluster). While it is very important for the plant or main flower stem to be properly conditioned, it is also important to condition the individual flowers separately after cutting (particularly the florets), using some of the same techniques even when the plant or main stem has already been conditioned. Table 3 on page 105 lists flowers that are commonly used individually.

Notes

Purchasing and Handling Specialty Flowers and Foliage

Notes

TABLE 3
FLOWERS COMMONLY USED INDIVIDUALLY

Cut from Blooming Plants	Cut Flowers
Kalanchoe (a cluster or inflorescence)	Agapanthus
Cyclamen	Alstroemeria
Geranium	Bouvardia
Azalea	Miniature Carnation (individual flower)
	Chrysanthemum, pompon (individual flower)
	Delphinium
	Hyacinth
	Larkspur
	Nerine
	Spray Rose (individual flower)
	Stock
	Tuberose

The use of individual flowers and florets is most common in corsage and bouquet work for weddings and proms. However, they may also be used in other aspects of design.

When using individual flowers or florets, it is most important for designers to remember that the same techniques are used on individual flowers and florets as for regular cut flower stems, including the following.

1. Plan ahead. Individual florets should not be used immediately after they are cut. A sufficient conditioning time of several hours or overnight should be allowed before use.

2. Cut off the flower or floret desired with a sharp tool. The flower or floret can then be moved to a shallow pan of warm water and a piece of stem cut off under water.

3. Place stems in a warm preservative solution that is in a small vase or container that offers support. Short-stemmed florets can be floated in a shallow container of warm preservative solution.

4. After a few hours, place the flowers or florets in the cooler to finish the conditioning or hardening off process, except flowers from blooming plants or chilling-sensitive cut flowers. The container may even be placed in a bag to help retain moisture. It should be kept in a safe place in the cooler, such as an upper shelf, to prevent damage.

Using Flowers from the Yard and Garden

This technique involves cutting materials and handling them so that they have the longest vase life possible. Commonly, materials from outdoors are collected hurriedly, in the heat of the day, or without regard to care and handling. As a result, they frequently wilt and die prematurely. Planning and proper procedures can prevent this from happening. A few examples of materials harvested from the yard and garden for use in design include annual and perennial flowers, blooming shrubs, evergreens, cattails, and even garden fruits and vegetables.

The use of materials from the yard and garden can provide a casual, country garden look and add unique shapes and textures to designs. Unusual materials found in yards can be unique, one-of-a-kind pieces that are well-suited to some contemporary and naturalistic designs. The florist may be tempted to cut materials from fields and roadsides. However, this is not suggested because it can interfere with nature's balance and may be illegal.

The same techniques that apply to commercial floral products also apply to materials from the yard and garden, including the following.

1. Plan ahead. These materials should not be used immediately after being harvested. They need a conditioning time of several hours to overnight.

2. Just as other crops grown in fields or greenhouses, carbohydrate (food) levels are highest at the end of the day, so try to harvest products in the late afternoon or early evening.

3. Take a bucket of pre-mixed preservative solution out to the cutting area. Cut off materials with a sharp tool, and place them immediately into solution (do not hold them in the hands or lay them on the ground until all materials are collected). Actually, cutting the stems under water first, immediately after harvest, and then

Notes

Purchasing and Handling Specialty Flowers and Foliage

placing them in preservative solution is best. Fruits and vegetables can be gathered in baskets or bags and misted with water. Inspect all materials closely for insects before taking them into a floral shop.

4. Take materials immediately inside; do not let them sit out in the hot sun. Leave floral crops in preservative solution and keep them out of the cooler to condition for at least 2 hours, then place them in the cooler for 6 hours to overnight before use (tropical materials should not be placed in the cooler). Fruits and vegetables can be placed in a plastic container or bag, misted with water, and placed immediately into a regular refrigerator (not the floral cooler) for several hours to overnight.

5. Materials should be used as soon as possible after the conditioning period instead of being stored.

Specific Flower Pointers

The abundance of unique flower species is part of nature's beauty, but it is also part of a florist's challenge. The basic care and handling techniques are applicable to all flowers, but each flower species has its own unique peculiarities based on genetics, structure, and natural growing environment; therefore, there are unique pointers for each species. Experience is one way to learn flower pointers. After a while, the powers of floral observation and knowledge improve, and the florist becomes aware of the unique personalities of specific types of flowers. This section offers information about specialty flowers that tend to cause problems and evoke questions.

Alstroemeria

The optimal stage at which to purchase alstroemeria **(see Figure 4.3)** is when the stems have at least one bud open in a cluster with other buds beginning to open. When all flowers in a cluster are fully open with the anthers shedding pollen, the flowers are more mature than desirable. Quality hallmarks are flowers with good color rather than fading and no signs of bruising or a transparent look to the petals; firm, green foliage with no signs of limpness, yellowing, mottling, bruising, or other damage; and firm, straight stems with no signs of bruising damage or stem ends that are browning and soft. The florist should check two

Figure 4.3 Alstroemeria

things: cultivar name, because there are differences in appearance and performance, and previous treatment. These should be checked because the use of ethylene-reduction solutions, such as STS and leaf color stabilizers to reduce post-harvest yellowing, are recommended at the grower level. Alstroemeria are often suspected of causing contact dermatitis, so it is helpful to wear gloves when handling. The lower foliage should be removed during processing. Some florists remove all of the foliage, but if quality product is purchased, this should not be necessary. Re-cutting is essential, especially underwater cutting if the flowers have been shipped dry.

If not previously treated with STS or another ethylene-reduction treatment, flowers can be treated at this time (usually for 1 hour, depending on the product). All flowers should be placed in warm preservative solution and should be kept out of the cooler for 1 or 2 hours, or longer if they were dry for an extended period or if further bud opening is desired.

Alstroemeria can be held this way in the cooler for up to a week, but some maintenance is required. Yellowing leaves and faded blossoms should be removed, stems should be re-cut every couple of days and placed in fresh solution every few days. If individual florets are used in a specialty design, such as wedding work, they should be cut off and conditioned separately for several hours or overnight even if the main stem has already been conditioned.

Bouvardia

The optimum stage at which to purchase bouvardia *(see Figure 4.4)* is when they have tight clusters with florets showing color and a few florets opening. Other hallmarks of quality are firm flowers with no signs of wilting; firm, green foliage with no signs of yellowing, browning, or wilting; and straight, firm stems with clean ends free of browning and mushiness. The florist should check two things at this point: cultivar name, because there are differences in appearance and performance, and previous treatments. These should be checked because reduction treatments, such as STS, are recommended for use at the grower level.

Figure 4.4 Bouvardia

Bouvardia are wilt-sensitive, so they must be removed from boxes and processed immediately upon arrival in the shop. Lower leaves should be removed, and stems must be re-cut, preferably under water. Some florists prefer to remove all foliage at this point because the foliage sometimes wilts and dies before the flowers; however, with careful selection and attention to care and handling details, this does not always have to be the case.

Purchasing and Handling Specialty Flowers and Foliage

Bouvardia need maximum water uptake and minimal water loss. If not previously pre-treated with STS or a similar solution, bouvardia can be treated at this point. Many times, however, when bouvardia reach the retail level, immediate hydration may be more critical than ethylene protection. Therefore, they can be dipped in a stem-sanitizing solution or placed into a pH-modifying hydration solution for 30 to 60 minutes, depending on manufacturer's directions. All stems should be placed into warm preservative solution for the main conditioning process. They can be kept out of the cooler for at least 1 to 2 hours or longer if water stress recovery (exhibited by limpness) is needed. Some florists place flowers in a bucket, mist flowers, and cover the bucket with a sheet of plastic before placing in the cooler.

Bouvardia need a constant supply of water, and they need more than just misting. The stems should stay under water. They should never be brought out of the cooler and left lying on the design bench until needed. Keep them in a vase or bucket of solution. If individual florets are used, they should be cut off and conditioned separately for several hours or even overnight.

Calla

Try to purchase callas (not true lilies) at the stage that is needed *(see Figure 4.5)*, because continual opening is minimal. Developmental stage is indicated by the spadix; flowers on the spadix should not be releasing pollen at the time of purchase. The spathe may be slightly curled back. Other hallmarks of quality are: a spathe with good color that is firm, clean, and free from bruising or tip browning; and firm, straight stems that are free from splitting and curling at the tips.

Callas must be handled gently to prevent bruising. Stem ends should be re-cut, preferably under water. Note: calla stems are slimy inside and can create a slippery surface if stem ends remain on the floor.

Stem splitting or curling is often a problem and an attempt should be made to prevent it at this time. It is widely believed that it is best for the grower to put callas in a sugar-based solution and for the wholesalers and retailers to keep them in plain water. If previous treatment is unknown, the florist can place callas in preservative solution overnight and then transfer them to plain water. During initial conditioning, they can be left out of the cooler for 1 or 2 hours. Like hybrid lilies, rapid turnover is recommended, because prolonged storage of more than a few days at cool temperatures can cause desiccation (drying out). If a cooler which is kept at 40 to 42 degrees Fahrenheit is available, callas should

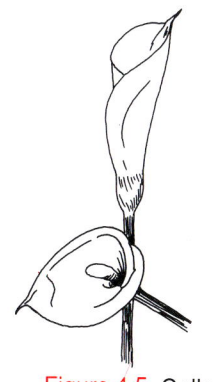

Figure 4.5 Calla

be kept in it. Some florists keep them out of the cooler in a cool spot away from traffic if they will be used in 1 or 2 days, such as for wedding work. Callas should be kept in a tall container that offers support. They should be stored alone or in an uncrowded environment to prevent bruising.

Since callas will not open much more on their own, they can be gently encouraged to open to a more desirable stage for design work. To encourage opening, place the flowers under warm water to moisten them *(see Figure 4.6a)*; place both thumbs in the flower and gently press outward *(see Figure 4.6b)*. Gently fill the flower with cotton at this point *(see Figure 4.6c)*; let the cotton remain in the flower for 1 or 2 days. Remove the cotton before designing, displaying, or selling callas *(see Figure 4.6d)*.

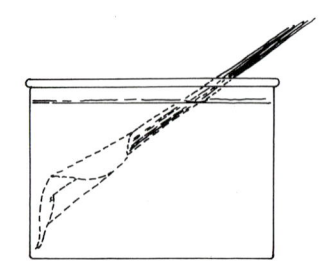

Figure 4.6a Calla Opening Technique

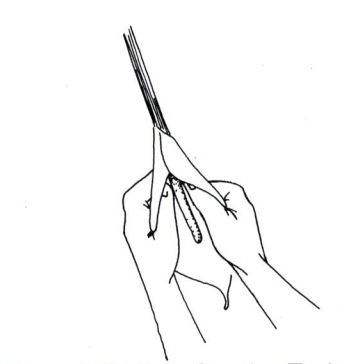

Figure 4.6b Calla Opening Technique

Figure 4.6c Calla Opening Technique

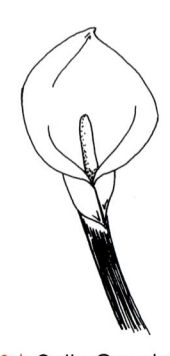

Figure 4.6d Calla Opening Technique

Field-grown or Garden-type Flowers

Field-grown or garden-type flowers are annual and perennial flowers that are grown outdoors and are at peak supply in the summer. Examples include astilbe, delphinium, dahlia, marigold, and zinnia *(see Figures 4.7a through 4.7c on page 111)*.

Garden flowers should be purchased from growers who have a reputation for being knowledgeable and using up-to-date practices and products. If purchased through a wholesaler, the company should be familiar with the proper handling techniques for this specific group of flowers. There can be an advantage to purchasing locally-grown products because minimal shipping distance is involved. Usage or turnover should also be considered. Many of these flowers have limited storage potential (1or 2 days), and many of them are purchased at the open stage.

The flowers should be inspected and processed immediately because they tend to be wilt-sensitive. Field-grown flowers tend to bring along traces of outdoor production, such as soil, debris, bacteria, and microbes, especially on foliage and stem tips. The lower foliage must be removed and stems re-cut; underwater cutting is most beneficial. Stem-sanitizing dips can be very helpful, followed by conditioning in warm preservative solution. Allow flowers to condition out of the cooler for 1 or 2 hours; place them in the floral cooler to complete conditioning for a total time of 6 hours to overnight before use.

Never bring flowers out of the cooler and allow them to sit dry on the design bench. Keep the stems in solution. Check buckets daily and remove any foliage that has fallen off into the water.

Purchasing and Handling Specialty Flowers and Foliage

Figure 4.7a Field-grown or Garden-type Flowers - Marigold

Figure 4.7b Field-grown or Garden-type Flowers - Dahlia

Figure 4.7c Field-grown or Garden-type Flowers - Zinnia

Figure 4.8 Gardenia

Gardenias

The purchasing of gardenias *(see Figure 4.8)* which are often used in wedding designs requires careful planning. Gardenias should be purchased when the blooms are open, but with the center not exposed. The flowers should be clean and bright white with no signs of browning or wrinkling on petals or on the protective wax peeling away from the petals.

Gardenias must be processed immediately upon arrival in the shop. If shipped loosely, the blooms should be covered with damp cotton and wrapped loosely in plastic or placed in a corsage bag and box and placed back in the cooler immediately. If shipped in special packaging, the box should not be opened until flowers are needed. Once the box is opened, the flowers that are not needed right away can be misted with Crowning Glory® or a similar product to minimize water loss. They should be covered with plastic and placed back in the cooler until needed. Gardenias can be kept in the original protective packaging (never opened) in the cooler for up to a week (inspect daily for signs of browning). Once a package is opened, flowers should be used as soon as possible.

Plan designing carefully, because once arranged, gardenias will only last approximately 2 days. During design, hands and blossoms should be kept moist to prevent browning of flowers (work with a bowl of water nearby and continually spray the flowers). Once designed, the arrangement should be misted, carefully packaged, and placed in the cooler immediately. An anti-transpirant, such as Crowning Glory®, can be used instead of water misting to minimize water loss and wilting.

Gerbera

The optimal stage at which to purchase gerbera *(see Figure 4.9 on page 112)* can be indicated by the center of the inflorescence which is actually a ring of disc flowers similar to that found in chrysanthemums. The center should not be fuzzy and full of pollen. Only one or two outer rows of the center flowers should be showing pollen. Other quality hallmarks are firm petals free of bruising and discoloration, especially at the tips, and firm, straight stems free of bruising or dark, soft ends. The florist should find out cultivar name, because there are differences in appearance and performance.

Water and cleanliness are especially important for gerberas in all care and handling procedures. Gerberas have fuzzy stems which attract debris and bacteria (slimy stems are an indication of bacterial growth and possible stem-clogging). Gerberas are also wilt-sensitive and should be removed from boxes and processed before hardier flowers. Stem ends must be cut to remove bacterial contamination; underwater cutting is preferred. Some suppliers use plastic straws or stem braces to provide support. Otherwise, note that it is not a requirement to wire gerbera at this point. Proper care and handling will help promote strong, straight stems. Commercial solutions are a safer choice than self-made mixes. Gerberas should then be placed in a clean bucket of fresh preservative solution. Gerberas should not be placed in a short container that does not provide support. The stem ends should also not touch the container bottom where bacteria may be lurking. The stems can be suspended in a container by securing a chicken wire grid over the top. After a 1 or 2 hour conditioning period out of the cooler, they must be put in the cooler to finish conditioning for several hours. Note that gerberas are sensitive to fluoride in the water, which can cause tip burn. If water is heavily fluoridated and tip burn is a problem, non-fluoridated water (but not softened) can be used for gerberas.

Gerbera stems in display containers or storage buckets can be re-cut every couple of days. When designing, gerberas should never be taken out of the cooler and laid on the design bench; they should always remain in solution. In vase arrangements, there should be an ample supply of preservative solution. Generally, gerberas do not last as long in foam-based floral arrangements; therefore, these designs should be constructed immediately before needed instead of 1 or 2 days in advance. These arrangements should have an ample water supply at all times.

Figure 4.9 Gerbera

Iris

The optimal stage at which to purchase irises **(see Figure 4.10)** is when the bud is emerging from the sheath approximately 1 1/2 inches and showing good color. Irises that are fully open will not last as long, and tight green buds still in the sheath will not open. Other quality hallmarks include firm petals with no signs of drying out, such as brown or shrivelled tips, and green foliage with no excessive yellowing, mottling, or brown tips. The florist should find out cultivar names, because there are differences in appearance and performance. Purchasing should be carefully planned as well. Minimal storage is dictated; longer storage is difficult due to the tendency of irises to dry out and not recover. (For example, do not buy flowers on Monday if they are not needed until Thursday.)

Figure 4.10 Iris

Purchasing and Handling Specialty Flowers and Foliage

The key to processing irises is preventing drying out. Remember that imported products, in particular, are likely to have been out of water for a few days. All irises should be unpacked and processed immediately after delivery. Lower foliage should be removed, and stems should be re-cut underwater to maximize water uptake.

Irises are flowers for which preservative use does not have the drastic benefits that it does with other flowers (although it does not harm them). Irises can be placed in warm preservative solution for conditioning, although some florists prefer plain water. The solution does not need to be ice cold or up to the necks of the flowers; several inches of solution is adequate. The goal is to hydrate the flowers quickly and effectively. Stems should not be overcrowded in buckets; room should be left for flowers to open. Flowers can be left out of the cooler for 1 or 2 hours, or longer if opening is encouraged. Once opening has started, cool temperature is the key for holding.

In the cooler, irises should be kept away from direct exposure to fans (to prevent drying out). For designing, stems should never be brought out of the cooler and kept dry on the design bench. They should always remain in solution. If second blooms on a stem are ever observed the mature bloom should be removed as it withers because it takes away nourishment that the second bloom can use. Irises can be manually opened for design purposes by gently peeling back the green sheath to expose the petals which can then gently be pulled or blown open.

Lilies (Asiatic and Oriental)

The purchasing of lilies **(see Figure 4.11)** should be carefully planned, because prolonged storage is not recommended. The optimal purchase stage is when buds show distinct color, as opposed to all of them being tight and green. Stems may have one or two flowers that are partially open. Other hallmarks of quality include strong, straight stems with tips that are clean and free from browning or mushiness and firm, green foliage that is free from mottling and severe yellowing. The florist should find out cultivar name, because there are differences in appearance and performance (attempt to obtain a full-color reference chart from suppliers). Also, find out about previous treatments. Grower treatments to prevent leaf yellowing and ethylene damage can be enormously beneficial.

Care should always be taken to prevent bruising of flowers and foliage. The lower leaves should be removed and stems re-cut, preferably under water. Some florists prefer to carefully cut off exposed anthers at this time to prevent pollen staining.

Figure 4.11 Lily

If lilies are not pre-treated, STS or another ethylene-reduction treatment can be used at this time for 1 hour. The lilies should then be placed in preservative solution. The use of plain water or half-strength preservative is not necessary to prevent leaf burning, but the preservative must be measured carefully at the normal rate to ensure that excessive or inadequate amounts are not used. Buckets should not be overcrowded, lilies must be given room to open. Lilies can be left out of the cooler for 1 or 2 hours or longer to encourage bud opening.

Lilies can be kept in the cooler; however, they should be used quickly, because they tend to discolor and the petals become transparent looking after a few days in the cooler (varies with cultivar). If there are multiple coolers in the shop, keep lilies in one in which the temperature is kept near 40 degrees Fahrenheit. If there is a recurring problem with petal discoloration, purchasing and handling should be reviewed to check for overstorage or ethylene problems.

Orchids

When purchasing orchids *(see Figure 4.12)*, it is of prime importance for the florist to request species (or cultivar) and color according to design needs. He should make sure that the supplier keeps the orchids in a cooler that is kept at an appropriate temperature for tropicals to prevent chilling damage. Purchases should be planned carefully. If there is a special cooler for chill-sensitive flowers in the shop, orchids can be stored in it for up to a week. Otherwise, it is best to purchase them 24 to 48 hours before needed, especially in hot, dry areas. For spray orchids, stems should have flowers open to within a few inches of the tip. Cymbidium sprays should have all flowers open. Single or corsage orchids should be well formed with no signs of limpness, bruising, or brown edges.

Orchids should not be placed in the regular cooler immediately upon arrival in the shop. Stem ends should be checked first. If they are already in water tubes, they can be removed from tubes and the ends re-cut, fresh water added to the tubes, and stems placed back into the tubes. If stem ends are wrapped in moist cotton, they can be re-cut and placed into water tubes. Dendrobium *(see Figure 4.13)*, oncidium, and cymbidium sprays can be cut and conditioned in buckets in a cool area of the shop; however, they should not be overcrowded in the buckets. Some florists prefer to soak sprays first (particularly dendrobium, but not oncidium), especially if they are located in a dry area. To do this, the sprays can be soaked for 10 to 20 minutes in water,

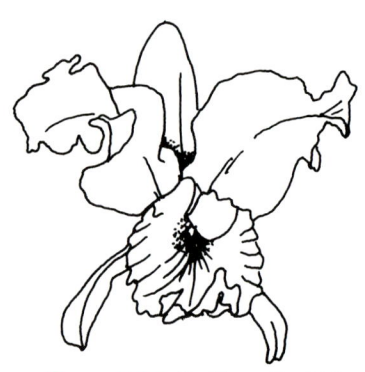

Figure 4.12 Cattleya Orchid

Figure 4.13 Spray Orchid (Dendrobium)

Purchasing and Handling Specialty Flowers and Foliage

then removed and allowed to drip dry. Stems may be placed in a bucket or wrapped loosely with tissue (not placed back in sleeves) and put in boxes for holding.

Refrigerating orchids always requires careful consideration. If a cooler which is kept at 50 to 55 degrees Fahrenheit or 85 percent or higher humidity is not available, cymbidiums can be placed in a cooler at 40 degrees Fahrenheit for short periods if kept in water tubes and protective packaging (i.e., plastic bags or shredded paper inside a shipping box). Other orchids can be kept in boxes, preferably in a cool, damp area of the shop (a warm and dry location is not recommended). Dendrobium and cymbidium orchids in buckets should never be placed in a cooler without protection. The florist must closely monitor orchids during the holding period to watch for limpness and browning. He should ensure that there is a sufficient amount of solution in buckets and water tubes on a daily basis. To revive orchids that might have become prematurely limp prior to designing (such as cattleya, cymbidium, and phalaeonopsis), float them in lukewarm water for 10 to 20 minutes just prior to using them in design work. When designing with orchids, handle them with care and take precautions to prevent bruising and spotting. For example, do not touch the calyx or throat of cattleya orchids; handle phalaeonopsis with particular care. Designs which contain orchids should be carefully packaged in shipping boxes (insulated boxes are ideal). Boxes used for packaging designs which contain orchids should not be precooled. Likewise, they should not be allowed to sit in a hot delivery vehicle.

Roses

The optimal stage at which to purchase roses **(see Figure 4.14)** is when buds show full color and are just starting to crack open; the petals should be beginning to pull away from the bud. Other hallmarks of quality are firm flowers that have outer petals intact with no black spots or tearing and with good color for the particular cultivar (no bluing or purpling in red or pink cultivars, greenish tones in yellows, or muddying of white colors); firm, straight stems with no signs of breakage or damage; firm, deep green foliage; and the absence of insect damage and disease, such as powdery mildew on leaves or botrytis on flowers. Find out about any previous treatments when purchasing, such as whether or not any hydration treatment was applied by the grower or wholesaler and if the flowers were held dry or in solution at the wholesale level or not. Also, find out cultivar name. This can provide specific information about the appearance and

Figure 4.14 Rose

performance of particular products, which can be particularly useful for wedding work and for planning storage.

Roses are wilt sensitive; therefore, they must be removed from shipping boxes before other crops. Do not remove all foliage from the stems, because leaves can help prolong life. However, leaves that will be below the water line should be removed at this time. Thorns can be removed but only if stems will be placed in preservative solution, which will help prevent microbial contamination of the areas where the thorns were removed. Leaves and thorns may be removed with gloved hands or a tool. If a tool is used, it must be used with care so the stems will not be scraped open (strippers with sharp metal teeth and knives that are used improperly can cause damage to the stems).

Some florists prefer to remove the guard petals - the outer protective layer of petals that is just pulling away from the bud - at this time. Removing guard petals at this point is helpful if roses will be sold as cash-and-carry items. In other cases, guard petals can be removed just prior to preparation for design or sale. Only the outer layer should be removed, unless some inner petals show damage or discoloration. If too many petals are removed, the flower will resemble a tight, little ball and will not open correctly. Remember that roses are sensitive to ethylene (although not as sensitive as carnations). If the florist knows or suspects that a serious ethylene problem exists while in transit or while in the shop, roses can be pre-treated with STS for 1 hour instead of with hydrating solution. This must be done with caution, however, and only in extreme situations.

Before cutting, make sure stem ends are even (there may be a difference of a few inches between stem ends of different flowers, depending on the way roses are packed in a bunch). Re-cut stems with a sharp floral tool designed for cutting. Underwater cutting in warm water is preferred and is very beneficial, especially when flowers have been shipped and stored dry since harvest. Proper care and handling steps can eliminate the need for wiring by promoting water uptake and strong stems.

A pH-lowering hydrating solution is a recommended pre-treatment to begin with to promote maximum water uptake, especially if flowers have been shipped dry or if the shop has experienced problems in the past. Treatment time is 30 to 60 minutes out of the cooler. Flowers should then be transferred to a warm preservative solution and placed in the cooler to harden off to make a total conditioning time of 6 to 12 hours before selling or using in design. Conditioning in a dark cooler - the "dark treatment" - has been found to help maximize uptake and prevent future bent neck. When placing roses in buckets for any

Notes

Purchasing and Handling Specialty Flowers and Foliage

treatment, the buckets should not be overcrowded or there will be tangling and breakage of stems. Extra care should be taken with pastel-colored roses because they tend to bruise more easily.

As part of daily maintenance, the solution level should be checked and foliage that has fallen off into the solution should be removed. Stems may be re-cut (under water not necessary) every couple of days. If premature wilting and bent neck are observed, revival techniques explained in the "Quick Revival" section can be used. During the design phase, roses should never be removed from the cooler and placed on the design bench dry. They should always remain in solution. Boxed flowers should be taken directly from the preservative solution in the cooler and packed with stem ends inserted into water tubes or a small block of preservative-soaked foam material. The box can be wrapped with cellophane or placed in a large plastic bag to help maintain high humidity. Boxes should always be refrigerated at 34 to 36 degrees Fahrenheit until delivery or sale, especially if made up a day or two in advance. (Be sure to tell customers to carry boxes with the "head end up" to prevent bruising). For roses in vase arrangements, there should be an ample supply of preservative-treated solution of the correct proportion. Do not sprinkle a small amount of solution in the vase and then fill it with water. For foam-based arrangements, the foam must be completely saturated with preservative solution. It should not be soaked by sprinkling preservative on top and pouring water over it.

Stephanotis

Stephanotis *(see Figure 4.15)*, which are often used in wedding designs, should be bright and waxy looking with no bruises or browning when purchased.

After inspection, place flowers in the packing material and carton once again, mist them with water, and put them in the cooler. Stephanotis can be kept in protective packaging for up to a week (open daily in the cooler to allow for ventilation and inspection).

Design time should be carefully planned because after being used in designs, stephanotis last only 1 or 2 days. Additional conditioning prior to design can help ensure the longest life possible. Condition by submerging in water for a few hours, especially after wiring (the flowers can be laid in a shallow dish of water with wired stems sticking out). The finished design should be misted with water, carefully packaged, and placed in the cooler immediately.

Figure 4.15 Stephanotis

Tropicals

Tropicals *(see Figures 4.16a through 4.16c)* are a varied group that includes crops grown in tropical conditions, such as anthuriums, birds of paradise, ginger, and heliconia. Most of these crops typically bear brightly-colored inflorescences that are not the true flowers. They are bracts from which the true flowers grow. Their native tropical environment - warm, humid conditions - is an important key to their care. The shipping and shop environment are frequently less than ideal, however, so optimum vase life is often not realized. The pointers listed below will assist florists in ensuring longer vase life for tropicals as a group.

Since there is such variability among species, ordering tropicals must be done carefully. The key is asking questions and utilizing specific information to prevent confusion and disappointment. For example, instead of just asking for ginger or heliconia, specific cultivars should be requested. There is a tremendous difference in appearance and performance among cultivars. Even with anthuriums, there is an assortment of forms, sizes, and colors. It helps to ask suppliers for booklets and posters with color pictures for easy identification and quick reference. The florist should also make notes regarding availability, because some cultivars are available year-round, while many are only available for a short time. Finally, one popular option is assorted boxes or packs which enable the florist to experiment with various crops at the same time.

The timing of purchases and the amounts of tropicals purchased should also be carefully planned. Since there is a tremendous variance in availability, a 2 to 3 week pre-order time frame is suggested if the needs are known in advance, particularly for a wedding or party. This provides the supplier with enough time to check on and plan for availability and to notify the florist if a particular cultivar will not be available. Also, since tropical flowers have very specific requirements that cannot always be optimally met, they should be purchased in minimal quantities to promote quick turnover. The florist who wants or needs to handle a large quantity of tropicals would be wise to purchase a special cooler for storing tropicals to optimize handling and display (there are some dual-temperature coolers available that offer two temperature sections in one unit, such as 50 to 55 degrees Fahrenheit and 34 to 36 degrees Fahrenheit). When purchasing tropicals, the florist should watch for limp, dull, or off-color anthuriums or other crops that have soft or rubbery inflorescences with signs of severe bruising, cracking, black spots, or brown tips.

Figure 4.16a Tropicals - Ginger

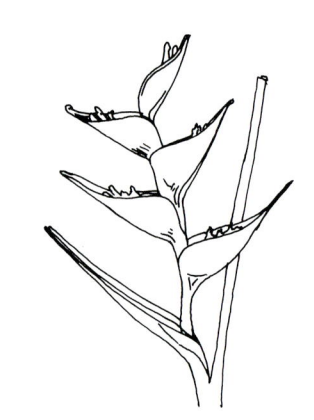

Figure 4.16b Tropicals - Heliconia

Figure 4.16c Tropicals - Bird of Paradise

Purchasing and Handling Specialty Flowers and Foliage

Notes

Yellowing, spotted, or damaged foliage should be removed. Actually, for heliconia and ginger, all foliage should be removed because it will not last as long as the flowers. It is usually left on to protect the inflorescences during shipping. If foliage is needed for design, it can be removed and conditioned separately or purchased separately. Next, all stems should be re-cut; underwater cutting is particularly beneficial. There are conflicting reports about the step which involves soaking flower heads in water for 20 to 60 minutes, followed by periodic misting. These techniques may be beneficial to any florist or even essential in warm, dry areas, particularly for anthuriums. Each florist should test them to determine what is best for his particular operation. If flowers are usually shipped directly from the grower, soaking may be even more important. If soaking is used, immerse stems and bracts in room temperature water for 15 to 30 minutes before use. Care should be taken to prevent flower damage and to make sure that water does not sit in the bracts of the flowers, particularly heliconia and ginger, or rotting may occur. The soaking technique should not be used on feathery, fuzzy, soft-petalled, delicate types of inflorescences. All stems whether soaked or not can be placed in lukewarm solution (not extremely hot or cold) for conditioning. Preservative is most beneficial to birds of paradise, with varying benefits to other flowers (although it is not harmful). After harvest, the actual uptake of solution by heliconia is minimal; however, it is beneficial to keep the stems in solution to prevent them from drying out.

Tropicals should never be placed in a regular floral cooler. They thrive in warm, humid conditions, which are comparable to their native environment. If the florist does not have a tropical cooler which is kept at 50 to 55 degrees Fahrenheit, the flowers can be kept in a room as close to those temperatures as possible. The temperature should be constant and flowers should not be placed in a hot window, drafty area, or next to a heat source. A piece of light, clear plastic can be placed over the flowers to help retain humidity. When a cooler especially for tropicals is available, they can be held in sealed plastic bags to retain humidity and freshness for a few days (check daily for signs of rotting), then the flowers should be processed and conditioned as described above. Tropicals frequently have thick, heavy stems; therefore, floral foam with a firm texture should be used in design work for best results. If multiple stems are used, additional support, such as chicken wire, may be necessary. Some florists prefer to use a leaf gloss to add sheen and to prevent moisture loss. Care must be taken not to use heavy, oily products, however, which may actually attract dust buildup and inhibit air and water exchange, especially on fuzzy or harry inflorescences. Misting with water and storing in a humid environment is recommended. For birds of paradise, heliconia, and ginger, the decorative bracts may be washed prior to design to remove nectar and fungicide residue. Birds of paradise may also be opened manually by soaking bracts in water at room temperature for approximately 20 minutes, making a small slit in the top of the pod, reaching in with thumbs, and gently pulling the flowers out into a fan or bird shape.

Tulip

The optimal stage at which to purchase tulips **(see Figure 4.17)** is when the bud is fully colored but still tight. Greenish, tight buds with little true color will not open well or last long. Open flowers with centers will have minimal life. Other quality hallmarks are firm, green foliage with minimal yellowing and mottling and firm, straight stems that are not spindly or limp.

Tulips are wilt sensitive and blow open quickly; therefore, they should be unpacked immediately and removed from the shipping box upon arrival in the shop. If short-term storage (less than 3 days) is planned, flowers should be left tightly wrapped, placed in water, and taken immediately into the cooler. The bunches can also be stored dry for a few days by keeping each bunch tightly wrapped in a horizontal position at 34 to 36 degrees Fahrenheit in the cooler (storage will not be successful at warmer temperatures). For unique design situations where the bulb is attached, the flowers can be kept dry in an upright position in the cooler. For immediate design and sale, tulips should be conditioned at room temperature before use. They also must remain wrapped or they will assume whatever shape they are in when absorbing water, such as droopy or bent. To condition, re-cut stems, wrap tightly in plastic or damp newspaper, if not already wrapped, and place in cool or lukewarm (not hot) water. Place in the cooler immediately and allow them to condition for 4 to 6 hours before using. Flower preservative can be used in the conditioning solution; however, it is not as beneficial as with some other flowers. Above all, never condition tulips with fresh cut daffodils, because daffodils exude a sap that can be harmful to tulips. Tulips can be combined with daffodils after the daffodils have been conditioned separately. To help control stem elongation in tulips, keep arrangements which contain tulips cool and do not make them several days before needed. Wiring will not stop stem elongation, but some designers use a U-shaped loop just under the flower and wrap the wire around the stem to help keep the flower within the lines of the arrangement.

Figure 4.17 Tulip

Purchasing and Handling Specialty Flowers and Foliage

Notes

An assortment of tips for controlling opening and extending life circulate among designers, such as piercing the stem below the flower head and applying egg whites, light glue, or a finishing spray. These may have isolated success but are not proven to be universally beneficial. Above all, for best results, it is important to purchase flowers at the right stage and to keep them in cool temperatures.

Specialty Cut Foliage Techniques

Specialty cut foliage techniques are procedures used to revitalize products that have been in storage, to add finishing touches to products, etc. These techniques should be used in addition to basic care and handling techniques. They do not replace them, although both types are geared toward promoting quality and longer-lasting products.

Soaking

Soaking can provide some revitalizing benefit to certain types of foliage, especially if they have been dry stored or are showing signs of water stress (limpness) upon receipt. Some types of foliage that are commonly soaked are Boston fern, boxwood, smilax, oregonia, galax, and ivy. Soaking is done by submerging the entire leaf or stem in a tub of warm water. Even when soaking is completed, it is still important to re-cut stems and condition properly to allow water uptake into the stem.

Glosses, Waxes, and Sprays

There is a host of commercial products available for cleaning, protecting, and providing a finishing touch. Some plant shine and cleaning compounds can be beneficial because they remove pesticide residues. These products must be selected with care, however, because some sprays are oil-based and leave an oily film on the leaf surface that attracts dust and dirt. Other products are formulated to minimize water loss, including anti-transpirants.

Leaf cleaners and shines may be used for cleaning, as well as aesthetic purposes. There are varying results with some of the other products, however. The anti-transpirants, in particular, may offer some benefit in dry situations (such as an arrangement that will be placed in a hot, dry house during the holidays), but they should always be used in addition to, not instead of, other care and handling procedures. The material should be applied after storage and design steps have been completed.

Cuttings

Like flowers cut from blooming plants for designs, foliage may be cut from green plants, for use in tropical arrangements, for example, particularly in last-minute situations. A list of plants more commonly used this way include: English ivy, prayer plant, syngonium, Boston fern, sword fern, monstera, dracaena, croton, and nephthytis. To use this method, both plant and cutting must be properly conditioned. The steps include:

1. Plan to take the leaf or stem cuttings the day before they are needed.

2. Water the plant several hours before cuttings will be taken.

3. Cut leaves or stems off with a sharp tool, leaving as much stem as possible.

4. Allow stems to condition in warm preservative solution for several hours or overnight before use.

Specific Foliage Pointers

Like flowers, different types of foliage have peculiarities and unique needs, based on genetics, structure, and natural growing environment. Specific pointers for specialty foliage popular for advanced designs are highlighted next.

Ming Fern, Plumosa, Sprengeri, and Tree Fern

When purchasing ming fern, plumosa, sprengeri, or tree fern, it is critical to look for signs of drying out, including yellowing and abscission, or shedding **(see Figures 4.18 through 4.20 and Figure 4.21)**.

Stems should be re-cut, preferably under water, and placed in warm preservative solution. These types of foliage should not be stored dry in boxes, because they can dry out or develop mold if there is too much moisture in the boxes. They can be kept in buckets of solution, with plastic bags placed over them to help retain moisture, for up to a week.

Figure 4.18 Tree Fern

Figure 4.19 Sprengeri

Figure 4.20 Plumosa

Figure 4.21 Ming Fern

Purchasing and Handling Specialty Flowers and Foliage

Boston Fern, Maidenhair Fern, and Sword Fern

When purchasing Boston fern *(see Figure 4.22)*, maidenhair fern, or sword fern, the foliage should be firm and green with no signs of yellowing, limpness, or browning leaf edges. Maidenhair fern is very short lived (approximately 3 days), so it should be delivered the day before it is needed to allow for conditioning time.

These types of foliage are wilt-sensitive and should not be allowed to dry out. Remove them from shipping boxes before other types. The stems must be re-cut, preferably under water. If they are showing signs of water stress, they can be soaked in a tub or sink for 1 or 2 hours, then placed in solution, or they can be placed directly into the solution and stored this way in the cooler. Buckets can be covered with plastic to help increase humidity directly around the foliage.

Figure 4.22 Boston Fern

Ivy

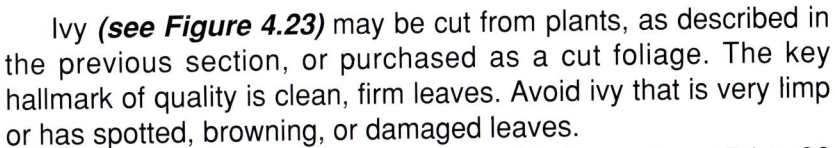

Ivy *(see Figure 4.23)* may be cut from plants, as described in the previous section, or purchased as a cut foliage. The key hallmark of quality is clean, firm leaves. Avoid ivy that is very limp or has spotted, browning, or damaged leaves.

If in good condition, ivy can be stored in the cooler at 34 to 36 degrees Fahrenheit in moisture-retaining plastic bags after purchase. Simply mist water in the bags and seal them. Open bags and mist with water daily. After storing or cutting from a plant, however, ivy must be conditioned. If it is limp, it can be submerged in warm water for 1 or 2 hours and placed in warm preservative solution; otherwise, it can go directly into the solution. Ivy can actually be stored for weeks if it roots; however, it will fade in color and gloss if it is kept in the cooler for this extended period.

Figure 4.23 Ivy

Galax

The quality of galax *(see Figure 4.24)* can be quite variable. Hallmarks of quality are firm, clean, glossy, round-shaped leaves with no limpness, browning edges, mottling or other blemishes. During the fall months, the leaves exhibit a reddish-green cast.

Galax can be stored dry in shipping cartons or bags in the cooler. Before designing, stems should be re-cut and conditioned in water for several hours, especially if showing signs of limpness after extended storage. Stems can also be stored in solution in the cooler if they will be used within a few days.

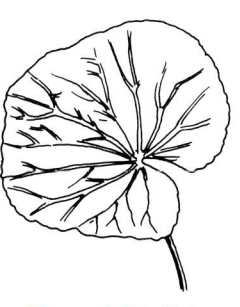

Figure 4.24 Galax

Care and Handling in Design

Notes

The care and handling process does not stop once flowers are stored in the cooler. It must continue through the design phase to ensure that floral arrangements are constructed and handled with care. There are a variety of steps and precautions which can be followed by designers to extend the life of fresh flowers for consumers. The following section highlights these techniques and procedures.

General Design Tips

The care and handling of floral products when designing requires the use of common sense. The following care and handling points for fresh flowers should be remembered and followed.

1. Flower and foliage stems should be inserted at least 1 1/2 inches into the floral foam to ensure maximum water uptake. (European designers insert flowers all the way to the bottom of the container to ensure proper hydration.)

2. Heavy stems require a deeper insertion to provide stability.

3. Inverting a flower to create a specific look in a design will eliminate its ability to drink.

4. The flowers in a design that are closest to the water line (i.e., depth placements and focal flowers) will last longer in the design than those that are farther away from that water line (i.e., the perimeter of the design).

5. If, during the process of inserting a flower, a flower stem has become bent, that flower will no longer hydrate properly. A flower with a bent stem should be removed and re-cut, then re-inserted into the arrangement to allow for proper water uptake.

6. If a flower has a weak stem, or requires additional stability because it is brittle, wiring for support is suggested. Wires can be inserted into the calyx of the flower and wrapped gently around the stem, or they can be laid parallel to the stem and secured to the

Purchasing and Handling Specialty Flowers and Foliage

stem with floral tape. A wooden pick can be used to support a flower, but the flower itself still needs to be completely inserted into the foam or the water of the container to allow it to drink properly.

Design Aids

There are a number of basic floral supplies which may be used to help extend flower life in designs. Often, the minimal amount of time required to use these products can add one or more days of life to an arrangement. Design aids frequently used for advanced arrangements are described here.

European Extenders

The European floral design market developed a means of extending the outer edges of a design with a mechanical tool called a European extender *(see Figure 4.25a)*. An inverted cone extended on a steel rod allows a floral designer to create additional height or width in an arrangement. Segments of the design are placed into the cone; the rod is then inserted into the overall design to increase the size of the arrangement *(see Figure 4.25b)*. The water level in this type of extender must be checked daily.

Bamboo Extenders

The way in which bamboo grows makes it an ideal natural extender for use in the floral industry. The stem structure of bamboo is divided into watertight chambers. By cutting open one of the chambers and exposing the interior structure of the bamboo, water can be placed in the chamber and flowers can be designed in the bamboo itself. *(See Figure 4.26)* This type of designing can be done in a horizontal or vertical direction, depending upon the circumference and the overall height of the bamboo structure. These chambers run in succession approximately 6 to 7 inches apart throughout the stem structure of the bamboo.

Sprays and Dips

Finishing sprays and dips are used to seal flowers and minimize water loss so flowers will stay firm and bright for longer periods of time. These sprays and dips are especially useful for designs created in advance and designs created with wilt-

Figure 4.25a European Extender

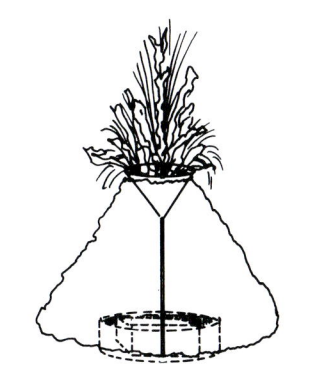

Figure 4.25b European Extender

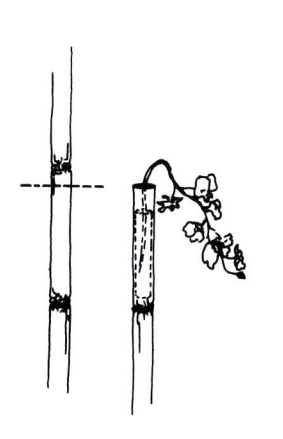

Figure 4.26 Bamboo Extender

sensitive flowers. They should only be applied to fresh, firm flowers. Do not apply to those that are already wilted. Allow sprays and dips to dry before packaging flowers or placing them in the cooler. Following is a discussion of finishing sprays and dips.

- Aerosols, such as Design Master Clear Life and Floral Life Clear Set, are sprayed on to seal pores and minimize water loss.

- Light glues are used to prevent petals from shattering, including Floral Life Mum Tite and Oasis® Mum Mist. Note: If the special sprays listed above are not available, a light mist of glitter glue can be used. Spray glues made for other purposes, such as photo mounting, should never be used. They will damage flowers.

- Liquid anti-transpirants, such as Crowning Glory®, may be used as sprays or dips that coat flowers or foliage and minimize water loss. These sprays can help prolong life if used properly by covering all surfaces rather than simply misting the flower. Read label directions on anti-transpirants before using.

- Self-made glue dip is made by mixing one part white glue, such as Elmer's Glue-All™, to three parts water. Flowers are dipped into this mixture to seal and prevent shattering of flowers, such as chrysanthemums, and prevent browning on other flowers, such as gardenias.

- Self-made gelatin sealer is made by dissolving one envelope of flavorless gelatin in 1 cup of boiling water. Allow the mixture to cool to room temperature, then paint it onto the backs of delicate flowers and set them in the cooler to stiffen.

There are several tips for using special finishing sprays and dips other than water.

- Do not apply to flowers that are already wilted.

- Remove items from the cooler and allow them to dry completely before application.

Notes

Purchasing and Handling Specialty Flowers and Foliage

Figure 4.27a Water Well for Spring Flowers

Figure 4.27b Water Well for Spring Flowers

Figure 4.27c Water Well for Spring Flowers

Figure 4.28 Re-shaping Allium

- Items with moisture-free surfaces can be dipped once or misted with several light coatings.

- Items should be allowed to dry completely after application before they are packaged and returned to the cooler or prepared for delivery.

- Treated items should not be oversprayed with water.

Design Techniques for Special Flowers

Specific types of care may need to be taken with different types of flowers. Following are some suggested tips for the handling of flowers with specific needs.

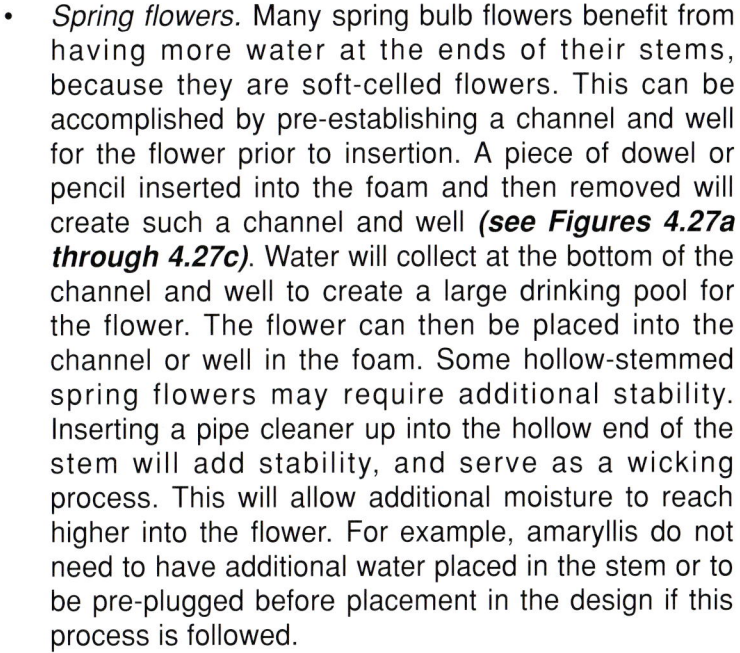

- *Spring flowers.* Many spring bulb flowers benefit from having more water at the ends of their stems, because they are soft-celled flowers. This can be accomplished by pre-establishing a channel and well for the flower prior to insertion. A piece of dowel or pencil inserted into the foam and then removed will create such a channel and well *(see Figures 4.27a through 4.27c)*. Water will collect at the bottom of the channel and well to create a large drinking pool for the flower. The flower can then be placed into the channel or well in the foam. Some hollow-stemmed spring flowers may require additional stability. Inserting a pipe cleaner up into the hollow end of the stem will add stability, and serve as a wicking process. This will allow additional moisture to reach higher into the flower. For example, amaryllis do not need to have additional water placed in the stem or to be pre-plugged before placement in the design if this process is followed.

  At no time should another flower stem be inserted into a flower for stability or to increase length in a flower for design. This practice increases the chance that the existing flower stem will not be properly inserted into the foam or water source.

- *Allium.* If the side of a head of allium becomes crushed, place the stem firmly between the hands and rotate the stem back and forth with a rolling motion *(see Figure 6.28)*. This gentle shaking of the flower head will loosen and assist in re-plumping the flower head.

Advanced Floral Design

- *Alstroemeria.* Remove lower leaves from alstroemeria before designing. The individual florets can be removed when used in corsage and wedding work, but they should be individually conditioned prior to use.

- *Amaryllis.* Some florists rub amaryllis stems in salt to prevent curling; however, this technique is not supported by research.

- *Astilbe.* Whenever possible, design astilbe in a direct water source rather than floral foam.

- *Bird of Paradise.* Often birds of paradise are purchased in tight bud form, and will not open rapidly enough for designing purposes. Blossoms may be opened by gently placing one thumb on either side of the opening of the flower and gently maneuvering the thumb into the sheath and under the flower itself and lifting it out of the protective pod **(see Figures 4.29a and 4.29b)**. Blossoms may require maneuvering from side to side, from tip to stern to free them from the pod.

- *Bouvardia.* Whenever possible, design with bouvardia in a direct water source instead of floral foam.

- *Calla.* Some florists rub the stems of callas in salt to prevent curling; however, this technique is not supported by research. If using callas in a wedding design, spray the ends of the stems with Floral Life Clear Set to eliminate seepage. The seepage from this flower will stain satin, and the stain is not removable.

- *Cornflower.* Cornflowers can be dipped in a solution of water and Elmer's Glue All™. This will add stability to the petals and keep them from shattering. The mixture is one part glue to three parts water.

- *Dahlia.* By turning a dahlia upside down and dropping a few drops of wax at the base of the stem and where the flower connects to the stem will add stability to the flower as it is used in design **(see Figure 4.30)**.

- *Flowering Branches.* Flowering branches must be allowed to open before being placed in a design.

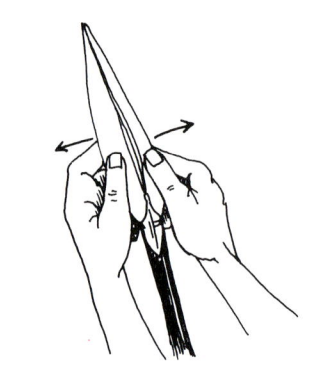

Figure 4.29a Bird of Paradise Opening

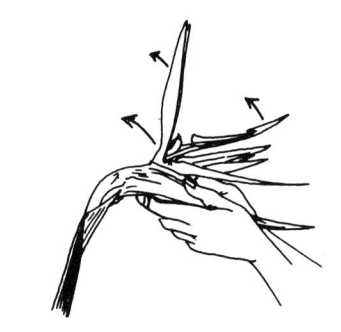

Figure 4.29b Bird of Paradise Opening

Figure 4.30 Sealing Dahlia Petals

Purchasing and Handling Specialty Flowers and Foliage

Figure 4.31 Splinting a Gerbera

Figure 4.32 Hyacinth Stake

Figure 4.33a Iris Opening

Figure 4.33b Iris Opening

- *Gardenia.* Gardenias brown easily if handled or touched. When designing with gardenias, keeping the hands and the surface of the flower moist will assist in retarding the browning or bruising of the petals.

- *Gerbera.* Whenever possible, gerbera should be designed in water instead of foam. Pre-wiring for stability or support is suggested for gerberas. The splinting wiring technique is used for this purpose. A wire is inserted into the calyx of the flower and gently spiralled around the flower stem all the way to the bottom *(see Figure 4.31)*. The stem may then be taped with light green floral tape for a more finished look.

- *Ginger.* Whenever possible, design with this product in a direct water source instead of floral foam.

- *Gloriosa or Glory Lily.* Gloriosa lilies require retention in a sealed plastic bag prior to and after being used in design. This flower should not be removed from the plastic bag until it is being placed in a design.

- *Gypsophila (Baby's Breath).* If the stem structure becomes bent during design, it must be removed, re-cut, and then re-inserted into the floral foam to allow for proper hydration or solution uptake.

- *Hyacinth.* Hyacinths must often be supported with a hyacinth stake when placed in a design. The flower head itself is frequently too heavy to be supported by the natural stem alone. A hyacinth stake should be inserted up into the stem structure and clipped to the desired stem length before the flower is inserted into the floral foam *(see Figure 4.32)*.

- *Iris.* The manual peeling of the sheath assists in the opening of the iris. This can be done by gently cracking the sheath in the center and peeling it backwards approximately halfway down the blossom bud *(see Figures 4.33a and 4.33b)*.

- *Lilac.* Use the entire stem of the lilac as a whole. Do not remove individual flower clusters from the woody stem.

Notes

- *Lily.* The stamens on lilies should be removed; once they mature, they give off a yellow or rust brown pollen that will stain clothing and skin. Individual blossoms can be removed from the main stem and used in design, but each should be conditioned individually first. Withered buds and excess leaves should be removed, because they tend to yellow and wither before the existing flower withers.

- *Marigold.* Remove foliage from marigolds before insertion into a design. Flower heads should be supported when necessary by inserting a #22-gauge wire up into the stem. Clip the wire and flower stem to the desired length before insertion into the floral foam.

- *Poinsettia.* Poinsettias emit a milky sap when cut, which can make them difficult to use in designs. Some new varieties have little, if any, sap flow. These poinsettias can be conditioned in a solution of 2 teaspoons of 10 percent liquid chlorine bleach per gallon of water (10 percent is made by mixing one part bleach to nine parts water). For old varieties with heavy sap flow, place the poinsettias in plain water for 1 hour. Then place the stems in 90 percent chlorine solution for 10 seconds. Following either process, the stems should be conditioned in the manner used to condition other flowers.

- *Pussy Willow.* Pussy willow is often harvested before the catkins themselves emerge from the hard-cased covering, which protects them on the stem structure. This covering should be removed for complete exposure of the catkins on the stem. Placing the thumb at the base of the catkin where it joins the stem, gently push up and away from the stem itself. This should allow the catkin to become free of the protective covering.

- *Tulip.* Tulips will continue to elongate when placed in a design. The designer must compensate for this by leaving space in the design for the tulip to continue to extend or by selecting another flower to be used in its place. Cool temperatures help inhibit elongation of tulips in a design.

Purchasing and Handling Specialty Flowers and Foliage

Notes

Flowers for Long-lasting Designs

Some flowers are known for their longevity in design. Flowers that have a long-lasting quality should be used as frequently as possible when the specific order does not restrict it, such as for corporate accounts or standing accounts. The geographical location of a shop also may have a bearing on the length of life of a specific floral combination. All flowers to be used in the flower shop should be tested out of the cooler to determine their design life. This is a test that can be done at random during specific periods of the year when temperature and humidity may change drastically at the shop location. Conducting such a test is simple. Design a basic arrangement, incorporating the flowers which will be available on the market for the next 6 to 8 weeks. Place the arrangement on the design floor and check the progression of life for each flower on a daily basis. This type of test should give the floral designer better insight into the expected life span of his products in the consumer's home.

Long-lasting Flowers and Foliage

Following is a list of flowers that are known for their long-lasting quality when designed in floral foam. Most types of foliage are long lasting with a 7 to 14 day or longer vase life. Exceptions to this rule are noted on the following list of short-lived foliage.

Long-lasting Flowers

Agapanthus	Heliconia (some species)
Allium	Liatris
Alstroemeria	Lily
Anthurium	Miniature Carnation
Brodiaea	Oncidium Orchid
Chrysanthemum	Ornithogalum (Star of Bethlehem)
Cymbidium Orchid	Protea (all varieties)
Dendrobium Orchid	Prunus
Eryngium	Standard Carnation
Feverfew	Statice
Forsythia	Strelitzia (Bird of Paradise)
Gladiolus	Tuberose
Heather	Wax Flower

Short-lived Flowers and Foliage

Certain flowers and foliage are wilt sensitive or temperature sensitive and do not last long when designed in floral foam.

These floral items should be avoided when designing arrangements which must last for several days or longer. Following is a list of flowers and foliage that are best suited for designing only in water or in foam-based arrangements for short-term use.

Short-lived Flowers

Acacia	Lilac
Anemone	Narcissus
Astilbe	Peony
Bouvardia	Phalaenopsis Orchid
Calla	Phlox
Camellia	Poppy
Cattleya Orchid	Queen Anne's Lace
Cornflower	Ranunculus
Cosmos	Rose
Euphorbia	Scabiosa
Gardenia	Stephanotis
Gerbera	Tulip
Iris	Violet

Short-lived Foliage

Boston Fern
Caladium
Gorse
Magnolia
Maidenhair Fern
Oregon Fern
String Smilax

Storing Designs

Once a design has been completed, the design must be stored until it is ready for delivery. Examine the design closely. Check for broken stems, bits and pieces of floral product that are not properly inserted into the foam, or anything that is out of place. These items should be replaced or removed prior to storage. The water level should be checked in the container prior to storage. Pre-greening of a container or completion of a floral design should never take place more than 24 hours prior to the time the design is needed for delivery. Any additional time that a design or a container is greened over and above 24 hours shortens the length of time the consumer will be able to enjoy the arrangement. Placing the design in the cooler should be done carefully. Adequate space should be provided to allow for ventilation between the design and the other items in the cooler. This space will also ensure that the flowers will not become damaged or broken in storage. When possible, floral designs

Notes

Purchasing and Handling Specialty Flowers and Foliage

Notes

should be stored away from cut flowers. A specific area of the cooler should be designated for the storage of floral designs. This area should have well-ventilated shelves that are deep enough to accommodate the depth of a container, as well as the height of the overall arrangement. The shelf should be perfectly flat without a lip on the front edge. If there is a lip on the front of the shelf, arrangements should be slightly elevated when placed on the shelf. If there is not enough room for a design to clear the shelf above it, the line flowers may be damaged. A lip on the edge of the shelf also requires that arrangements be tipped slightly, which will increase the likelihood of water being spilled in the cooler. This can create an additional mess in the cooler, as well as a loss of the water source to the arrangement.

A floral shop owner should strive for a good working relationship with the wholesalers he or she buys from. When both the wholesaler and the florist have a mutual understanding, both can benefit from the relationship. A florist has the responsibility to order products far enough in advance for the wholesaler to obtain them in a timely fashion. It is the wholesaler's responsibility to provide the freshest, best quality products available. Purchasing quality flowers and foliage should be one of a florist's primary business objectives.

Quality flowers are cut at the proper stage of development and shipped to the supplier quickly. A supplier will care for the flowers and foliage in the appropriate manner so that the fresh products are of the best quality that a florist can purchase. It is then up to the florist to care for and handle those flowers and foliage in the proper manner so that the consumer can have the opportunity to purchase quality, long-lasting flowers.

More is involved in care and handling than water and coolers. It involves combining different skills in order to deal with specific crops and special situations. In the floral industry, there are always new species and cultivars of flowers on the market and new shipping and handling challenges. Likewise, in the shop, there are always questions or problems which often arise that are related to specific crops or how-to steps.

A florist should realize that the quality of the flowers and foliage he or she sells is just as important as their price. Poor quality, cheaply-priced flowers do not encourage repeat purchases. Products of high quality that are fairly priced will encourage repeat business and help ensure the success of a florist's business.

Advanced Floral Design

Notes, Photographs, Sketches, etc.

Purchasing and Handling Specialty Flowers and Foliage

Notes, Photographs, Sketches, etc.

Mechanics and Specialty Techniques

Chapter
5

Mechanics are the foundation upon which floral designs are constructed. Christian Dior, one of the greatest fashion designers of this century, has often been quoted, "Without proper foundation, there can be no fashion." Advanced designers would be wise to heed these words. Proper mechanics, like proper foundations, permit floral designers to excel.

This chapter is designed to provide advanced florists with more knowledge in the area of mechanical techniques, including the mechanics of topiaries, wall hangings, and glass containers, as well as painted finishes. Although these techniques are useful in a variety of situations, there are always some designs which require customized mechanics. In these cases, designers should adapt the techniques herein or engineer original mechanics to accommodate each arrangement.

Floral Foams

Water-absorbent, plastic foams, commonly used in basic design, are the primary foundations for advanced floral design as well. Foams are available in pre-cut blocks or specialty-cut foams; therefore, a wide selection is available to florists. As a result, time and money are saved because waste, material costs, and labor are reduced. In addition to the standard rectangular block, cylinders, squares, pre-molded cages, and wreath forms are also available.

Specialty Foam Products

The European Designer Collection by OASIS® was developed to stimulate designers' creativity by offering a wide selection of floral mechanics. Outlined in this section are some products that might lend assistance to designers.

Advanced Floral Design

Pre-caged Floral Foam

Pre-caged floral foams are cut to a specific size and covered with a molded plastic cage. The cage helps secure stems and keep the foam intact. The cages also have pre-formed holes in the plastic frames which facilitate wiring or nailing to surfaces. Pre-caged floral foams include the following.

- Corso™ Holder - A plastic cage which is 3 inches by 4 1/2 inches by 4 1/2 inches. It holds one-half brick of floral foam and has hinged wings to facilitate attachments to wreaths, posts, and poles. **(See Figures 5.1a and 5.1b.)** *Tip: Use as a mechanic for wedding pews where elaborate floral designs are desired.*

- FLORACAGE® Holder - A plastic cage which measures 3 inches by 4 1/4 inches by 3 1/2 inches. It has a handle which makes it ideal for use in designing standing or hanging sprays and candelabras. *Tip: May also be used as a mechanic for holiday swags and can be positioned on a door.*

- FLORACAGE® Grande Holder - A large, plastic cage which measures 4 1/2 inches by 7 inches by 3 1/2 inches. It has a handle which makes it ideal for use in creating large sprays and wedding arches. *Tip: Handle could by removed to allow the cage to be used in a disposable centerpiece for a party.*

- Place-It™ Holder - Small, round holder which measures 3 inches by 3 1/2 inches in diameter. It is used to secure arrangements to non-porous surfaces, such as wood, metal, glass, and plastic, using a unique vacuum (suction cup) device. *Tip: May be used on a car window as a wedding decoration.*

- Place-It™ Grande Holder - A larger, version of the Place-It™ Holder, it measures 3 1/2 inches by 3 1/2 inches by 3 1/2 inches in diameter. *Tip: May be used to secure an arrangement to a mirror, thereby adding a unique feature to a wedding or party.*

- IGLU® Holder - Small, all-around utility holder which measures 2 1/2 inches by 2 5/8 inches in diameter. It can be placed in a section of a container. **(See**

Figure 5.1a Pre-caged Floral Foam - Corso™ Holder

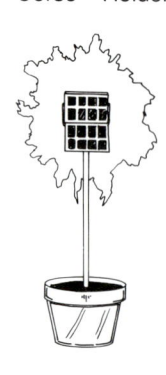

Figure 5.1b Precaged Floral Foam - Corso Holder™ in a Topiary

Figure 5.1c Precaged Floral Foam - IGLU® Holder

Figure 5.1d Precaged Floral Foam - IGLU® Holder in a Topiary Arrangement

Mechanics and Specialty Techniques

Figures 5.1c and 5.1d on page 138.) Tip: IGLU® Holders are ideal for use in party work when the containers will not be returned.

- IGLU® Grande Holder - A larger version of the IGLU® Holder which measures 3 1/4 inches by 3 3/8 inches in diameter. It has a unique cell-structured foam that holds larger stems and is excellent for dramatic centerpieces, candelabras, large wreath clusters, and topiaries. *Tip: May also be used to create multiple clusters on an arch.* **(See Figure 5.1e.)**

Figure 5.1e Precaged Floral Foam - IGLU® Grande Holder

RAQUETTES®

RAQUETTES® are pre-cut, rectangular blocks of floral foam wrapped in thin plastic and positioned on a rigid foam board. They are available in two sizes: 18 inches by 4 inches by 3 inches and 27 inches by 4 inches by 3 inches. The perforated, nonremovable poly cover prevents moisture loss. The rigid plastic bottom gives support and makes RAQUETTES® ideal for large, elongated arrangements, as well as sympathy sprays.

Wreath Rings

These pre-formed rings allow designers to create circular wreath-type designs in floral foam. They are available in two styles.

- Ring Set Holders - Sequentially-sized foam rings, 12 inches, 8 1/2 inches, 5 1/2 inches, and 3 1/4 inches in diameter, typically used for table-top centerpieces.

- Individual Wreath Ring - Single foam wreath ring, 15 inches in diameter, which is ideal for large sympathy pieces or centerpieces. **(See Figure 5.2.)**

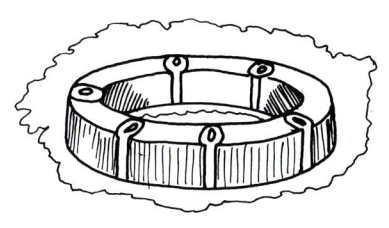

Figure 5.2 Individual Wreath Ring

Specialty-Cut Foams

Specialty-cut foams provide designers with a unique selection of pre-cut foams designed to fit popular containers or for use in custom design work.

- Designer Block - Oversized, water-absorbing floral foam in a 12-inch by 9-inch by 6-inch block, ideal for elaborate floral displays, such as designs for lobbies, stages, ballrooms, and business exhibits.

Advanced Floral Design

- OASIS® #5, #5 Super Cylinders, and #6 Cylinders - Used for bowl arrangements, they help eliminate the need for cutting down larger foam blocks. These cylinders are made to fit containers of many different sizes. The #5 cylinder is 3 inches in diameter by 2 1/2 inches in height; the #5 super cylinder is 3 inches in diameter by 3 3/16 inches in height, and the #6 cylinder is 4 inches in diameter by 3 3/16 inches in height.

- Micro Brick - A small, pre-cut block of floral foam, which measures 3 inches by 3 inches by 4 inches. It is commonly used for everyday arrangements because it fits most common containers.

- Filler Stix - An alternative to shredded styrofoam, Filler Stix can be used alone as a mechanic or packed around foam bricks when extra support or water retention is needed. Available in 10 cubic foot cases.

- Mini-Deco™ - Small foam pad which measures 1 7/8 inches in diameter. It is placed on durable self-adhesive plastic backing which allows it to be stuck almost anywhere. May be used to attach fresh flowers to many things, such as hats, packages, or champagne or wine bottles.

Contouring Foam

While pre-cut floral foams are time efficient and provide a standard mechanic, designers most often use standard floral foam, cutting it to the desired dimension. It is important to remember that the mechanic should be as small as possible while still providing adequate support. Foam edges should be contoured to eliminate squareness. In addition, designers should leave a water reservoir to facilitate watering. *(See Figure 5.3.)*

Contouring Tips:

1. Place foam in container; sculpt edges so that water runs freely to the side reservoir.

2. Insert a knife into the foam and carve to create desired pockets, ponds, steps, slopes, or valleys. *(Figure 5.4)*

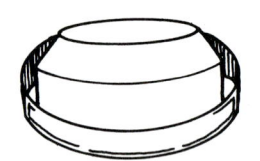

Figure 5.3 Inserting Foam in a Container

Figure 5.4 Contouring

Mechanics and Specialty Techniques

3. Area may be carved to provide pockets where stones can be lodged.

Securing Foam

It is essential for foam mechanics to be attached securely. Methods such as pan melt glue, waterproof tape, and floral clays can be useful. Other common techniques are described in the Redbook Florist Services' *Basic Floral Design* textbook. When securing foam, it is important to start with a clean, dry container. Advanced techniques are described below.

Floral Clay

Floral clay, previously used as a mechanic in designing with dry flowers, is used to anchor mechanics in modern fresh flower designs.

1. Stretch floral clay using both thumbs and index fingers. Do not roll in palms of hands. Oils in the hands cause the clay to lose its stickiness.

2. After stretching, form clay into a circle or donut shape and press onto an anchor pin.

3. Press anchor pin into desired location within container, turn, and press to the right. To release, twist anchor pin to the left.

4. Place wet floral foam on anchor pin, and secure and tape by lasso method (see below).

5. Clay may be removed with lighter fluid; therefore, it should never be adhered to a surface with a delicate finish.

Lasso Taping Method (Figure 5.5)

The lasso technique is a taping method which allows designers to secure blocks of floral foam without crossing the foam surface. ***(See Figures 5.5a through 5.5d on pages 141 through 142.)***

1. Secure an anchor pin in the desired corner of the container.

2. Place presoaked floral foam on top of the anchor pin.

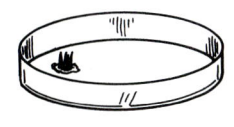

Figure 5.5a Lasso Taping Method

3. Using clear waterproof tape, adhere tape to the side of the container and wrap it around the foam section.

4. Return to original point of adhesion; secure by crossing over the point.

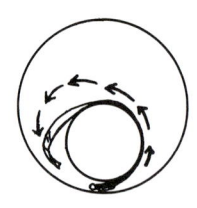

Hot Melt Glue

Floral foam and many types of caged foam can be successfully secured for party work using hot melt glue. Refer to Redbook Florist Services' *Basic Floral Design* textbook for applications.

Stabilizing Large Stems

The sizes of some stems and arrangements make it necessary for additional mechanical security. The following techniques may provide the security needed.

Foil-wrapped Chicken Wire

1. Wrap wet floral foam in florist foil (not polyfoil). Fold edges down; cut away selvage to avoid overlapping foil.

2. Set foil-wrapped brick in container; place chicken wire over the top, and secure with waterproof tape.

3. Insert a heavy-stemmed flower through the chicken wire holes, penetrating the foil. If necessary, clip the chicken wire to make the hole larger.

4. Adhere waterproof tape over the original tape location; loop it around the large stem, and secure the tape to the opposite side of the container.

Mass Design Extensions (Figure 5.6)

Floral designers may need extra height when constructing large English-style bouquets or massive arrangements for churches.
Floral extensions can add extra height to massive designs. The extensions may be made by attaching a plastic cemetery bouquet holders to a plant stakes using the following steps.

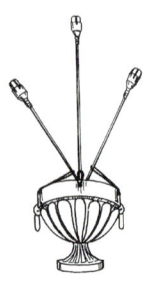

Figure 5.5b Lasso Taping Method

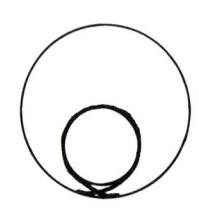

Figure 5.5c Lasso Taping Method

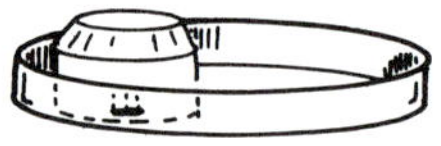

Figure 5.5d Lasso Taping Method

Figure 5.6a Making Mass Extentions Step 1

Figure 5.6b Making Mass Extensions Step 2

Mechanics and Specialty Techniques

1. Secure holder to plant stake using waterproof tape. *(Figure 5.6a on page 142.)*

2. Insert extensions into floral foam which is already secured in the container. Use the lasso taping method around the extension ends if extra security is needed. *(Figure 5.6b on page 142.)*

3. Fill extensions with floral foam and secure. *(Figure 5.6c)*

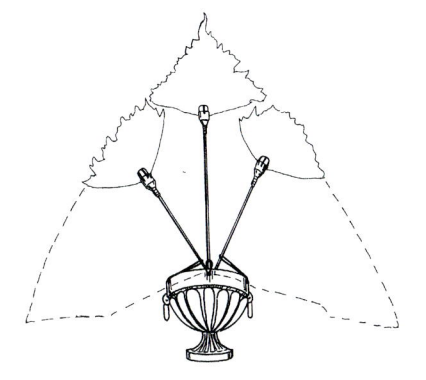

Figure 5.6c Making Mass Extensions Step 3

Columnar Design Frame *(Figure 5.7)*

This mechanic can be used in several ways. The most common method is to design a large, flat-backed, oval-shaped arrangement. It can also be a solid column of flowers or foliage on both sides.

1. Using plaster of Paris, secure a wooden board in a stable container. Make sure the container is heavy enough to support the height and weight of the board before and after flowers are added. If the support container is not strong enough, the board will fall over.

2. Hammer a single nail into one side of the board; center it near the top. Drop down several inches and secure another nail into the board. Continue down the length of the board until reaching the bottom. *(Figure 5.7a)*

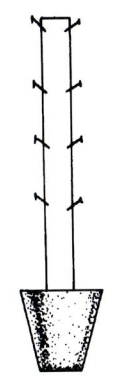

Figure 5.7a Making a Columnar Design Frame Step 2

3. Hang FLORACAGE® Holders or FLORACAGE® Grande Holders on the nails by the holes in the handles. *(Figure 5.7b)*

4. If necessary, secure the base of each cage around the wood post with chenille stems to prevent the cages from rocking.

5. Design a columnar arrangement so that there is no visible separation between the foam cages. *(Figure 5.7c on page 144.)*

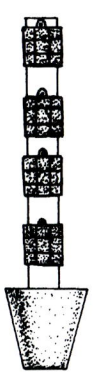

Figure 5.7b Making a Columnar Design Frame Step 3

Advanced Floral Design

Kenzan

Kenzan, often referred to as needlepoint holders or pin frogs, is a common mechanic used in the ikebana style of floral designing. Kenzans are available in a wide variety of shapes and sizes. The best kenzans are from Japan and are characterized by a pre-molded rubber bottom that holds them in place. Less expensive kenzans without this rubberized base may be secured using floral clay.

With the influence of oriental style in the United States, this mechanic has become increasingly important to commercial floral artists. It might be used for in-store displays or exhibit work. However, designs created in kenzans cannot be delivered easily; therefore, they are not a useful substitute for floral foams.

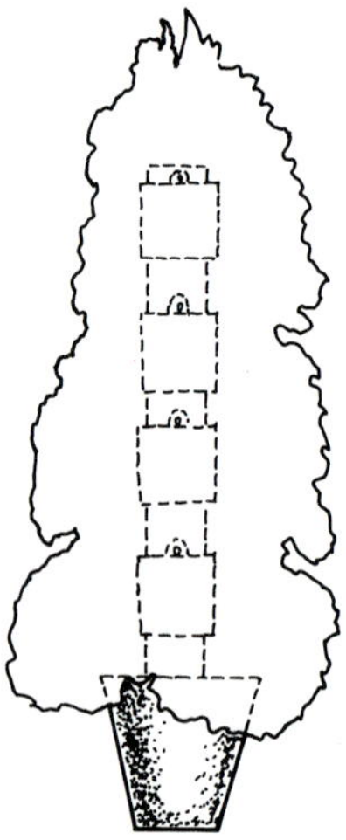

Figure 5.7c Making a Columnar Design Frame Step 5

Cutting Material for Kenzan Insertion *(Figure 5.8)*

It is important to know how to cut branches and stems correctly before securing them in a kenzan.

- Flowers and grass-like stems should be cut straight across at the stem end. *(See Figure 5.8a.)*

- Heavy flowers with soft stems and those with thin, soft leaves should be cut horizontally to a desired angle. *(See Figures 5.8b and 5.8c.)*

- Branches should be cut at a slant with a sharp point like a wedge, and the cut end must face the opposite direction from which the branch is tilting at the bottom portion. *(See Figures 5.8d and 5.8e.)* If the branch is thick, it should be split after cutting. *(See Figure 5.8f.)*

- Large bamboo, thick and wide leaves, and thick branches are best if cut so that a wedged portion is left. *(See Figure 5.8g through 5.8i.)*

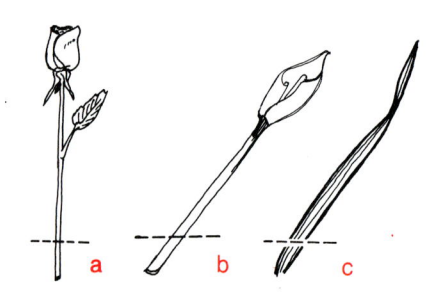

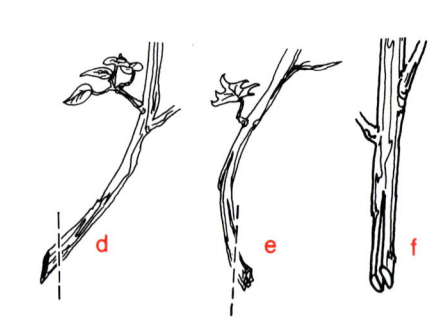

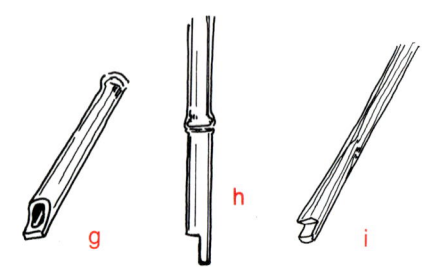

Inserting Cut Materials Into Kenzan *(Figure 5.9)*

After material has been appropriately cut, the following insertion techniques will be useful.

1. Insert the stem point into the kenzan between steel needles. Try not to insert the stem directly onto the needles. *(Figure 5.9a on page 145.)*

Figure 5.8 Cutting Material for Kenzan Insertion

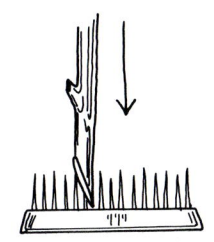

Mechanics and Specialty Techniques

Figure 5.9a Inserting Material into Kenzan Step 1

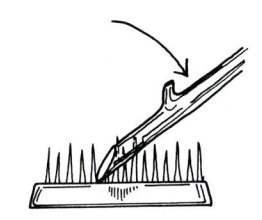

Figure 5.9b Inserting Material into Kenzan Step 2

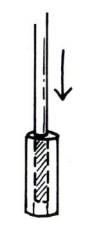

Figure 5.9c Inserting Material into Kenzan Step 3

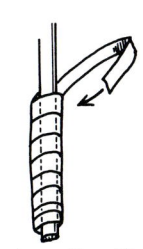

Figure 5.9d Inserting Material into Kenzan Step 3

Figure 5.9e Inserting Material into Kenzan Step 3

2. Tilt the stem in the desired direction by pushing the stem end toward the needles. *(Figure 5.9b)* Apply pressure to the base of the branch or stem to avoid breakage.

3. If a branch or stem is thinner than the space between the needles, apply one of the following techniques.

   - Cut a short, thick stem from another plant material and insert the slender stem into it.

   - Wind floral tape or tissue paper around the slender stem to make it thicker.

   - Tie another short twig to the slender stem or branch securely. (Kobayashi, 30) *(Figures 5.9c through 5.9e)*

Kubari

Kubari is the method of creating a mechanic using branches for security. These methods are indicative of traditional ikebana style arrangements, and are not intended to be seen; however, in commercial floral design, many of these techniques are visible and enhance designs. Some examples are listed below.

1. Partitioning is the method of dividing the container or vase into smaller sections. *(Figure 5.10)*

   - Single-bar Fixture - Cut a small twig slightly longer than the diameter of the mouth of the container, and wedge it in at a point approximately 1/2 inch down from the top edge of the vase. Place all material into half of the space. Floral foam could be wedged using this method. *(See Figure 5.10a on page 146.)*

   - Cross-bar Fixture - If more division is desired, apply a cross-bar fixture; using the method above, cross one twig over the other. *(See Figure 5.10b on page 146.)*

2. Wedging, as the name implies, is the method of positioning a branch to hold either stems or floral foam in place. *(Figure 5.11)*

Advanced Floral Design

a. Wedge a wishbone-shaped branch horizontally into a cylindrical container to hold material. **(Figure 5.11a.)**

b. Split approximately 2 inches through the diameter of two branches and wedge half of one branch through half of the other on an angle and place inside the container. **(Figure 5.11b.)**

c. Insert a hyacinth stake through a piece of floral foam that is smaller than the container; wedge impaled foam into the container to create a floating effect.

Glass Container Mechanics

Glass, one of the floral industry's most common container materials, offers a wide range of creative expression. Below are examples of mechanical techniques which can be used to design arrangements in glass containers.

- A square glass container wedged with corkscrew willow divides the space of the container and allows for placement in segregated sections. **(See Figure 5.12a.)**

- Rocks or marbles positioned in a glass container to one side of the design can be effectively used as a stabilizing mechanic. **(See Figure 5.12b on page 147.)**

- An IGLU® Holder adhered with floral clay to the top of the glass cylinder allows the creation of a floral design which enhances the beauty of the glass. **(See Figure 5.12c on page 147.)**

- Foam mechanic can be concealed within a glass container using the following method.

  1. Cut foam slightly smaller than the container; wrap with a ti leaf or galax leaf, and secure the leaf with a greening pin.

  2. Place the covered foam on a secured anchor pin in the container.

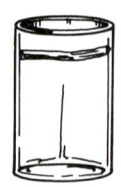

Figure 5.10a Kubari Partioning

Figure 5.10b Kubari Partioning

Figure 5.11a Kubari Wedging

Figure 5.11b Kubari Wedging

Figure 5.12a Designing Arrangements in Glass Containers

Mechanics and Specialty Techniques

- Wrap foam in sheet moss, and secure it to the bottom of a glass container by wedging and impaling it on an anchor pin.

Candles

When candles are used in advanced designs, they are often placed on the same level and grouped together. In addition to adding unity, this allows the candles to create more impact within the design. Candle use and placement are discussed in the Redbook Florist Services' *Basic Floral Design* textbook. However, the following points are also applicable to candle use in advanced designs.

- Review city and state laws governing the use of candles. Many large cities require candles to be enclosed in a glass covering or hurricane.

- Check the burning time of each type of candle used. The diameter of the candle will determine how long the flame will last. This can be of particular importance when candles are used in wedding or party designs. Florists can predict how long candles will last; therefore, possible safety hazards can be determined.

- When grouping candles together in an arrangement, make sure the space between each candle is sufficient to keep the candles from simultaneously melting each other.

- Extremely tall designer candles may be secured by attaching three 4-inch picks to the base with waterproof tape and inserting them into floral foam. Standard candle caddies are not recommended for this purpose because they are too shallow to support the height of tall (24 inches to 36 inches) candles.

- Votive candles should always have a small amount of water placed in the bottom of the cup. Water adds a safety measure and facilitates cleanup, allowing the wax to be easily removed.

Figure 5.12b Designing Arrangements in Glass Containers

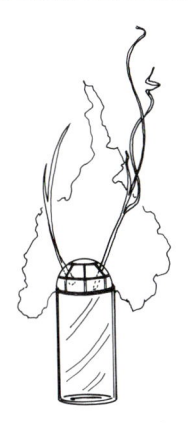

Figure 5.12c Designing Arrangements in Glass Containers

Advanced Floral Design

Wall Hangings

Floral wall hangings, appropriate for commercial accounts and special clients, are becoming increasingly popular in the industry. They vary between mounted sculptures of interesting plant materials and collages of many colors and textures. Some appropriate mechanics for wall hangings consist of styrofoam, wood, canvas, metal grids, and foam board. Below is a suggested method for constructing a permanent wall collage.

Permanent Collage on Canvas *(Figure 5.13)*

1. Obtain a piece of mounted canvas. Finish edges by nailing lightweight molding into the canvas wood frame.

2. Adhere wire hanger or picture frame hooks to the back of canvas.

3. Adhere silk and dried floral materials in patterns with pan melt glue and/or a glue gun.

4. If desired, chalk or pencil may be used to sketch a pattern before materials are attached.

Figure 5.13 Constructing a Permanent Wall Collage

Suspended Designs

Suspended designs can add interest and drama to almost any room. They may be as simple as a Christmas pomander ball or complicated pieces of artwork made of chiselled wood. The ensuing descriptions are examples of suspended designs.

Suspended Styrofoam Globe or Carved Dry Foam Design

1. Obtain styrofoam of desired size, or carve an appropriate shape out of floral foam.

    a. If a large, dry floral foam globe is desired, glue four bricks together with pan melt glue.

    b. Carve to form a globe.

2. Attach a cord, fishing line, or raffia to the globe by tying two sections equally spaced and joining at the top. Knot cord, leaving enough length for desired suspension.

Mechanics and Specialty Techniques

3. Using pan melt glue, adhere material to the surface of the globe. Consider using the shapes of continents as a guide for arranging.

4. If fresh flowers are desired, dowel small holes into the globe and insert water picks.

5. To add movement, attach corkscrew willow to the outside, using a greening pin. Willow adds movement and reinforces the shape of the globe.

6. Insert flowers into filled water picks, if desired.

7. Securely suspend the globe from an appropriate location.

Suspended Sculptured Wood with Cluster *(Figure 5.14)*

1. Procure an interesting piece of wood.

2. Experiment to find the best position of balance and shape.

3. Drill completely through wood, making one to three small holes from which the suspension support can be attached. The number of holes needed depends on the size and weight of the wood.

4. Secure either chains, ropes, or cords through the holes in the wood. The choice should be made based upon the support needed.

5. Mount IGLU® Grande Holder or another desired mechanic after suspension support is attached.

6. Secure foam mechanic by drilling holes and wiring or by gluing with pan melt glue. If using an ILGU®, nail directly through the holder's precut holes.

7. Hang the sculpted piece of wood prior to designing, if possible.

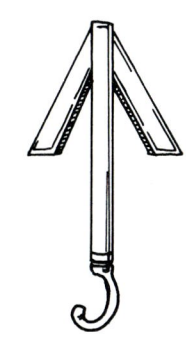

Figure 5.14a Constructing Suspended Designs

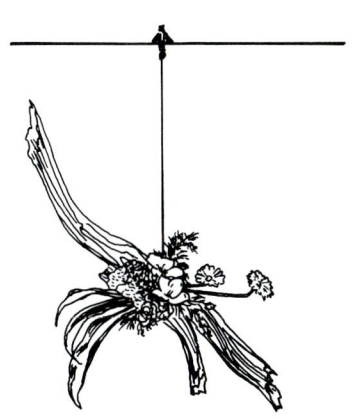

Figure 5.14b Constructing Suspended Designs

Topiary Trees

Topiary trees have a classic appearance and have long been used as outdoor decorative plants. They have become increasingly popular as indoor decorations and are often used for parties and weddings. While a true topiary may be found in many shapes, the most popular is the globe-shaped form which is placed on top of a branch or dowel fixed in a garden-type container. The following steps explain how to construct a permanent topiary prop that needs only to have the floral foam changed in order to reuse it.

Topiary Prop *(Figure 5.15)*

1. Select a dry branch, one that is not too twisted, or use a dowel.

2. Place branch, dowel, or PVC pipe in a plastic nursery pot or papier maché container. Keep the proportion of the branch in mind when selecting pot size.

3. Pour plaster of Paris solution around the branch, filling the container to within 1 1/2 inches of the top. **(Figure 5.15a.)** Do not use a pottery container to mount the branch, because pottery will crack when the plaster expands during the setting process.

4. When the branch is secure, place an IGLU® Grande Holder or sculpted floral foam wrapped in chicken wire on top of the branch.

   To Attach IGLU®

   Remove cutout center from the bottom of the holder, cover cutout section with an even layer of floral adhesive, and impale on branch or dowel. **(See Figure 5.15b through 5.15d on pages 150 and 151.)**

   To Attach Wet Foam Wrapped in Chicken Wire to PVC Pipe *(Figure 5.17)*

   a. Place a ring of floral clay a few inches down from the top of the PVC pipe.

   b. Impale the foam pack on the PVC pipe, pressing gently until the pack rests on the floral clay.

5. Set the topiary form in a decorative container.

Figure 5.15a Constructing a Permanent Topiary Prop

Figure 5.15b Constructing a Permanent Topiary Prop

Figure 5.15c Constructing a Permanent Topiary Prop

Mechanics and Specialty Techniques

Figure 5.15d Constructing a Permanent Topiary Prop

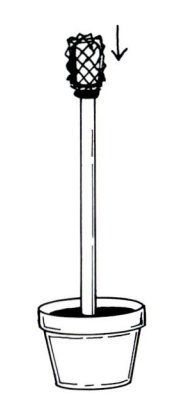

Figure 5.15e Constructing a Permanent Topiary Prop

Special Finishes/Container Coverings

Adding a decorative touch to a container or prop can be a wonderful way to increase the value of an inexpensive piece. Outlined below are some methods for producing an appealing countenance for common surfaces.

Faux Finish

Faux finish is the process of creating a false image on a surface, such as a wall, table, or container, using paint. These replications may imitate such things as marble, wood, and stone, or they might simply be textured, fantasy-type painted surfaces. A true painted finish is a labor-intensive process. Most often, this process is too time consuming to be viable for commercial florists. However, a painted finish may be obtained using floral spray paints. Listed below are several methods of creating this effect.

Verdigris

This finish adds a greenish blue coating on copper or its alloys. To obtain this finish:

1. Mist gold-colored container with water.

2. Lightly spray copper on misted surface.

3. Over spray teal colored floral spray paint on container and let dry.

Distressed Neguro Nuri

This finish creates a traditional look characterized by a red overcoat, worn away to reveal a black coat underneath.

1. Spray a container with three coats of black floral spray paint. Let each coat dry completely.

2. Spray a coat of orange-red floral spray paint over the top.

3. Rub with a towel before the paint dries to partially reveal the black underneath.

Sponged Coating

1. Mist desired color of floral spray paint on the container.

2. Immediately blot with a sponge.

Faux Marble

1. Spray three or four colors of floral spray paint into a bucket of clean water. Select colors that resemble different types of marble.

2. Swirl container into water letting it randomly pick up spray paint.

3. Allow container to dry before using.

Gilding

1. Spray gold paint on the surface of a bucket of water.

2. Swirl the container or desired article in paint.

3. Allow to dry before use.

Photographic *(Figure 5.16)*

1. Hold a leaf or another object with a distinct shape in front of a container or backdrop.

2. Mist the leaf with the desired color.

3. Remove the leaf, leaving an imprint of the leaf on the surface.

Figure 5.16 Photographic Finish

Leafwork *(Figure 5.17)*

Leafwork is the technique of layering on a larger scale. It can be used to cover a container or as a design in itself.

1. Neatly remove leaves from stems.

2. Position leaves at the top of a container. Adhere with floral adhesive. Do not use too much floral adhesive or burning or browning may result.

Figure 5.17 Leafwork Finish

Mechanics and Specialty Techniques

Notes

3. Progressing in one direction, glue leaves end over end, always covering the stem.

4. The process is continued until the desired surface is covered.

Bark, Moss, Blossoms

Materials, such as bark, moss, and blossoms, can be applied to the surface of a container or wreath.

1. Moss - Pin strands of moss to the surface or adhere with floral spray adhesive.

2. Bark - Adhere strips of bark with hot glue; overlap the ends to keep it neat.

3. Blossoms - Remove stems completely from blossoms. Adhere to desired surface with floral adhesive.

Designers should study and apply traditional techniques, continually test new products, and, through personal research, expand their methods of creating new mechanics. Developing a keen interest in the meticulous construction of mechanics will enable designers to achieve floral design excellence. The keys are security and aesthetics. As long as the mechanics used provide a stable foundation which is well hidden, the mechanics of the design will be strong.

Advanced Floral Design

Notes, Photographs, Sketches, etc.

Mechanics and Specialty Techniques

Notes, Photographs, Sketches, etc.

Advanced Design Styles

Chapter 6

*T*he art of using all of the principles and elements of design is the wonder of all floral designers. Each artist is inspired by the available materials, the environment, the mood, and perhaps other art forms. The creativity of each floral artist is developed over a period of time by observing historical examples, by experimenting with various media, and by learning from mentors or colleagues.

In the advanced design styles discussed in this chapter, one can see the connection to either an historical period or a phenomenon of nature. Changes in attitudes and lifestyles have also influenced floral design styles. Evidence of these influences on floral design is noted.

Floral designs can be divided into three major groups: mass arrangements, linear arrangements, and a combination of both linear and mass. In a mass arrangement, the outer edge of the design forms a shape and the floral material is placed within that shape. The individual blossoms are less important than the design as a whole. A linear arrangement is one in which each flower stem is used individually to create the lines of the design. Space is as important as the floral material in a linear design. Each flower must be placed with great care so as not to interfere with the strength of the line being created.

Many advanced designs fit into the third category and are a combination of linear and mass designs. The crescent design, for example, is a linear-shaped design with a strong crescent line; however, the line can be created with a mass of floral blossoms. Vegetative and landscape designs can be line designs, mass designs, or a combination of the two styles. The phoenix design is a mass arrangement with a strong linear thrust shooting out of its center.

As each style is examined, the specific designs will illustrate this division between mass and line. The relationship between styles will also be explored. The arrangements discussed in this chapter represent only one way to create each style. A basic knowledge of the techniques and principles of each style will provide a solid foundation upon which floral designers can expand and explore the creative world of floral art.

Mass Designs

In mass designs, floral materials are placed within a specific shape. Flemish arrangements, Biedermeier arrangements, and country bouquets are examples. Instructions for creating Flemish and Biedermeier arrangements follow, along with descriptions of English, French, and American country bouquets.

Flemish

The passion for collecting flowering plants during the late seventeenth century has remained unsurpassed. The gentry of the European community took great pride in their floral collections. They hired men to maintain the greenhouses and artists to capture the blossoms on canvas. As the gentlemen traveled the world, they often carried these portfolios of floral drawings with them. They were anxious to share and trade with others they met on their journeys.

The artists themselves painted massive arrangements using the various flower "catalogs." These large arrangements are not likely to have actually existed because the floral materials within them did not necessarily bloom at the same time. The artists did accurately depict the stem lengths of the actual flowers; therefore, those materials at the top of the design would have actually had the longer stems. Pieces of fruit and/or various insects were always included in the paintings.

The Flemish arrangement as a floral design style is an interpretation of the paintings of the seventeenth century. Flemish arrangements are usually oval in shape, most often include at least one piece of fruit, and have a combination of flowers that do not always appear harmonious. The arrangements suggest a sense of opulence much like the image of the European gentry and burgeoning upper class who craved such botanical collections.

To develop a better understanding of this style of floral design, one should search out the paintings of this period either in books or museums. After becoming more familiar with the original paintings, one will be able to "paint" a Flemish arrangement with actual floral materials.

Notes

Advanced Design Styles

Notes

This style of design is frequently used in hotel lobbies or in other areas where large displays are needed. Silk or permanent arrangements in this style can be used effectively in homes. In front of a mirror in an entryway is only one of the many appropriate locations for such a grand design.

Designing a Flemish Arrangement *(Figure 6.1)*

Following is one of the many ways to create a Flemish style floral design. Similar materials may be substituted; however, fruit, a bird's nest, a preserved butterfly, or shells should be included. This style of arrangement is usually three sided, and the back of the arrangement is normally placed against a wall or mirror. However, the back of the mechanics should be finished with foliage. The floral arrangement should reflect the strong colors in the paintings from this period. Choose colors such as reds, oranges, and dashes of yellows; save pastel colors for a different style.

Materials Needed

- Urn-shaped container
- Bird of paradise
- Three stems of French tulips
- Five stems of open roses
- One stem of star gazer lilies
- Three stems of Madonna lilies
- Two gerbera daisies
- Six cornflowers
- Three peonies
- Maidenhair fern foliage
- Ivy
- One fresh lime

Design Steps

1. Secure enough presoaked floral foam into the container so that the foam extends approximately 2 inches above the lip of the container. Cover the floral foam with a piece of chicken wire to give added strength to the floral foam. Secure the chicken wire with waterproof tape.

2. Place the bird of paradise slightly off center of the middle of the floral foam. The flower should be 2 times the height of the container. *(Figure 6.1a)*

3. Insert one French tulip to the left and one to the right of the bird of paradise to establish an oval perimeter. *(Figure 6.1b)*

4. Insert two roses, each approximately one-quarter of the height of the arrangement and at the widest point of the imaginary oval outline. *(Figure 6.1c)*

5. Let one stem of the Madonna lily drape down on one side of the arrangement. Place another French tulip on the opposite side, but do not allow it to drape as dramatically as the Madonna lily. This would make the outline too perfectly symmetrical. *(Figure 6.1d on page 161)*

6. With the outline established, add the remaining flowers in a random pattern to fill in the oval shape. Place some of the flowers deeper within the arrangement to create depth. Again, avoid a symmetrical appearance; attempt to create freer, more natural movement within the design.

7. Add the maidenhair fern, and let the ivy trail down over the container edge. *(Figure 6.1e on page 161)*

8. Pierce a wooden pick into the lime, and cover the area where it was pierced with melted wax. Insert the pick into the floral foam near the lip of the container.

Biedermeier

Taken from an historical period (1815-1848) in Germany and Austria, the Biedermeier arrangement was in response to a time

Figure 6.1a Flemish Arrangement Step 2

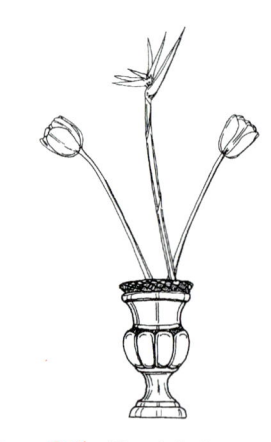

Figure 6.1b Flemish Arrangement Step 3

Figure 6.1c Flemish Arrangement Step 4

Advanced Design Styles

Figure 6.1d Flemish Arrangement Step 5

Figure 6.1e Flemish Arrangement Step 4

of industrial revolution. As the masses became more affluent, they shared in the admiration of the beauty of flowers and were able to afford to grace their homes with fragrant bouquets. A forerunner of the American Victorian tuzzie muzzie, the Biedermeier bouquet was characterized by a compact, circular form.

Most identifiable are the Biedermeier bouquets which consist of concentric circles of flowers. Each ring of flowers typically uses only one variety of floral material, and each ring is different from the others. The color and textural contrasts of different materials used in each ring adds to the visual interest of each design.

Another interpretation of the Biedermeier design employs the same circular compact form. The materials are not placed in concentric circles, but they are used in a planned pattern. The American Williamsburg design and the traditional centerpiece form are examples of the development of this style. American designers are considered to have mastered this style with a feeling of warmth and comfort reminiscent of American homes.

It is also interesting to note that European designers most often created this arrangement with one or two colors. Their preference was expressed in soft tone on tone bouquets. American artists' love of color is often demonstrated in their use of strong and multiple colors.

The Biedermeier arrangement is particularly suited for use as a table centerpiece. The all-around design can be flanked with candles and used as a dining room centerpiece. This type of arrangement is also attractive on low coffee tables which allow the full impact of the design details to be easily admired. A Biedermeier design in a porcelain teacup would make an ideal special for Mother's Day.

Designing a Biedermeier Arrangement (Figure 6.2)

Materials with a rounded shape are preferable in the Biedermeier arrangement. In addition to floral products, many unusual forms of material can be used to develop the concentric circles. Nuts, kumquats, pods, brussel sprouts, quail eggs, and a variety of foliage forms can all be incorporated successfully. As will become apparent, a large quantity of material is necessary to complete this design.

Materials Needed

- Round compote container

- Six stems of miniature carnations

- Four stems of statesmen or yellow button chrysanthemums

- Four stems of alstroemeria

- Six rosebuds

- One open rose

- Pittosporum

- Baby's breath

Figure 6.2a Biedermeier Bouquet Step 1

Design Steps

1. Fill the compote with floral foam to a height of 3 inches above the rim. With a knife, contour the outer edges of the foam to create a more circular form. *(Figure 6.2a)*

2. Secure the foam into the container with waterproof tape.

3. Beginning at the lower edge of the container, place a ring of miniature carnations. Cut the stems to lengths of approximately 2 inches, and insert until the flower heads rest against the foam surface. *(Figure 6.2b)*

4. Place a ring of statesmen chrysanthemums above the miniature carnations.

5. Use small pieces of pittosporum to separate the two rings of flowers by inserting a light layer of foliage. *(Figure 6.2c)*

6. Continue adding rings with the additional floral materials. The baby's breath and pittosporum can be used to create additional separation between rings and to add texture to the design.

7. Finish the design by placing one open rose in the very top. *(Figure 6.2d)*

Figure 6.2b Biedermeier Bouquet Step 3

Figure 6.2c Biedermeier Bouquet Step 5

Country Bouquets

In the floral design arena, English country, French country, and American country bouquets are floral arrangements which

Figure 6.2d Biedermeier Bouquet Step 7

Advanced Design Styles

Notes

are reflections of styles of interior design and furnishings. The designs are obviously influenced by the historical contributions of the three different national lifestyles and have made great impact on contemporary design trends. As a floral designer, it is important to become familiar with the characteristics of these bouquets so that when asked to provide decorations for a particular home, one will be able to determine which style to use.

Country bouquets are always circular in form, American country bouquets are the tightest or most closely spaced, and French country bouquets are the loosest or most airy. The following discussion will further clarify the differences and provide some insight into the development of these styles.

English Country

The English country design style developed from the rural cottages, which were built to house the poor working class needed by the gentry to maintain the large estates and manors. Often these people had been displaced when the gentry confiscated their lands to create their own large estates.

These cottages were minimal in space and were usually built of stone or brick. Frequently, they were old farm buildings that had been converted into several cottages under one roof. The appearance of oversized beds in small rooms with very low ceilings, the doubling of one room to act as both kitchen and living room, and the lack of smooth wall space on which shelves could be built contributed to the cluttered, haphazard look characteristic of this style.

Romanticized by nineteenth century writers, this idyllic lifestyle represented a "return to the wholesome way of life and a rejection of the grime and uniformity of industrialized Britain." (Miller, 41) Because few changes had taken place in this rural environment for hundreds of years, this style also came to represent comfort, stability, mellowness, and gentleness. Nothing was dramatic, manicured, or deliberately decorated. John Richardson, a writer and critic, wrote that English country is a "simultaneous look of relaxed elegance and benign neglect." (Gilliatt, 18)

The fabrics and wall coverings of this style are best represented by those of William Morris, a notable English textile and wall paper designer. The use of repetitive flowers, birds, or trellis patterns on dark backgrounds produced a busy, almost indistinguishable pattern. The overall look of color and pattern was more important than the individual flowers within. The colors ranged from the favorites of the Victorian era, including deep crimson, rich maroons, and dark greens, to the lighter more natural tones of the blues, sage greens, ochres, and golds of a later period.

The floral arrangements of the English country style should

reflect the gardens surrounding the cottages. Floral designers strive to create vases of flowers that appear to have just been picked and that fill a room with life and color. The containers should be either simple glass vases, pieces of crockery, or baskets as yet unused for yarns or sewing needs. All are based on a natural presentation of floral materials. Glass vases may be designed without the use of floral foam. When the container is something other than a vase, the use of floral foam is acceptable but not always necessary.

    The flowers should be a combination of garden materials. The fullness of the bouquet is graceful, yet unassuming. The individual flowers are not the most important element, but the overall display should convey a feeling of warmth and elegance. The colors should be pastel and not dramatic. The Victorian preference of using only one variety of flower in a vase is still a frequent choice. However, the two extremes are often used, and in another area one might use a grand bouquet of many different types of materials. Regardless, the colors should still be subdued, and the materials should be a combination of garden materials.

French Country

    French country reflects a slightly different environment. This style was influenced by the region of Provence, France; this area in France's deep south is bordered by both the Rhone river and the Mediterranean sea. Unlike the dark, somber interiors of English country cottages, French interiors reflect the bright blue skies and rich colors of this Van Gogh country. (Miller, 59) Van Gogh discovered in these hills the "combinations of burnt oranges, bitter lemons, cobalt blues, and sunflower yellows." (Miller, 59)

    The country homes of this French style are more likely to date back to medieval times and might be built of local stone and/or red clay. Shutters were often painted in turquoise (said to repel flies), and these bright colors were taken inside the homes. Walls might be painted buff, mustard yellow, and/or dusky red. When a strong color was used in one room, the next room would be painted white to give the eye a rest.

    Similar to the English country, fabric featuring repetitive patterns of fruit, birds, or flowers were used; however, the backgrounds were bolder in color. The Mediterranean colors of mustard yellow, cherry red, and deep russet were fashionably exhibited.

    The interiors of French style homes were much less cluttered than the English; therefore, each piece of furniture or accessory became important. French style floral arrangements are still full bouquets, but the colors are stronger and bolder. The bouquets also reflect the more open interiors and the less cluttered look. As

Notes

Advanced Design Styles

Notes

a result, space becomes an acceptable part of the design. This lightness in form is interpreted with a more casual style of arranging the flowers in the vases. Larger arrangements are taller and more willowy, but not necessarily more massive.

American Country

American country is the most diversified of all the styles. As America developed, the styles of the homes depended on the location. The settlers used the material that they found near them to build their homes. Consider the New England salt box home, made from the plentiful wood and weathered by the salty air, or the southwestern adobe home, made from the clay of the earth. The abundance of wood in the Americas and the use of that wood in both homes and furniture was reflected in American country interiors. Also abundant was cheap paint, which was made from milk and pigments. As a result, Americans became known for their use of color.

Many other elements of American country were inspired by the traditions of the original motherlands. Therefore, the Cape Cod cottage was patterned after the English cottage, and the southern plantation homes were reminiscent of English estates. The interiors of all American country homes were more sparse than their English counterparts, and function and economy were the most important aspects.

Floral designs typical in American country homes were also dependent on available material. Great bouquets of "wildflowers" were common, and changes in the weather encouraged the drying of materials so that arrangements could be enjoyed all year. Americans became adept at drying and collecting natural materials, a feat in which they continue to excel.

The Colonial Williamsburg arrangement is the most well known of the American styles. This tight, compact arrangement of floral materials is similar to the Biedermeier arrangement in shape and form. It is considered the forerunner of the funeral set pieces, and Americans are considered the masters of the style. These bouquets often combine natural grasses and wildflowers with garden-grown varieties. This combination of fresh and dried materials was and is uniquely American.

The differences between the English country, French country, and American country design styles are very subtle. All are round in shape, all use garden materials, and all reflect a certain amount of nature. In her book *Period Flower Arrangement*, Margaret Fairbanks Marcus writes "too often we are tempted to make compositions so consciously styled that our conception of eighteenth century forms cannot be mistaken. But there are English, French, and American variants of the eighteenth century spirit. Too elegant an arrangement may well look French, one too heavily loaded may be mistaken for English Georgian. A happy medium can be found." (Vance, 34) Table 4 shows a comparison of the differences and qualities of the three country bouquet styles.

Table 4

Comparisons of Differences and Qualities of Bouquet Styles

	English Country (Figure 6.3)	French Country (Figure 6.4)	American Country (Figure 6.5)
Shape	Round	Round, edges less defined	Round
Quantity of Material	Very full, almost crowded	Moderate, light and airy	Full, compact and dense
Colors	Light pastels, i.e., pinks, lavendars, soft blues, one or two per arrangement	Bold, earthy colors, i.e., mustard yellow cherry red, turquoise, and deep russet; several colors used in same arrangement	Very colorful, unlimited
Materials	Garden flowers; some wild materials	Garden flowers and/or elegant hybrid flowers	Garden flowers, dried flowers and fruit

Linear Designs

The Japanese art of arranging floral material is known as ikebana. Arrangements created in the ikebana style of design, along with its many schools, are excellent examples of linear designs. Following are instructions for creating various designs in the line-mass style.

Ikebana

This ancient practice developed from the religious tributes offered before the statue of Buddha. "Legend suggests that the very first flower arrangements were created from storm-scattered branches and flowers which the monks rescued and put in water to give them a few hours more life." (Royal Horticultural Society, 152)

There are many schools of ikebana; ikenobo is the oldest

Figure 6.3 English Country Design Style

Figure 6.4 French Country Design Style

Figure 6.5 American Country Design Style

Advanced Design Styles

Notes

school of floral design and the sogetsu is one of the largest and newest schools. The sogetsu school's modern interpretation of the traditional basic principles is more suited to Western tastes. The relaxed approach of this school is less intimidating than the more classical approach of other schools. There are two fundamental styles of arranging in the sogetsu school: moribana and nageire. Moribana covers all of the arrangements designed in low, shallow containers and nageire includes those in tall, upright containers.

The influence of the Japanese style of floral design is increasingly noticeable as one becomes more familiar with such styles as parallelism, new convention, and all other types of linear designs. The need to study the natural growth patterns and growth environments of flowers and foliage is reflected in the European vegetative and landscape styles. A familiarity with the various styles of ikebana makes it easier to master advanced naturalistic design styles.

Rules of the Sogetsu School

There are three main placements used in ikebana arrangements of the sogetsu school: shin (heaven), soe (man), and hikae (earth). These symbolic names also have a deeper interpretation, shin referring to spiritual truth, soe being the harmonizer, and hikae representing material substance. "The significance is that man, in his flower arranging, is supposed to harmonize spiritual truth with material substance." (Coe, 43)

Shin/Soe/Hikae Proportions

Standard-sized Arrangements:

    Shin = the width of the container plus the depth times 1.5
    Soe = three-fourths of shin
    Hikae = three-fourths of soe

Large Arrangements:

    Shin = two times the sum of the width and depth of container
    Soe = three-fourths of shin
    Hikae = one-half of soe

Small Arrangements:

Shin = the width of the container plus the depth
Soe = three-fourths of shin
Hikae = three-fourths of soe

The measurements are used in both the moribana and nageire styles of design; however, in the nageire style, they indicate the length of the placement above the rim of the container. Additional length must be allowed for the stem that will actually be placed inside the container.

In all arrangements, the stems are placed at specific angles. These angles are 10 degrees, 45 degrees, and 75 degrees, and they are measured from an imaginary line rising from the point where the shin is placed in the kenzan. *(See Figure 6.6.)*

The tips of the branches can face anywhere within a 180-degree radius of the stem angles. *(See Figure 6.7.)* To achieve a three-dimensional look, the material should also lean toward the front. The Japanese explain that the front of the arrangement is like the south, a direction where the sun is strong and growth is plentiful; the back is like the north, an area with sparse and undeveloped growth.

See Chapter 5 for information on kenzans and kubari - mechanics for holding stem placements in ikebana arrangements.

Following are some of the requirements of all ikebana arrangements.

- Designs are based on curved, not straight lines.

- One must first determine the length of the shin, and then all other lines are measured against that line.

- All material tends to be positioned forward.

- Changes in angles result in a multitude of variations of style.

- Material with unique imperfections are desirable.

Designing an Upright Moribana Arrangement *(Figure 6.8)*

Moribana arrangements are considered more natural styles, which reflect nature and the growth patterns of the materials used within the designs. "Moribana stresses the pictorial rather than the design element in Japanese flower arrangement." (Coe, 40)

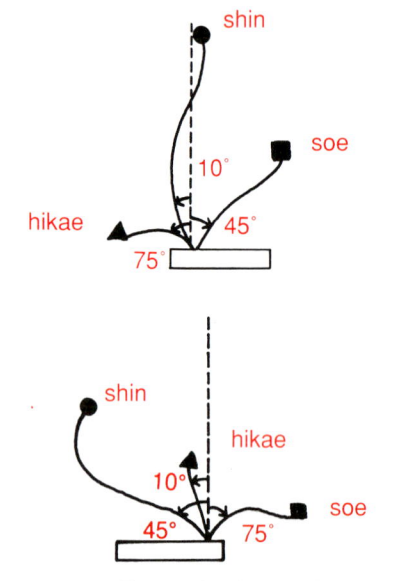

Figure 6.6 Proper Angles for Shin, Soe, and Hikae

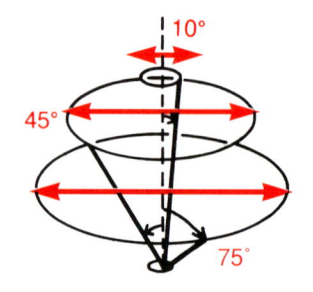

Figure 6.7 180° Radius for Tip Placement

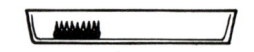

Figure 6.8a Upright Moribana Arrangement Step 1

Advanced Design Styles

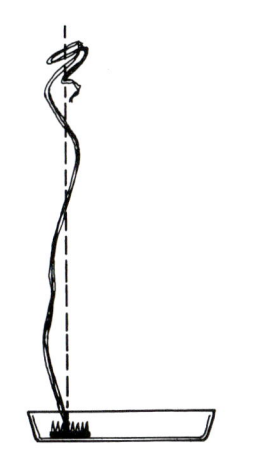

Figure 6.8b Upright Moribana Arrangement Step 2

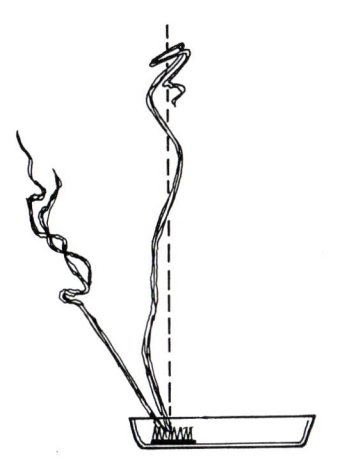

Figure 6.8c Upright Moribana Arrangement Step 3

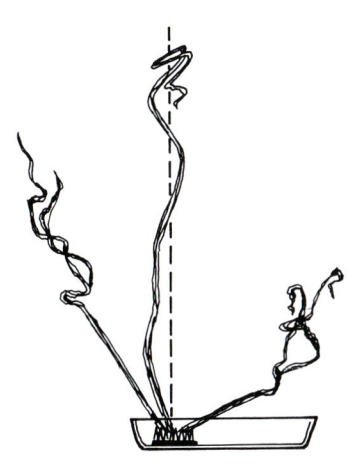

Figure 6.8d Upright Moribana Arrangement Step 4

Materials Needed

- Low, flat ceramic dish
- Kenzen (pin holder)
- Three stems of star gazer lilies
- Curly willow - three branches with character and movement
- Galax foliage

Design Steps

1. Position the kenzan in the container. If a lightweight kenzan is used, use a bit of floral cling to secure the pin holder in place. Place the kenzan to the left of the dish, never directly in the center. In the Japanese art form, lines are never absolutely straight and most of the time placements are not made in the direct center. *(Figure 6.8a)*

2. Imagine a line rising vertically from the center of the kenzan. Point the bottom of the first piece of curly willow (shin) so that it creates a 10-degree angle with the imaginary line. *(Figure 6.8b)* The dotted line represents the imaginary line.

   Design Note: For stem length refer to the previous discussion on proportions, page 167.

3. The second stem of curly willow (soe) is placed to the left of shin at a 45-degree angle to the imaginary line. *(Figure 6.8c)*

4. The third stem of curly willow (hikae) is placed to the right of the kenzan at a 75-degree angle to the imaginary line. *(Figure 6.8d)*

5. The three stems of lilies will repeat this same pattern; the length of the lilies should be shorter than the curly willow so they will not detract from the main lilies. The lilies will be contained within the center of the curly willow branches. Ensure that all materials lean slightly

toward the front of the design for added depth and dimension. **(Figure 6.8e)**

6. The galax leaves are placed at the base of the kenzan to hide the mechanics and to reinforce the lines of the design.

Designing a Slanting Nageire Arrangement *(Figure 6.9)*

Nageire translates to "thrown in;" however, this term is misleading. The nageire arrangements only appear to be thrown together. They are, in fact, very meticulously designed. These arrangements in tall, slender containers are particularly suited to Western tastes and look spectacular in entry halls, on tables, or anywhere a dramatic statement is needed.

Without the use of floral foam, these arrangements are difficult to transport. Although floral foam would never be used in the traditional Japanese arrangement, its use is suggested in the nageire style, as long as it is not visible to the eye when completed.

Materials Needed

- Tall, narrow ceramic container
- Forsythia branches
- Three blue irises

Design Steps

1. The nageire style of design does not use a kenzen; therefore, another form of mechanical stability is necessary. One such technique involves placing two or more branches inside the container in a crossbar fashion. **(Figure 6.9a)** These crossbars will help hold the weight of the materials used in the design, and they will secure the placement so the stems can be placed at the proper angles.

2. Using a well-shaped forsythia branch as the shin, place the branch toward the right front edge of the container with its tip at a 45-degree angle to an imaginary vertical line rising from the center of the vase. **(Figure 6.9b)**

Figure 6.8e Upright Moribana Arrangement Step 5

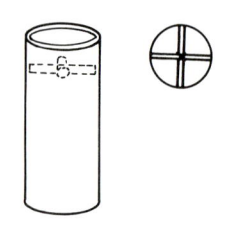

Figure 6.9a Slanting Nageire Arrangement Step 1

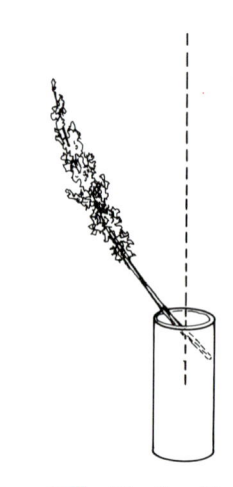

Figure 6.9b Slanting Nageire Arrangement Step 2

Advanced Design Styles

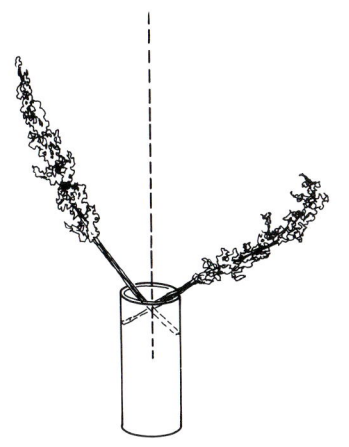

Figure 6.9c Slanting Nageire Arrangement Step 3

Figure 6.9d Slanting Nageire Arrangement Step 4

Figure 6.10 Parallel Design

3. Using another forsythia branch as the hikae, place the branch to the left front with its tip at a 75-degree angle. Remember to follow the previous guidelines to determine the proper length of all material. **(Figure 6.9c)**

4. The three irises will be grouped to create the soe line. Place all three at the same 10-degree angle, but stagger their heights. This placement should resemble a parallel placement. Supplemental pieces of forsythia may be added to enhance and unify the design. **(Figure 6.9d)**

Parallelism

The design technique of placing stems in a container with each stem parallel to one another and at a 90-degree angle to the rim of the container is taken one step further in the linear design style known as parallelism. In this design style, all stems are placed parallel to each other, most often at 90-degree angles to the rim of the container. **(See Figure 6.10.)** (In a diagonal design, the stems are still parallel to each other; however, the angle to the rim is changed.) European floral designers developed this linear floral art form to the height of its creativity in the late 1980s. The drama of the clean, strong lines with the spacious voids of equal importance was radical to a floral design world more comfortable with mass form arrangements.

Although the initial placements were not difficult, the floral artists found themselves developing many new techniques to complete the arrangements, especially at the base. Layering, pavéing, clustering, pillowing, and terracing were all techniques developed to finish parallel designs. This development of additional design techniques will continue to play an important role in the world of floral design for generations to come.

This style of design is often used as centerpieces on long tables. The required voids in the design allow for height without obstructing the view of guests sitting on either side of the table.

New Convention

Taking the parallel design one step further by adding a horizontal plane creates the design style known as new convention. In this style, vertical lines are reflected with horizontal lines, which are also parallel to each other but at 90-degree angles to the vertical lines. These horizontal lines are much

Advanced Floral Design

shorter than the vertical lines. Since they are meant to be reflections and not duplicates, less material is used and not all of the vertical lines are reflected. The intensity of these strong, clean lines adds drama and power to the design.

Interpretive new convention is used in funeral design work, stage or altar decorations, and as table centerpieces. The look is strong, structural, and dramatic as opposed to soft, flowing, and romantic. This style might be interpreted as more masculine and, therefore, particularly appropriate for a man.

Designing a New Convention Arrangement *(Figure 6.11)*

New convention arrangements may be one-sided or all-around. These instructions are for an all-around design. For this arrangement, choose materials with as little curvature as possible in order to achieve straight and parallel lines. Choice material might include pussy willow, gladiola, snap dragons, birds of paradise, and ginger.

Materials Needed

- Flat, shallow, rectangular dish
- Ten stems of liatris
- Twelve pink roses
- Seven purple china asters
- One bunch of equisetum
- Sheet moss, lotus pods, galax leaves, stones, and/or reindeer moss

Design Steps

1. Place a block of floral foam into the container so that it is 1 inch above the rim of the container. Use waterproof tape to secure the foam.

2. Place five stems of liatris on the left-hand side of the floral foam. Each stem should be approximately 1/2 to 1 inch away from the others. The heights of the liatris should be staggered in the manner of the golden cut referred to in Chapters 2 and 3. *(Figure 6.11a)*

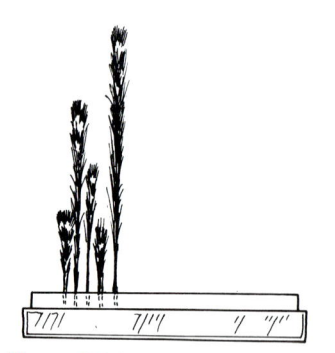

Figure 6.11a New Convention Arrangement Step 2

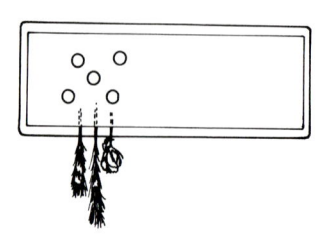

Figure 6.11b New Convention Arrangement Step 3

Advanced Design Styles

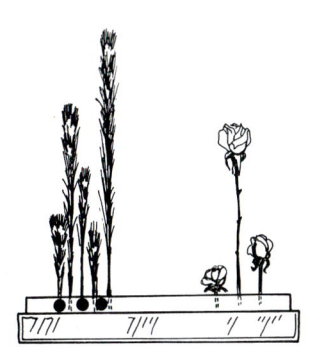

Figure 6.11c New Convention Arrangement Step 4

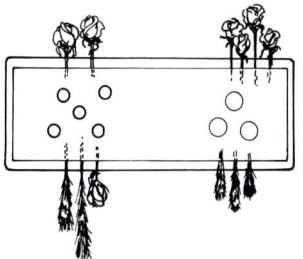

Figure 6.11d New Convention Arrangement Step 6

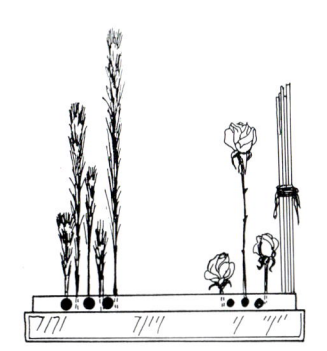

Figure 6.11e New Convention Arrangement Step 7

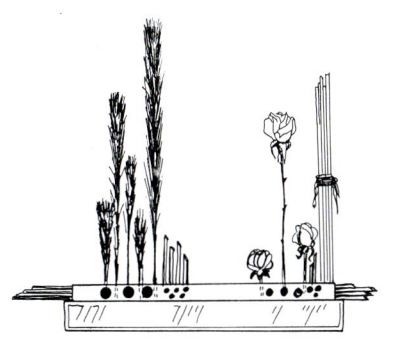

Figure 6.11f New Convention Arrangement Step 7

3. Looking down at the arrangement (bird's eye view), place two stems of liatris parallel to the work table and at right angles to the original group of liatris. Add one rose parallel to this group and shorter in length. *(Figure 6.11b on page 172)*

4. In the center of the floral foam toward the right end of the container, position roses parallel to each other and at right angles to the rim of the container. Stagger the heights so that one rose is very tall (yet not as tall as the tallest liatris on the other side) and two are very short. *(Figure 6.11c)*

5. Place three stems of liatris that are rather short in length at right angles to the roses over the lip of the container.

6. Place two of the roses at right angles to the group of five liatris and in backward directions over the lip of the container. Place the other four roses at right angles to the group of three roses at the opposite end of the container toward the back of the arrangement. *(Figure 6.11d)*

7. Hold several stems of equisetum tightly together and bind with a piece of raffia. Then insert the unit into the floral foam on the far right side of the container. *(Figure 6.11e)*

8. Cut several other stems of equisetum into 2 inch pieces with both ends cut on sharp angles. Use these pieces both vertically and horizontally in the basing of the design. *(Figure 6.11f)*

9. Using the layering technique, insert four stems of asters in the base of the container between the vertical liatris and the vertical roses. Place the other three stems of asters parallel to the tall unit of equisetum, staggering the height and placing the asters in a spiraling fashion around the equisetum. *(Figure 6.11g on page 174)*

10. Using the remaining materials, complete the base of the design by layering, pillowing, terracing, and/or pavéing.

Line-mass Designs

Line-mass designs are a combination of Oriental and European continental designs. Following are instructions for constructing three types of line-mass designs: a Hogarth curve arrangement, a crescent arrangement, and a phoenix arrangement.

Hogarth Curve

The Hogarth curve is based on an artistic line developed by William Hogarth. Hogarth, an English artist (1697-1764), wrote about the "Line of Beauty," theorizing that all artistic beauty developed from this line. (Professional Floral Designer, 41) This line is best described as an elongated lazy S. Hogarth also signed his paintings with a symbol that looked like a lazy S. (Royal Horticultural Society, 110) In floral design, the crescent shape begins at the top and is reversed at midpoint and cascades down the front of the container in the reverse direction. The upper curve should be one and one-half times the length of the lower curve. The upper line can lean back as long as it remains balanced; however, the more upright the line, the more dramatic. The lower curve should lean slightly forward, toward the viewer. The upper and lower curves should appear to be one continual line.

The Hogarth curve is a classical style which, after mastery, can be interpreted in a contemporary manner. In the classic use of this style, the arrangement usually stood in a niche or against a wall. The container was always a tall pedestal because half of the arrangement must fall below the rim of the container. The use of floral foam is very important. The stems of the bottom curve must be inserted upside down. The beauty of this particular design style is in the grace of line and movement. It is best achieved using material with natural curves, such as Scotch broom, freesia, and pussy willow.

Hogarth curve designs are frequently placed on fireplace mantles or in front entry halls framing mirrors. This style of design can also be used in funeral work; the standing basket will provide the pedestal container. The line can also be developed into an easel spray.

Designing a Hogarth Curve Arrangement *(Figure 6.12)*

Any flower that has a natural curve in its stem may be used to develop this style of arrangement. The calla lily, for example, is frequently chosen by designers. Snap dragons, Stars-of-

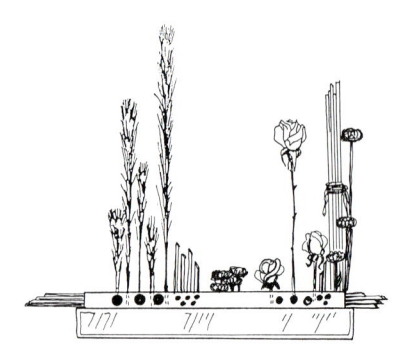

Figure 6.11g New Convention Arrangement Step 9

Advanced Design Styles

175

Figure 6.12a Hogarth Curve Arrangement Step 2

Figure 6.12b Hogarth Curve Arrangement Step 3

Figure 6.12c Hogarth Curve Arrangement Step 4

Bethlehem, anthuriums, and dendrobium orchids are other alternative materials.

Materials Needed

- Tall pedestal container
- Twelve roses
- One bunch pussy willow
- Plumosa fern or sprengeri
- Pittosporum (variegated)

Design Steps

1. Fill the container with floral foam that rises 4 inches above the rim. Secure the floral foam with waterproof tape. For large designs, added security may be provided by placing chicken wire over the foam.

2. Using the bending technique, carefully manipulate each pussy willow branch until it exhibits a graceful bend. Create an outline of a lazy *S* with these branches. The top curve should be one and one-half times the length of the lower curve. To ensure good balance, each tip of the *S* should touch but not cross an imaginary vertical line running through the center of the container. *(Figure 6.12a)*

3. Add the roses, beginning with the smallest blossoms, near the tips of the *S*. Stagger the flowers back and forth in a stair-stepped fashion along the line to create depth. The focal area of the design should be developed where the two curves meet. Larger flowers should be grouped closely in this area to create a broadened center. *(Figure 6.12b)*

4. The plumosa fern is used to repeat the *S* curve. Each piece of fern may need to be trimmed so that instead of adding clutter to the design, the material will reemphasize the graceful lines. Place the pittosporum in the center of the arrangement to add bulk and depth and to cover any visible mechanics. *(Figure 6.12c)*

5. This is a one-sided arrangement; therefore, the back of the design must be finished by covering the floral foam with enough greens to hide the mechanics.

Crescent

As the name suggests, the outline of this arrangement will form a crescent or "sliver of a moon" shape. This style was developed during the French rococo period and was a change from the lazy *S* shape of the English artist William Hogarth. This design style was popular in the Victorian era and was often positioned to frame either a mirror or a statue.

The crescent design can be created with either a linear form or by using mass material grouped to suggest the crescent lines. The length of the curves are dictated by the measurement of the container. The high curve will be the usual measurement of one and one-half the length of the container, and the lower curve should be one-half or three-fourths the length of the high curve.

When using the linear form, complete control over the materials must be maintained, and the use of mechanics to assist in this control is sometimes necessary. The linear material, such as liatris, snapdragons, or callas, will continually repeat the crescent shape of the design. When flowers such as gerberas or anthuriums are used, wire support may be needed to control stem angle and position. Such a support may be provided by laying a wire alongside the flower stem. Do not twist the wire around the stem. Using stem tape, tape the wire to the stem while keeping the wire as straight as possible. The flower can then be bent into graceful curves.

The mass style of a crescent design is accomplished by using materials that are not important by themselves. The way the materials are grouped together and controlled visually produces the crescent shape.

To develop the crescent shape, materials such as snapdragons, bells of Ireland, Scotch broom, and miniature calla lilies are excellent choices. With the use of the bending techniques explained in Chapter 2, it can be ensured that the stems have graceful bends capable of defining the crescent shape. Miniature carnations, roses, and freesia can be used to create the mass needed to develop the crescent line. The center of the arrangement must remain "scooped out" so that the crescent shape is clearly defined.

Notes

Advanced Design Styles

Designing a Crescent Arrangement *(Figure 6.13)*

The following example of a crescent design illustrates the linear form of this design style. The same crescent line can also be developed using a greater number of blossoms of smaller flowers, such as miniature carnations. By massing the miniature carnations along the crescent line, an arrangement can be developed using mass rather than a line of flowers and stems.

Materials Needed

- Oval, shallow container
- Five anthuriums
- One king protea
- One-fourth bunch of Scotch broom
- Five red ti leaves
- Sheet moss

Design Steps

1. For this arrangement, select a shallow, oval-shaped container. The oval shape of the container will be repeated visually in the arrangement of the flowers. Cut a piece of floral foam that is approximately one-third the surface area of the container. The height should be only about 1 inch above the edge of the container. Use pan melt glue to secure the dry floral foam to the far left side of the container. Soak the floral foam thoroughly.

2. Use the bending technique to create graceful curves in each piece of Scotch broom. Using the proper measurement (one and one-half times the length of the container), take the first piece and insert it in the left side of the floral foam in an upright fashion. The second piece of broom should be two-thirds the length of the first and should be placed in the right side of the foam so that it visually connects through the foam to the first piece, creating one continual crescent line.

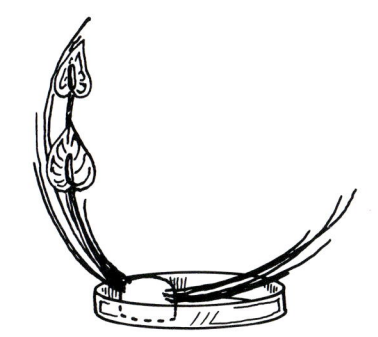

Figure 6.13a Crescent Arrangement Step 4

3. Using the remainder of the Scotch broom, strengthen the crescent line with both depth and weight. Stagger the heights of the pieces of the Scotch broom.

4. Using the wiring technique explained earlier, wire and tape all five anthuriums. Once this is done, gingerly shape the stems with the thumb and index finger so that the stem has a very graceful curve as demonstrated in the illustrations. Note that two stems will curve toward the left and three stems will curve toward the right. *(Figure 6.13a)*

5. Place the tallest anthurium (also the smallest) just to the right of the higher curve of Scotch broom. The next flower will be placed so that it is slightly shorter and echoes the line of the first flower. *(Figure 6.13b)*

6. Place the remaining three anthuriums in the same pattern, only on the opposite side and facing the first two stems. The tallest of the three should be one-third the height of the first anthurium placed in the design, and the other two should be shorter than the one before. *(Figure 6.13b)*

7. Place the king protea with the bottom of the flower head on the surface of the floral foam at the base of the stems of anthurium on the left-hand side. *(Figure 6.13c)*

8. Use ti leaves to repeat the pattern of the lines of the anthuriums. Trim them so that their size is proportionate to the arrangement and shorter than the anthurium stems. *(Figure 6.13d)*

9. Use the moss to cover any visible floral foam, making sure that the moss is positioned low, similar to a bed of grass.

Phoenix - An Interpretive Design Style

This design style was influenced by the legend of the mythical bird, the phoenix, and developed by a panel of American floral designers. Like the phoenix rising from among the ashes, the floral stems rise up out of the base arrangement with a surge of strength and renewal. A mass arrangement is developed near the rim of a tall cylindrical container, and the

Figure 6.13b Crescent Arrangement Steps 5 & 6

Figure 6.13c Crescent Arrangement Step 7

Figure 6.13d Crescent Arrangement Step 8

Advanced Design Styles

Figure 6.14a Phoenix Arrangement Step 1

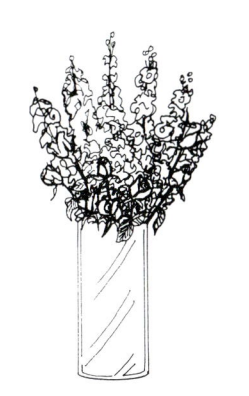

Figure 6.14b Phoenix Arrangement Step 2

Figure 6.14c Phoenix Arrangement Step 3

linear material shoots from the center of the mass to reach high above the mass design.

This style is commonly used in grand entry ways, on grand pianos, or on buffet tables. The height of the vertical material creates the illusion that the arrangement is much larger than it is in actuality.

Designing a Phoenix Arrangement *(Figure 6.14)*

This example is rather simple in form. A more complex mass arrangement of mixed floral material could be designed for the base and tall pussy willow or gladiolus could be used for the center grouping to create a vertical thrust. Foliage is unnecessary in this version of the arrangement.

Materials Needed

- Tall glass cylindrical vase with a narrow neck
- Twelve red roses
- One bunch of delphinium
- Five stems of monte casino aster

Design Steps

1. Fill the vase with preservative solution. No mechanics are needed to prepare the container. Arrange the roses in the vase with the heads of the roses rising just above the rim of the vase. *(Figure 6.14a)*

2. In the center of the ring of roses, place the entire bunch of delphinium. Place each stem individually so that there is space around each tall stem. *(Figure 6.14b)*

3. Place the monte casino in the middle of the delphinium. The monte casino should be taller than the delphinium. *(Figure 6.14c)*

Natural Designs

Natural designs feature flowers and other materials as they appear in nature. Following are instructions for designing a vegetative arrangement and a waterfall arrangement.

Advanced Floral Design

Vegetative and Landscape

Go for a walk in the woods, stroll through an English garden, or study the growth habits of any particular plant and an understanding of these natural design styles will begin to take shape. Nature is the inspiration and the floral designer's perception is the interpretation.

A vegetative design is a floral creation that simulates a small area of a growing environment. The floral materials are placed in the arrangement as they grow naturally. The taller growing materials are placed higher in the design; the shorter growing materials are placed lower in the design. The floral materials used would normally be found growing in the same environment at the same time of year. A good combination is tulips, irises, and daffodils, all of which are spring flowers that grow in a temperate climate. On the other hand, anthuriums should not be combined with tulips, nor lilacs with marigolds, because these materials are incompatible with each other.

A landscape design represents a slice of a designed garden. Just as many English gardens are sketched and planned so that the plantings will be a continual burst of color with taller material to the back of the garden and shorter, bushier plantings to the front, so is a landscape floral design planned and developed. Materials are added to represent man-made structures, such as walkways, throughout the garden, or rocks can be placed as if the garden were organized around such an object. The organization and development adds to the challenge of the floral artist.

To capture the essence of any of these natural design styles, floral designers need only observe the nature that abounds in the environment. Study the fields, the gardens, and the beauty of the products used everyday and the inspiration will flow.

Comparison of Vegetative and Landscape Designs

A vegetative arrangement is the most natural. It can be unkempt in appearance - wild as in nature. It can also be more controlled so that it appears to be a slice of nature. All materials must grow and/or bloom in the same climate at the same time of the year.

A landscape design is a more controlled arrangement. All of the materials are placed with attention to the design of the garden setting. It usually includes representation of a man-made structure (bridge or walk-way). All material must grow and/or bloom in the same environment at the same time of the year.

Notes

Advanced Design Styles

Designing a Vegetative Arrangement *(Figure 6.15)*

Any container that is in harmony with nature can be used for this design. Baskets, terra cotta pots, driftwood, and flat ceramic containers are good choices. The following idea is only one idea for creating vegetative design.

Materials Needed

- Burlap fabric
- Heavy-duty plastic bag
- Sisal rope
- Dogwood branch
- Three stems of lilac
- Five stems of daffodils
- Eight stems of grape hyacinth
- Rock
- Mosses
- Pieces of bark or driftwood

Figure 6.15a Vegetative Arrangement Step 1

Figure 6.15b Vegetative Arrangement Step 2

Design Steps

1. Place the plastic bag on top of the burlap fabric. Put a block of presoaked floral foam on top of the plastic and gather the burlap and plastic around the foam. With the surface of the floral foam exposed, tie the burlap and plastic with sisal rope. The natural rope form is important to the design style. *(Figure 6.15a)* Note: It may be necessary to add sand to the bag of burlap for stabilizing the weight of the branch material.

2. Insert the dogwood branch so that it appears to be growing out of the earth. The lines of the branch should also frame the rest of the arrangement. Observing the natural growth pattern of the branch is very important, and the placement of the branch must be thought out carefully. *(Figure 6.15b)*

3. On the opposite side of the dogwood branch, insert the three lilac stems to simulate a lilac bush. The stem length must be taller than any other material except for the dogwood branch. Attempt to visualize the way a lilac bush might look growing at the edge of a field. **(Figure 6.15c)**

4. Group the five daffodil stems under the dogwood branch at a height lower than the lilacs. When growing in the wild, the daffodils would not all point their heads in one direction. Try to emulate this natural growth behavior. For ease in inserting in the foam and for longer lasting ability, place a chenille stem inside the hollow stem of each daffodil. Push the chenille stem up as far as it will go without tearing the daffodil stem. **(Figure 6.15d)**

5. In the center of the design, make a low grouping of the grape hyacinths. Some will be taller than others, and some might even be bending toward the ground from the weight of their heads. Use the natural foliage for added reality. Before inserting, wrap the bottom of the stems with a very fine wire; this will make insertion easier. **(Figure 6.15e)**

6. Finally, using the remaining material, complete the basing and finishing details. The more natural and unkempt the base looks, the better in this particular design.

Figure 6.15c Vegetative Arrangement Step 3

Figure 6.15d Vegetative Arrangement Step 4

Figure 6.15e Vegetative Arrangement Step 5

Waterfall

The inspiration for this design style comes both from nature and from the wedding bouquets of the early 1900s. The lush, flowing, cascading bouquets with trails of ivy and flowers are romantic fantasies of brides of all eras.

This naturalistic example of a mass design illustrates that the individual parts are as important as the whole. This floral style invites the admirer to look at the design repeatedly so that the intimate details of the design can be appreciated.

A waterfall design is most effective when displayed on a tall pedestal. A spotlight can enhance the play of material to reflect light. Entry halls, museum displays, and hotel lobbies are a few of the places such designs can be used dramatically. Because of the intricacy of a waterfall design, it is not recommended for areas where there is a great distance between the viewer and the arrangement, such as in a church or stage setting.

Advanced Design Styles

Designing a Waterfall Arrangement *(Figure 6.16)*

The quantity of material used in a waterfall arrangement is totally dependent on the individual designer's preference and budget. The more material, the more layering that can be done. A low container or a basket could be used, but it would have to be displayed on a pedestal. Instead, a tall cylindrical container may be used to provide the height necessary for elevating the cascading flowers.

Materials Needed

- Tall cylindrical container
- Sprengeri fern
- Spray roses
- Monte casino
- Queen Anne's lace
- Bear grass
- Dendrobium orchids
- Yarn, fine metallic wire
- Feathers and other material that drapes or hangs

Design Steps

1. Fill the container with floral foam that rises above the rim approximately 4 inches. For an especially long waterfall, the foam might need to be raised higher.

2. Carefully consider the balance of this arrangement; add weight to the container if necessary for physical balance. Cover the foam with chicken wire for additional strength.

3. The stems of the floral material will be placed in the opposite direction of most arrangements - progressing from the bottom toward the top of the floral foam. *(Figure 6.16a)*

Figure 6.16a Waterfall Design Step 3

4. Begin with the longest pieces of foliage, and build layers of floral material from the floor to the top of the foam. The art of this design is not to follow a pattern, but to develop several layers of material with bits and pieces peaking out from underneath. The random flow of material is the goal in this style of design. Crossing lines add interest unlike traditional design styles. **(Figure 6.16b)**

5. The top of the design must also convey the feeling of falling water. The blossoms will not suddenly reach toward the sky, but must also cascade down the front surface of the design. The use of bear grass at this stage is recommended. Place the material so that a forward motion is achieved. If necessary, bend the material. **(Figure 6.16c)**

6. Add pieces of feathers, metal wires, glitter, or yarn among the layering for added texture and interest.

Miscellaneous Designs

Some design styles fit into no particular category. Some are actually design techniques used as a style. The following illustrates a few of these alternative styles.

Free-form Design

A free-form arrangement is one in which there is no specific geometric form. "Pattern rather than scenic effect is striven for and, where convenient, nature can be forgotten." (Coe, 86) The use of crossed stems, unheard of in classical design styles, is widely accepted. The floral material may flow in all directions, perhaps hanging down over the rim of the container or lying horizontally at the container's edge. Placements do not define a shape; they only form part of a pattern. The materials need not relate to each other in any symbolic rite; artists only need consider if they fit into the pattern he/she has envisioned. **(Figure 6.17)**

This design style also crosses into other design styles. For example, a vegetative arrangement may also be free-form, as if one were standing in the middle of a field that was recently pelted by heavy rains. Many of the stems might be broken by the rains, while others stand straight and tall.

Figure 6.16b Waterfall Design Step 4

Figure 6.16c Waterfall Design Step 5

Figure 6.17 Free-form Arrangement

Advanced Design Styles

Notes

Designers are uninhibited when designing a free-form arrangement. Their creativity and sense of artistry allows them to be totally free. Although this may imply that anything goes, when completed, the arrangement is pleasing to the senses and is not without artistic principles, balance being instinctual and an integral part of the design.

The application of free-form designs is unlimited. The environment should be taken into account and the customer open to unrestrained creativity.

Hand-tied Bouquet

European designers have brought this design technique to its mastery. This is actually a technique. All of the material is held in one hand until the bouquet is finished. At that time, the stems are bound with waxed string or raffia. The style could be Biedermeier, linear, structural, or free-form.

As the stems are held between the thumb and the index finger, the subsequent stems are placed in a spiraling fashion around the initial stems. In a hand-tied bouquet, it is necessary to first prepare the material to ensure that no foliage will fall beneath the binding point of the stems. All of this lower foliage should be removed from all material. The amount of material is only dependent upon the designer's desire and the budget of the consumer.

This fashion of designing a "bunch of flowers" has several advantages. First, one can create a much larger, fuller bouquet with the use of foliage and fillers. This can be very impressive to the consumer and profitable for the retailer.

Secondly, in Europe these bouquets are presented to a host or hostess as a house gift. The hostess needs to spend little time placing the flowers in a vase; therefore, she need not take time away from her guests to arrange the flowers.

Designing a Hand-tied Bouquet *(Figure 6.18)*

This type of bouquet can be constructed with an unlimited variety of flowers. Foliage is helpful in constructing this design in order to help space and maintain placement of floral materials.

Materials Needed

- Three callas
- Ruscus foliage

- One-fourth bunch of asparagus fern or plumosa fern
- Six pink roses
- Two stems of star gazer lilies
- Six stems of lavender freesia
- Bear grass

Design Steps

1. Place one calla in the left hand so that the stem rests on the palm and the thumb and index finger hold the material at a 45-degree angle. Place some of the ruscus around the calla. This helps both support and give space to the material.

2. Place a stem of long plumosa under and shorter stems over the calla. Be sure to bring all stems toward the calla stem in the same direction so that the stems of the additional material spiral around the calla and do not cross either themselves or the calla. **(Figure 6.18a)**

3. Add additional stems of flowers and foliage in a like manner. The top of the bouquet should become wider and the spiraling of stems more noticeable. **(Figure 6.18b)**

4. Continue to add material, placing it so that the material flows forward and downward. By turning the bouquet a quarter of a turn continually throughout the formation, the placements can be controlled and a pleasing shape be developed with a slightly cascading feeling in the front of the bouquet. **(Figure 6.18c)**

5. Lay one end of a piece of waxed thread under the thumb, and wrap the other around the stems at the binding point. Carefully lay the bouquet on a table, and tie the ends of the thread together. **(Figure 6.18d)**

6. Cut the stems so that the inner stems are slightly shorter than the outer stems. The stem length should

Figure 6.18a Hand-tied Bouquet Step 2

Figure 6.18b Hand-tied Bouquet Step 3

Figure 6.18c Hand-tied Bouquet Step 4

Figure 6.18d Hand-tied Bouquet Step 5

Advanced Design Styles

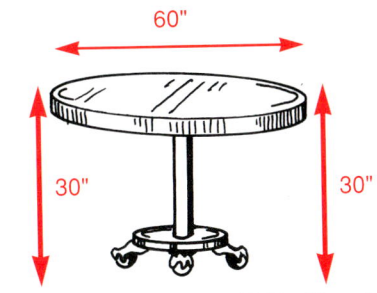

Figure 6.19a Leafwork Table Step 1

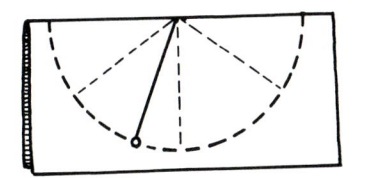

Figure 6.19b Leafwork Table Step 1

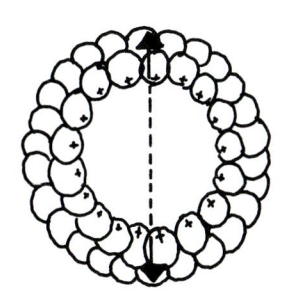

Figure 6.19c Leafwork Table Step 2

be approximately one-third of the height of the bouquet. If the design is well balanced and the stems cut properly, the bouquet should stand on a table without falling down.

Leafwork Table *(Figure 6.19)*

This technique creates unusual tablecloths of foliage. Various types of foliage can be used, although galax and salal are most commonly used. Each leaf will be attached to the base individually; therefore the stems of the leaves must be clipped to a short length.

Materials Needed

- Tablecloth or sheet (king size)
- Galax or salal leaves

Design Steps

1. Acquire an inexpensive tablecloth of the appropriate size or a piece of burlap which has been cut and pieced together to form the needed size. A king size sheet can also be used. Fold the sheet in half. Multiply the height of the table by two; adding the diameter of the table gives the needed length of the cloth. Divide that number by two. This number is the length of a piece of string needed. Tie the string to a pencil and, while holding the string in the center of the fold of the sheet, draw a half circle. ***(Figure 6.19a and 6.19b)***

2. Lay the cloth on a flat surface. Beginning at the bottom edge of the material, attach each leaf, by using either spray adhesive or sewing each leaf with florists thread. (Regular sewing thread may not be strong enough.) Slightly overlap each leaf with each placement. Go all the way around the circumference before moving toward the center. ***(Figure 6.19c)***

3. While working toward the center, be sure to overlap each leaf to hide both the stem and the mechanic (thread).

Topiary *(Figure 6.20)*

Those familiar with the formal gardens of England and France are most familiar with topiary trees. The trees are clipped into various shapes and then maintained with frequent clippings.

In the floral arena, topiary trees are ever popular. As centerpieces, they allow for great heights without interfering visually with guests on either side of a table. Topiary forms also make dramatic statements in church or cathedral settings.

Materials Needed

- A piece of curly willow branch 2 to 3 feet in height and at least 1 inch in diameter. (A wooden dowel with the same diameter could also be used.)

- One IGLU® Grande Holder or CORSO™ Holder

- Six-inch plastic flower pot (Do not use terra cotta at this stage. When topiary is completed, if terra cotta is the desired finished look, the plastic can be slipped into a terra cotta pot. If plaster of Paris is placed in a terra cotta pot, the pot will crack as the plaster hardens.)

- Plaster of Paris

- One bunch of spiral eucalyptus

- One bunch of tulips

- Boxwood

- Ten stems of orange enchantment lilies

Design Steps

1. Mix the plaster of Paris according to directions. Place the plaster in the plastic pot. (Do not be concerned about the holes in the bottom of the pot; the plaster should be thick enough to prevent running.) Position the branch carefully in the center of the pot. Remember that when the plaster hardens, the branch cannot be changed. While the plaster is still malleable,

Advanced Design Styles

Figure 6.20a Topiary Step 1

Figure 6.20b Topiary Step 5

ensure that the branch is centered and straight. The bottom of the branch should be cut straight across, while the tip should be fashioned into a point. *Tip: A piece of styrofoam can be glued to the bottom of the container before filling with the plaster. The dowel or branch can then be secured into the styrofoam until the plaster sets.*

2. If using the IGLU® Grande Holder, remove the cutout center of the bottom of the mechanic. Position either form of presoaked mechanic on top of the branch and tape the mechanic securely, using the lasso method. **(Figure 6.20a)**

3. Cover the mechanic with a piece of plastic so that the moisture will be effectively retained within.

4. Beginning with the eucalyptus, create an outline of the form around the mechanic. The center of the mechanic should be approximately two-thirds from the top of the finished design. Using the remaining floral materials, create an all-around mass design. The ends of the topiary may appear to be whispy, but the center should be dense and full. Create depth by placing floral material at different levels within the design.

5. The design can be finished with ribbons or any vining material. Attach the ribbons to the center of the mass, and twirl the streamers down the center trunk. Glue the ends to the bottom of the trunk, and let the ends cascade over the rim of the pot. Cover the outer side of the plastic pot with either fabric or sheet moss, or drop the plastic pot into another decorative pot. **(Figure 6.20b)**

There are a few floral designers who are so naturally talented that little study is needed. The majority, however, possess an artistic ability that can be developed into a fine art with study and practice. As in any art form, floral designers need to become familiar with the elements of design, the mechanics useful in the craft, and the classical study of the art form. With this knowledge, each designer can soar to new heights with his/her own creativity.

ns and Design

This chapter has introduced many different design styles and emphasized the main principles. However, designers must rely on their artistic abilities to put these principles into practice. For further instruction, seek out workshops with noted artists. With experience, designers should be able to fine tune their floral designs.

Ultimately, the most important factor is whether or not a designer's arrangements can be sold. When experimenting with new design styles, carefully monitor the reception they receive from consumers. (It may be necessary to educate consumers regarding alternate design styles.) Consumers are the final judges, and the profitability of a floral business must remain uppermost in every florist's mind.

Notes

Advanced Design Styles

Notes, Photographs, Sketches, etc.

Advanced Floral Design

Notes, Photographs, Sketches, etc.

Advanced Design Styles

Notes, Photographs, Sketches, etc.

Sympathy Design

Chapter 7

Advanced floral design expands elementary principles to create a more personalized expression of tribute, sympathy, or celebration. This chapter is designed to provide ideas from which advanced designers may glean knowledge and applications for developing personal creative potential. There is no universal formula for sympathy designs, because regional differences prevail. However, using personal empathy and sensitivity, the foundation for an application of the principles presented in this chapter may be found.

Casket Designs

As a center of interest, the casket cover may set the mood for the entire funeral service. In advanced design, florists have the opportunity to create designs that represent the personality, interests, or accomplishments of the deceased. The style of the cover will vary according to regional differences and the buyer's taste. The casket cover in advanced styles of design can be taller than traditional versions. The setup and transportation of arrangements of unusual heights, lengths, or sizes should be coordinated with the funeral home.

Casket Saddle Mechanics *(Figure 7.1)*

A plastic or metal casket saddle is most often used as the container or mechanic for a casket design. Presoaked floral foam is then placed in the saddle. Allow the foam to sit on a drain board before placing it in the saddle. This will prevent the foam from dripping at the funeral home.

Camouflaging the saddle base by gluing leaves or mosses to the exposed frame is suggested. *(See Figures 7.1a and 7.1b. on page 196.)* To add extra foam support, place chicken wire over the top of the presoaked floral foam. Add chicken wire to the surface of the foam only. Ensure that no wires touch the casket. Make sure wire ends are securely tucked into the saddle base leaving no ends exposed. Remember, exposed wire may cause injury. Use waterproof tape or wire to secure chicken wire and foam blocks to saddles. **(See Figure 7.1c.)**

An alternate method of giving extra support to the floral foam is to cover the foam with foil and wrap it several times with waxed string. The foil and the string give extra strength to the foam but are lighter than the chicken wire.

Casket Design Styles

Advanced style casket designs follow the same principles of design as the arrangements of the same name. For example, a vegetative casket cover is designed as if it were growing, just as a vegetative arrangement is designed as if it were growing. The primary difference is the mechanics.

Knowing the difference between design styles, such as vegetative, new convention, and abstract, will assist designers in selecting an appropriate style for a casket. Advanced designers should review Chapters 2 and 6 regarding techniques and design styles. Reviewing these chapters may reinforce the necessary principles and styles, as well as inspire designers to create interesting floral tributes.

Remember, Euro-styled (vegetative, new convention, etc.) arrangements and abstract arrangements may be characterized by grouping and clustering flower varieties. In addition, the base of the design may be layered, terraced, sectioned, framed, or the pavé process can even be applied. Advanced designers should feel free to add personal interpretations of these styles, because the designs must be modified in order to complement different casket styles. The following instructions and illustrations provide examples of how these principles may be implemented.

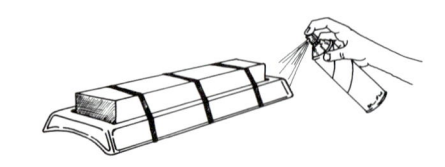

Figure 7.1a Casket Saddle Mechanics

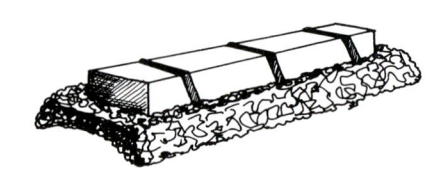

Figure 7.1b Casket Saddle Mechanics

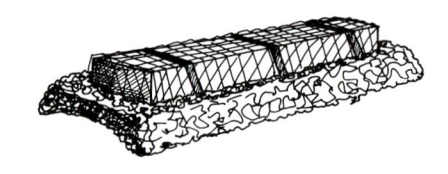

Figure 7.1c Casket Saddle Mechanics

Vegetative

Vegetative designs copy nature or mimic a look often associated with a natural environment. A casket cover in this style might give the appearance of growing by the waterside, in the forest, or in the desert. Grasses, mosses, stones, and driftwood are ideal materials to use on the base of such a cover. Impact is created when garden varieties, such as spray roses, tulips, ranunculus, and allium, are used. Following is an example.

Sympathy Design

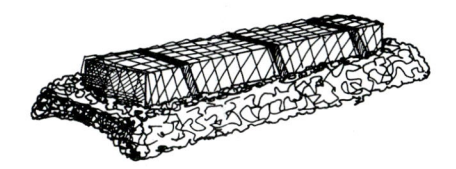

Figure 7.2a Designing a Vegetative Casket Cover Step 1

Figure 7.2b Designing a Vegetative Casket Cover Steps 2 & 3

Figure 7.2c Designing a Vegetative Casket Cover Step 5

Designing a Vegetative Casket Cover *(Figure 7.2)*

1. Use a double casket saddle with pre-mossed base. *(Figure 7.2a)*

2. Establish groups of vertical lines with separation between each group. Each group should be designed randomly as if it were growing. *(Figure 7.2b)* Staggering flower placements vertically is not recommended. Staggered flowers appear too designed for this styled. Material, such as iris, amaryllis, and horsetail, work well as vertical lines. Multi-branched materials, such as pompon mums and baby's breath do not usually work well, because their form does not create a good line.

3. Establish groups of horizontal lines using materials that will cascade down and drape over the casket. Ivy, bear grass, ti leaves, and bouvardia may work well as cascading lines. Again, materials should be grouped for impact, as well as reinforcement of the base of the design.

4. Use terracing, layering, or the pavé method between groups with galax leaves, processed mushrooms, and carnation heads.

5. Connect the groups with a textured base using flowers and foliage that will enhance each group. For example, if a line group is designed with white irises, perhaps the base flowers below the group could be white ranunculus. The white color of the ranunculus ties in with the irises, and the round shape pulls the eye down and creates a feeling of stability at the base. *(Figure 7.2c)*

6. Finish the design with moss and foliage.

New Convention

New convention designs can successfully be adapted to casket covers. While this style utilizes the parallel techniques, there are not only vertical groups but also horizontal groups juxtaposed at 90-degree angles. The horizontal groups should be a reflection of the vertical groups in the design. It should be possible to draw an imaginary rectangle or square around a new

Advanced Floral Design

convention arrangement. Techniques such as terracing, layering, and strong grouping are important to this style. A way of making a new convention arrangement more interesting is the use of framing, which may not only be angular, but contrastingly circular in form. In order to adapt to the shape of the casket, some cascading lines need to be incorporated into the design. Below is an example of a casket design inspired by new convention.

Designing a New Convention Casket Cover *(Figure 7.3)*

1. Place vertical and horizontal groups of flowers and foliage at 90-degree angles. Straight flowers or plant materials, such as liatris or flax, may be used to establish these lines. Remember to group materials by species. *(Figure 7.3a)*

2. Insert a few cascading lines. Ivy, asparagus, sprengeri, or other trailing materials will work well.

3. Moss, layer, and terrace between groups.

4. Add flowers of the same variety to each group, blending verticals and horizontals and joining with the base. Remember, the base of the design is the presoaked floral foam in the casket saddle or the point of connection for the vertical and horizontal lines.

5. Insert additional cascading materials, such as bear grass, to blend the design with the casket. *(Figure 7.3b)*

6. Finish by placing moss, foliage, or pods between the groups.

Waterfall

A revival of the late 1800s romantic cascading design, the waterfall design works particularly well as a casket design. The long, trailing materials accent the shape and give the cover a flowing effect. It is essential that the material literally looks as if it jumps from the center of the container and cascades to the desired length. Inside placement and depth are created by an overlay of materials. Typical of the waterfall style is the layering of one material over another to allow diversity. Generally, select smaller varieties of flowers and combine them with large amounts of foliage to achieve the "untidy" appearance of an waterfall. Bear grass, flat

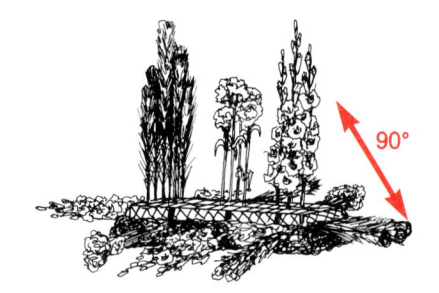

Figure 7.3a Designing a New Convention Casket Cover Step 1

Figure 7.3b Designing a New Convention Casket Cover Step 5

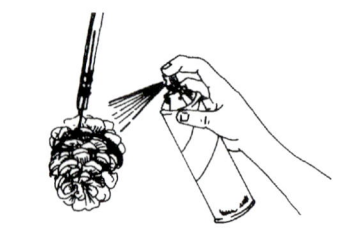

Figure 7.4a Designing A Waterfall Casket Cover Step 2

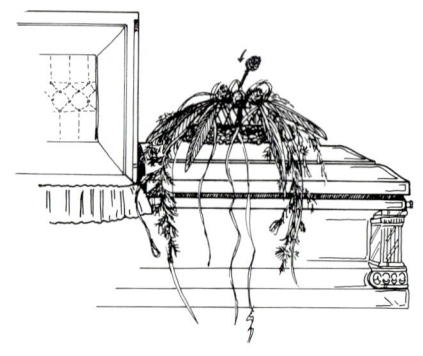

Figure 7.4b Designing A Waterfall Casket Cover Step 4

Sympathy Design

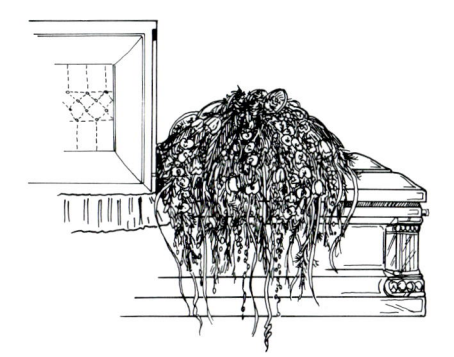

199

Figure 7.4c Designing A Waterfall Casket Cover Step 5

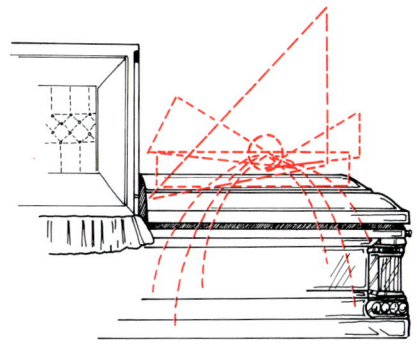

Figure 7.5a Designing a Landscape Casket Cover Step 1

Figure 7.5b Designing a Landscape Casket Cover Steps 4 - 6

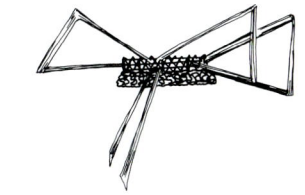

Figure 7.6a Designing an Abstract Casket Cover Step 2

fern, asparagus plumosus, conifer, vines, and twigs are used, as is the addition of ribbon, tulle, or copper wire as a decorative element. The first impression is that of little design style; however, it can be one of the most difficult styles of floral design to master.

Designing a Waterfall Casket Cover *(Figure 7.4)*

1. Begin with a casket saddle that has been covered with chicken wire and moss. Insert materials from the bottom of the foam to the top. Place the longest materials into the saddle first.

2. Insert pine cones or other pods to add seasonal variety. Secure by wiring to a pick and coating with spray glue on the underside. Next, place the cone or pod in the top of the design. The glue assists in adhering the cones/pods to the composition. *(Figure 7.4a on page 198)*

3. Place the cones or pods upright, like soldiers, so that they all angle slightly toward the front.

4. Continue to overlay materials, leaving pockets underneath to create depth and give character. *(Figure 7.4b on page 198)*

5. The top of the design must also convey the feeling of falling water. The blossoms should not suddenly reach toward the sky, they must cascade down the front surface of the design. Position materials so that a forward motion is achieved. *(Figure 7.4c)*

6. Copper wire or other reflective materials may be added or woven through the design to mirror the image of moving water.

7. Finish by filling with moss, foliage, or flowers.

Landscape

At first, vegetative designs seem quite similar to landscape arrangements. Upon close observation, the influence and discipline of landscape architecture is seen. The assembly of the materials and the techniques, such as terracing and layering, are essential. Placement of material often follows overlapping

Advanced Floral Design

geometric shapes. Often, taller flowers are placed in the back and shorter flowers in the front. In landscape designs, there is little staggering of stem lengths within the same cluster. Instead, staggered heights occur between the flower groups. Differences in height prevent rigidity in this style.

Appropriate flowers to feature in landscape designs are those that would actually be planted in a garden. Using only a combination of seasonal flowers in an arrangement provides a more authentic look. Stones, mosses, and branches can be used as part of the foundation of the arrangement. Often, this design contains a man-made structure, such as a fence or bridge. Once again, advanced designers must adapt the principles of a landscape arrangement to emphasize the curves of the casket.

Designing a Landscape Casket Cover *(Figure 7.5)*

1. In the mind or on paper, visualize the overall geometric shape desired. Break the overall shape down to smaller shapes to understand placement. *(Figure 7.5a on page 199)*

2. Place large branch material, such as corkscrew willow, slightly off center toward the rear of the design.

3. Establish a focal area with several large form flowers, such as king proteas or rubrum lilies.

4. Using the techniques of sequencing and grouping, reinforce horizontal lines using ti leaves on one side of the focal area and roses or ranunculus on the other. *(Figure 7.5b on page 199)*

5. Layering the base with galax leaves, cluster with roses or carnations, and terrace with mushrooms to reinforce vertical and horizontal lines. *(Figure 7.5b on page 199)*

6. Fill in with flowers and foliage; meld them to the curves of the casket. Ivy, trailing jasmine, or dendrobium could be used. *(Figure 7.5b on page 199)*

Abstract

Using nonclassical form, crossed stems, bold colors, geometric shapes, or strong textures, the abstract design style can be used to create an appropriate sympathy tribute. Leaving the traditional affords designers opportunities to use multiple focal

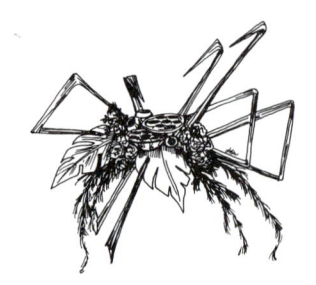

Figure 7.6b Designing an Abstract Casket Cover Step 5

Figure 7.7a Designing a Foliage Casket Blanket Step 2

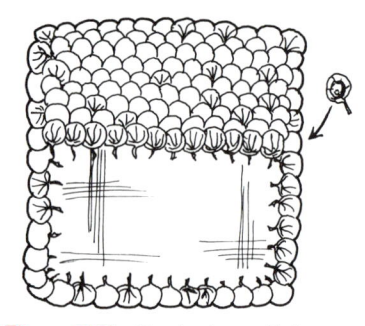

Figure 7.7b Designing a Foliage Casket Blanket Step 3

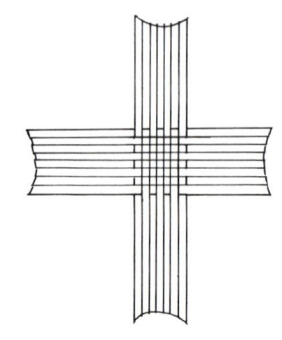

Figure 7.7c Designing a Foliage Casket Blanket Step 4

Sympathy Design

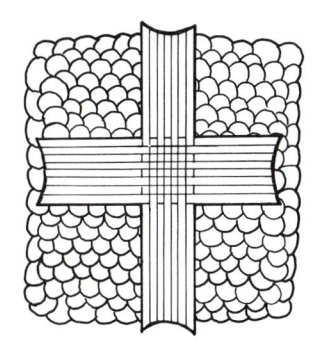

Figure 7.7d Designing a Foliage Casket Blanket Step 5

Figure 7.7e Designing a Foliage Casket Cover Step 8

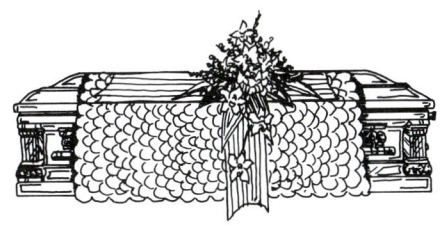

Figure 7.7f Designing a Foliage Casket Cover Step 9

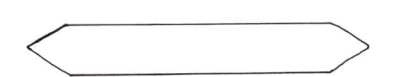

Figure 7.8a Designing a Casket Scarf Step 1

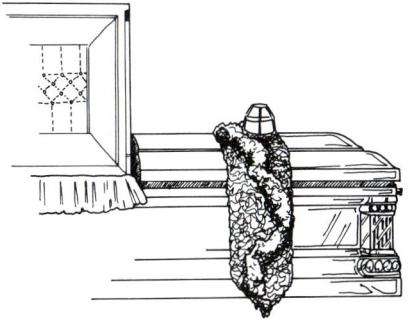

Figure 7.8b Designing a Casket Scarf Step 5

areas, contrasts, and natural materials in unusual ways. Care should be taken to balance the shape of the design with the contours and colors of the casket. This type of design would not typically be used in everyday situations, but should be reserved for the customer who desires a unique, expressive casket cover.

Designing an Abstract Casket Cover *(Figure 7.6)*

1. Insert the ends of long flax stems into the sides of a casket saddle which has had chicken wire applied.

2. Bend the flax into angles, and insert the tips into the top of the foam. *(Figure 7.6a on page 199)*

3. Add large, tropical leaves to cover the saddle.

4. Place pods, such as lotus, low in the focal area.

5. Cluster mass flowers and foliage between the pods to unite the sections of the design together. *(Figure 7.6b on page 200)*

6. Keep clustered materials sectioned according to variety. Do not mix the clusters or confusion is likely to occur.

7. Add additional flax or other line materials to give height to the design. These stems may be positioned to frame the focal area.

8. Finish with moss and foliage.

Casket Blanket

The casket blanket is usually considered a traditional design; however, this style can be updated by applying unusual materials and shapes. For example, instead of solid flowers, advanced designers might create a blanket out of layered galax leaves underneath a design of woven flax. (See leafwork described on page 65 in Chapter 3.) Plant materials can be secured to moss green burlap fabric with a floral adhesive. The burlap is strong enough to provide the mechanic while still allowing draping.

Designing a Foliage Casket Blanket *(Figure 7.7)*

1. Cut moss green burlap to approximately 6 feet by 6 feet.

2. Using floral adhesive edge, starting at the cover the blanket with galax leaves or other flat and round or oval-shaped leaves. *(Figure 7.7a on page 200)*

3. Glue leaves in neat rows, overlapping each leaf base with the tip of the next leaf in order to completely cover the fabric. *(Figure 7.7b on page 200)*

4. Weave flax stems under and over to create an asymmetrical woven structure. *(Figure 7.7c on page 200)*

5. Carefully pin or staple the woven flax to the center area of the blanket. *(Figure 7.7d on page 201)*

6. Attach a small, presoaked floral cage, such as an IGLU® to the center of the flax structure.

7. Secure the cage by piercing chenille stems through the burlap, leaves, and flax.

8. Place the ends of the chenille stems through the plastic holes of the cage; twist till secure, and clip excess chenille. *(Figure 7.7e on page 201)*

9. Finish the blanket by designing a contemporary line-mass accent in the caged foam. *(Figure 7.7f on page 201)*

Scarves

Scarves are normally constructed using fabrics such as satin, velvet, or moiré. A floral cluster is often wired and taped and then pinned into the fabric. An alternative to this method is using moss green burlap with a floral foam cage as the mechanic. This allows a broader variety of flower types to be used for this design.

Designing a Casket Scarf *(Figure 7.8)*

1. Cut burlap to the desired scarf length, width, and shape. Tapered ends of various kinds can be cut to add interest. *(Figure 7.8a on page 201)*

2. Heavily mist the burlap with spray glue.

3. Press Spanish moss or sheet moss onto the fabric.

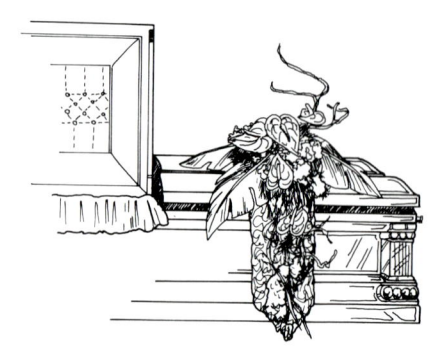

Figure 7.8c Designing a Casket Scarf Steps 6 & 8

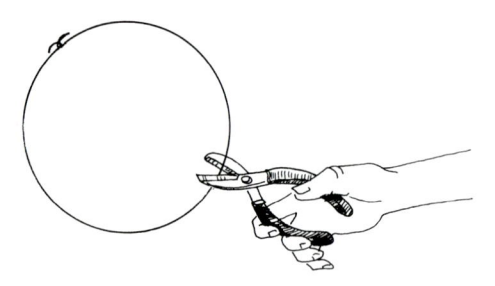

Figure 7.9a Designing a Children's Casket Cover Step 1

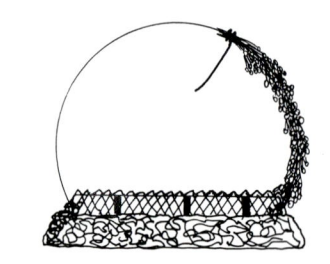

Figure 7.9b Designing a Children's Casket Cover Steps 2 & 4

Figure 7.9c Designing a Children's Casket Cover Step 7

Sympathy Design

Figure 7.9d Designing a Children's Casket Cover Step 10

Figure 7.9e Designing a Children's Casket Cover Step 15

Figure 7.10a Designing a European Funeral Wreath Step 1

Figure 7.10b Designing a European Funeral Wreath Step 2

4. Using pan melt glue, attach larger clumps of moss to the scarf to create a mosaic appearance and add interest.

5. Secure a presoaked floral cage to the center of the scarf, using chenille stems poked through the burlap. **(Figure 7.8b on page 201)**

6. Using twigs and leaves, establish the outline of the cluster. **(Figure 7.8c on page 202)**

7. Use large flowers or pods to establish a focal area.

8. Reinforce line and fill in with mosses, pods, or small mass flowers to finish the design. **(Figure 7.8c on page 202)**

Designs for Children's Caskets

Requiring special sensitivity, designs for children's caskets place unique demands on the creativity of designers. Capturing youthful qualities without diminishing the somber dignity of the occasion can be quite challenging. Incorporating a small toy or object common to children into the casket cover can be suitable if properly designed. The following example demonstrates one of the many ways that a children's accessory can be featured in a sympathy piece.

<u>Designing a Children's Casket Cover</u> **(Figure 7.9)**

1. Cut a 30-inch diameter wire wreath in half. **(Figure 7.9a on page 202)**

2. Insert the ends of one-half of the wreath into the sides of the chicken-wired casket saddle. **(Figure 7.9b on page 202)**

3. Twist the ends of wires which have had floral tape applied to them, around the ends of the inserted wreath, and wire through the chicken wire mesh to anchor the wreath frames.

4. Using #28 gauge paddle wire, garland filler material, such as heather, baby's breath, or tea tree, to the wreath frame. When garlanding, always place material end over end and advance in one direction, covering stem ends. **(Figure 7.9b on page 202)**

Advanced Floral Design

5. Make a bow with long streamers.

6. Attach the bow to one side of the wreath frame.

7. Baste the ribbon streamers into the wreath frame by attaching sections with wire. Leave space between each attachment to create the feeling of movement. *(Figure 7.9c on page 202)*

8. Lightly moss the top of the casket saddle.

9. Twist floral-taped wires around the legs of a teddy bear.

10. Attach the wired ends around 6-inch wooden picks. *(Figure 7.9d on page 203)*

11. Lay out the lines of a basic casket design emphasizing the cascade over the sides of the casket.

12. Group flowers on the top of the casket saddle. Keep them low and within the frame of the wreath.

13. Add cascading flowers and foliage.

14. Attach five to seven small bows with six loops each and long streamers to wooden picks. Bows should be made of the same ribbon as that used in the wreath garland.

15. Insert the picks into the top of the design. Let the ribbon streamers weep through the cascading section of the design. *(Figure 7.9e on page 203)*

Wreath Designs

Symbolizing the circle of life, wreaths are a traditional form of tribute. The continuous lines of a circle are pleasing because they signify the continuation of the life cycle. Used for centuries in many countries, they are a beautiful way to express sympathy and respect. The following designs provide various methods of wreath application.

Figure 7.10c Designing a European Funeral Wreath Step 3

Figure 7.10d Designing a European Funeral Wreath Step 4

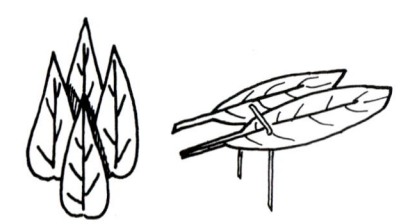

Figure 7.11a Designing a Triple-ring Foliage Wreath Step 1

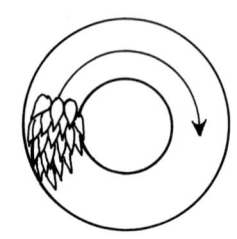

Figure 7.11b Designing a Triple-ring Foliage Wreath Step 1

Sympathy Design

Figure 7.11c Designing a Triple-ring Foliage Wreath Step 2

Figure 7.11d Designing a Triple-ring Foliage Wreath Step 7

Figure 7.12a Designing a Solid Wreath Ring Step 1

Figure 7.12b Designing a Solid Wreath Ring Step 2

Figure 7.12c Designing a Solid Wreath Ring Step 4

European-inspired

These wreaths are often designed using grouping and clustering to create a vegetative or landscape effect. They can be placed on the floor or on a wire easel with the top bent back to allow the wreath to sit nearly flat, but off the ground.

If a designer wishes to construct a wreath attached to an easel, the wreath can be secured to the easel at the top and sides using chenille stems or floral-taped wires.

Designing a European Funeral Wreath **(Figure 7.10)**

1. Lay a soaked floral foam wreath flat, and pin groups of moss randomly to the base. **(Figure 7.10a on page 203)**

2. Establish vertical lines with the placement of upright pods or small branches. **(Figure 7.10b on page 203)**

3. Reinforce vertical placements with groups and clusters of segregated varieties of flowers, foliage, pods, or mushrooms. **(Figure 7.10c on page 204)**

4. Wire the wreath to a metal easel that has been bent to create a resting area that is almost flat from which the wreath may be viewed. **(Figure 7.10d on page 204)** Note: Refer to the section regarding easels on page 212 of this chapter for frame bending technique.

Triple-ring Foliage Wreath

This can be a dramatic design when meticulously layered leaves are overlapped to cover the wreath form. The leaves provide a sleek, repetitive background. Advanced designers may capitalize on the color and texture of flowers when they are placed on a foliage-covered base. This design is constructed with three wreaths of different sizes of layered with foliage and wired together.

Designing a Triple-ring Foliage Wreath **(Figure 7.11)**

1. Working with three different sizes - small, medium, and large - use greening pins to attach leaves to the surface of each wreath. Make sure they are pointed in the same direction. Be sure to cover the stem ends with each placement. **(Figures 7.11a and 7.11b on page 204)**

2. Complete the leafwork around each wreath. **(Figure 7.11c on page 205)**

3. When leafwork is completed, carefully wire the three wreaths together so that they overlap. Keep balance and proportion in mind to achieve the desired shape. Use floral-taped wires only; plain wires may cut through the leafwork.

4. Using floral taped wire, attach caged floral foam near the joining point of the three wreaths.

5. Insert ivy or another cascading plant material into the foam to establish lines.

6. Position focal flowers in the center of the foam and reinforce with leaves, moss, and clustered flowers.

7. Incorporate ribbon, rope, or cording to add a draping feeling. **(Figure 7.11d on page 205)**

8. Finish with moss or leaves to hide mechanics.

Solid Wreath Ring

Typically, these wreaths are kept in the traditional category using carnations, gladioli, or chrysanthemum florets. However, using nontraditional floral materials, such as hydrangea blossoms, the principles of solid work can achieve a less contrived appearance. This wreath could be completely covered with hydrangea blossoms, and a cluster of flowers could be designed as a focal point.

Designing a Solid Wreath Ring *(Figure 7.12)*

1. Start with a saturated floral foam wreath. **(Figure 7.12a on page 205)**

2. Place hydrangea blossoms into the foam until wreath base is completely covered. **(Figure 7.12b on page 205)**

3. Using small branch material and several form flowers, such as amaryllis, establish a center of interest at the desired location on the wreath frame.

4. Incorporate a bow made of specialty ribbon, such as French-wired ribbon. **(Figure 7.12c on page 205)**

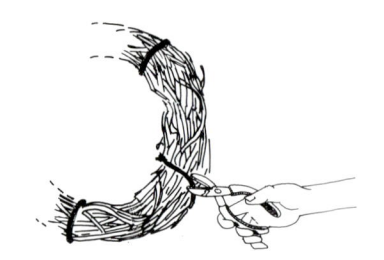

Figure 7.13a Designing a Composite Grapevine Wreath Step 1

Figure 7.13b Designing a Composite Grapevine Wreath Step 2

Figure 7.13c Designing a Composite Grapevine Wreath Step 2

Figure 7.13d Designing a Composite Grapevine Wreath Step 3

Sympathy Design

Figure 7.13e Designing a Composite Grapevine Wreath Step 6

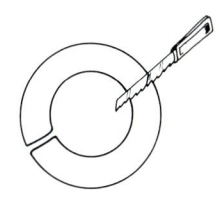

Figure 7.14a Designing a Modified Styrofoam Wreath Step 1

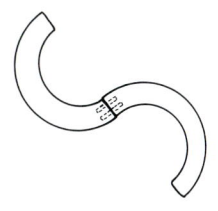

Figure 7.14b Designing a Modified Styrofoam Wreath Step 4

Figure 7.14c Designing a Modified Styrofoam Wreath Step 8

5. If allowed to dry in the foam wreath, the hydrangea may serve as a keepsake.

Composite Grapevine Wreath

In this type of design, designers can transform traditional grapevine wreaths into advanced designs by altering the shape to create a more abstract appearance. Basically, a form that is a traditionally closed is opened, and satellite clusters are used to add dimension.

Designing a Composite Grapevine Wreath *(Figure 7.13)*

1. Using wire cutters, clip any existing attachment wires on the grapevine wreath. *(Figure 7.13a on page 206)*

2. Pull the grapevine apart; and attach curled sections to a prepared easel using wire. *(Figures 7.13b and 7.13c on page 206)*

3. Using wire, attach a small, presoaked floral cage (such as an IGLU®) to each key section of grapevine. *(Figure 7.13d on page 206)*

4. Using crescent lines to reinforce the circular lines of the grapevine, place floral materials into the cages.

5. Establish focal areas in each accent area.

6. Use trailing flowers and foliage to visually connect each unit of the wreath. *(Figure 7.13e)*

Modified Styrofoam Wreath

Styrofoam affords designers the opportunity to cut and alter the shape of the traditional circle. By reorganizing the shape of the circle, new shapes, such as crescents and Hogarth curves, can be created. The construction of a styrofoam wreath is outlined below.

Designing a Modified Styrofoam Wreath *(Figure 7.14)*

1. Using a styrofoam saw, cut a styrofoam wreath in half. *(Figure 7.14a)*

2. Apply floral adhesive to one end of each wreath section.

3. Insert double-ended picks into the ends of the glue-covered wreath ends.

4. Place the two ends together to create an *S* shape. **(Figure 7.14b on page 207)**

5. Position the *S* on an easel.

6. Cover the styrofoam with leafwork.

7. Attach a small floral foam cage at the center of the *S*.

8. Design an accent cluster of flowers in an exaggerated *S*. **(Figure 7.14c on page 207)**

Braided Ribbon Wreath *(Figure 7.15)*

This wreath gives the impression of a multi-looped, satin rope. It is constructed by using a simple, three-strand braided ribbon of approximately 5 yards. **(See Figure 7.15a.)** The wreath can be created by making loops with the braid. The braids are circled five times and joined at the top. **(See Figure 7.15b.)** Attach a small, presoaked floral cage to the joining point, using floral-taped wires and twisting tightly to secure the cage. Special care should be taken to avoid dripping water from the caged foam onto the ribbon and causing damage. Flower clusters are designed in the foam to individualize the wreath. **(See Figure 7.15c.)**

Figure 7.15a Designing a Braided Ribbon Wreath

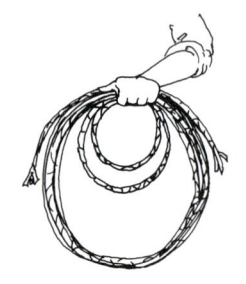

Figure 7.15b Designing a Braided Ribbon Wreath

Figure 7.15c Designing a Braided Ribbon Wreath

Easel Designs

Typically designed on a three-legged tripod of wire, wood, or brass, easel designs may provide a backdrop for a casket. Pillows, hearts, crosses, and sprays are traditional designs that can be altered to demonstrate advanced creative expression.

Sprays

Sprays are a popular funeral piece, even though they do not last as long as arrangements in water. Sprays make effective backgrounds and can range from simple to dramatic as the advanced principles are creatively applied. For those who desire, dried materials can be used to create a keepsake design that will remain after the funeral.

Figure 7.16 Designing an Easel Spray

Sympathy Design

To create an advanced spray design, visualize the floral cage and easel as a container. The designer should decide on an arrangement style and then apply the principles. Outlined below is one suggested method of construction.

Designing an Easel Spray *(Figure 7.16 on page 208)*

1. Attach a large floral cage to a prepared easel using wire.

2. Visualizing the easel and cage as a container, establish the lines of the desired design style chosen from Chapter 6.

3. Using mass or form flowers, establish a focal area.

4. Incorporate advanced techniques, such as grouping and layering, to individualize the design.

Composite Sprays

Designing composite easel sprays involves integrating components of traditional sprays while adding clusters and satellite sprays to enhance the main design. Following is an example for constructing an asymmetrical composite easel spray.

Designing a Composite Easel Spray *(Figure 7.17)*

1. Attach a large, presoaked floral cage to the upper portion of an easel and a smaller presoaked floral cage to the middle section of one easel leg.

2. Choosing an asymmetrical design style and keeping in mind that both sections constitute the design, establish the outline of the design. *(Figure 7.17a)*

3. Establish the focal area in the top spray. *(Figure 7.17b)*

4. Establish a smaller, secondary focal area in the bottom spray.

5. Strengthen the lines and focal areas with flowers, foliage, and moss.

6. Finish with ribbon or cording. *(Figure 7.17c)*

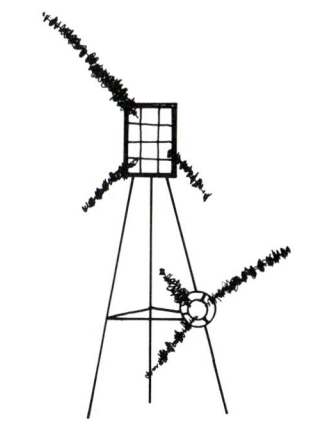

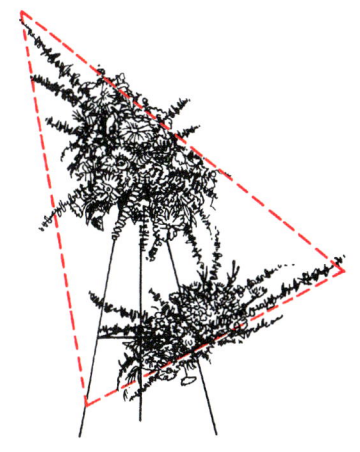

Figure 7.17a Designing a Composite Easel Spray Step 2

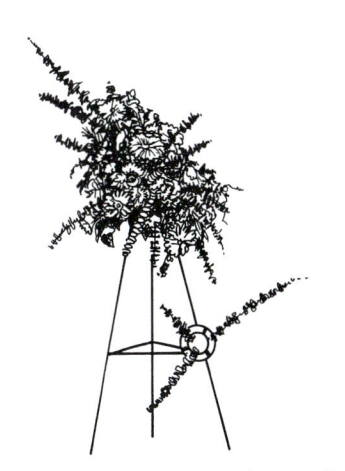

Figure 7.17b Designing an Composite Spray Step 3

Figure 7.17c Designing a Composite Easel Spray Step 6

Advanced Floral Design

Pillows and Hearts

As the traditional pillow or heart design is transformed into a contemporary, high style tribute, a variety of textures and colors can be used. The focal point may remain in the upper left corner, as traditional design dictates, but the pavé technique can be utilized to blend traditional material to achieve a more contemporary design. The pillow explained below may inspire designers to attempt advanced techniques on other traditional shapes, including the heart.

Designing a Contemporary Funeral Pillow *(Figure 7.18)*

1. Lightly moss a pillowshaped styrofoam base.

2. Glue fresh leaves to picks, using floral adhesive.

3. Outline the pillow base with picked foliage. **(Figure 7.18a)**

4. Working from the edges toward the upper left corner, layer and group foliage, moss, and flowers into desired patterns. Do not allow sections to mix. **(Figure 7.18b)**

5. Place roses or other flowers between sections of the pillow to further define areas.

6. Add a small floral foam cage to the focal area and design a floral cluster. **(Figure 7.18c)**

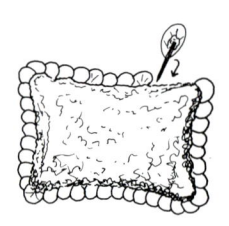

Figure 7.18a Designing a Contemporary Funeral Pillow Step 3

Figure 7.18b Designing a Contemporary Funeral Pillow Step 4

Figure 7.18c Designing a Contemporary Funeral Pillow Step 6

Horsetail Cross

A significant development in the designing of a cross can be the use of textures and materials. As an original religious symbol, the cross will take on new dimensions when unique materials, such as horsetail, pussy willow, and birch branches, are fashioned into the frame and design of the cross. In this design, a styrofoam cross is covered with horsetail. A presoaked floral cage is placed in the center of the cross and bisected by a horsetail ladder. Following are the instructions for constructing such a cross.

Designing a Horsetail Cross *(Figure 7.19)*

1. Lightly moss a styrofoam cross base. Position long stems of equisetum vertically to cover the main bar of the cross. Use greening pins to secure the horsetail in

Figure 7.19a Designing a Horsetail Cross Step 1

Figure 7.19b Designing a Horsetail Cross Step 2

Sympathy Design

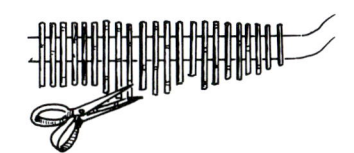

Figure 7.19c Designing a Horsetail Cross Step 3

Figure 7.19d Designing a Horsetail Cross Step 4

Figure 7.19e Designing a Horsetail Cross Step 6

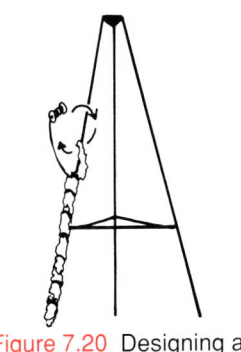

Figure 7.20 Designing a Moss-covered Easel

place. Clip the ends to keep them even. **(Figure 7.19a on page 210)**

2. Position short stems of equisetum horizontally to cover the cross bar. **(Figure 7.19b on page 210)**

3. String small pieces of horsetail on two #20 gauge wires. **(Figure 7.19c)** Clutch additional wires to the ends of each #20 gauge wire as length is needed.

4. Attach a medium-sized, presoaked floral cage to the center of the cross. **(Figure 7.19d)**

5. Position the horsetail fence diagonally into the floral cage, attaching with greening pins and wire.

6. Finish the cross by designing the central accent piece in the shape of a Hogarth curve. Be sure to establish a focal area and cover all mechanics. **(Figure 7.19e)**

Easel Variations

Wire, wood, and brass easels are commonly used. As creative thoughts are incorporated into designs, a variety of styles and materials may be used to create easels which coordinate and enhance the elements of the floral arrangement. Birch branches and bamboo can easily be fastened to form tripod easels.

Coordination of the easel and arrangement is essential so that they will not dominate or detract from the design. Applying covers to easels is another way to expand the traditional style. Using moss, twigs, and fabric can create an interesting easel to present designs. Following are several methods of covering an easel.

Moss-covered Easel *(Figure 7.20)*

1. Attach moss to the bottom of the easel using paddle wire.

2. Be sure to overlap enough moss to conceal most of the wire. **(Figure 7.20)**

Branch-covered Easel *(Figure 7.21)*

1. Lay the longest, largest branches against the easel and secure with wire.

2. Starting at the top of the easel, wire smaller branches to the frame of the stand. **(Figure 7.21)**

3. Working downward, overlap branch ends to conceal unsightly stem ends and wire.

4. If needed, glue bits of moss over wired joining points to conceal them.

Fabric-covered Easel *(Figure 7.22)*

1. Before starting, make sure the fabric is not too thick or stiff. Soft, supple material is best.

2. Starting at the bottom of the easel, roll and weave fabric around the easel frame. **(Figure 7.22)**

3. Secure with wire.

4. Ensure that the wire is covered by puffing fabric out to cover. **(Figure 7.22)**

Bent Easel *(Figure 7.23)*

1. Place a wire easel flat on a sturdy table with the hook facing down against the table top. **(Figure 7.23a)**

2. Hold on to the top portion of the easel; apply pressure to the midsection of the easel using the palm of the hand. Bend both sides until the easel top has desired tilt. **(Figure 7.23b)**

3. Attach a floral foam cage and design an arrangement in an upright form. **(Figure 7.23b)**

Bamboo or Wood Tripod *(Figure 7.24)*

1. Using an electric drill, drill a hole completely through three pieces of bamboo approximately one-fourth of the way down the stem.

2. Thread #22 gauge wire through the holes in the bamboo and twist very tightly to secure. **(Figure 7.24a on page 213)**

3. Spread the bamboo legs to create a tripod.

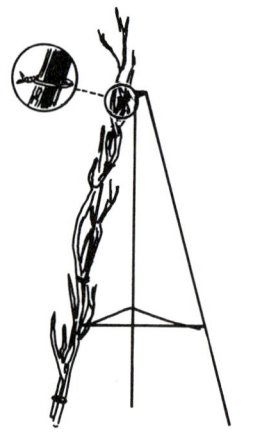

Figure 7.21 Designing a Branch-covered Easel

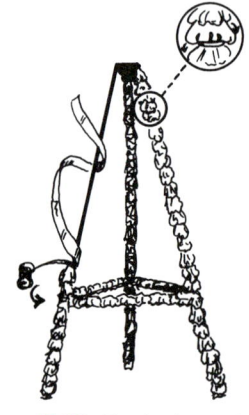

Figure 7.22 Designing a Fabric-covered Easel

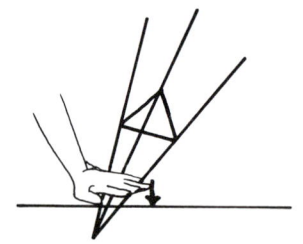

Figure 7.23a Designing a Bent Easel Step 1

Figure 7.23b Designing a Bent Easel Steps 2 & 3

Sympathy Design

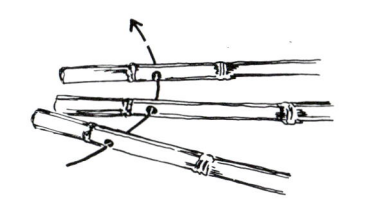

Figure 7.24a Designing a Bamboo or Wood Tripod Step 2

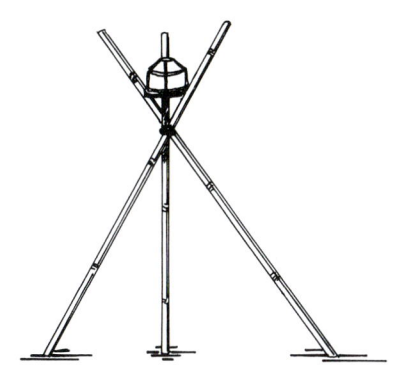

Figure 7.24b Designing a Bamboo or Wood Tripod Step 4

Figure 7.25 Abstract Vase Arrangement

Figure 7.26 Landscape Vase Arrangement

4. A floral cage or container may be wired or taped into the fork of the tripod. *(Figure 7.24b)*

Arrangements

As a comfortable medium for most designers, arrangements allow for infinite variations of design dynamics. Horizontal, vertical, symmetrical, asymmetrical, Euro-style, and abstract arrangements can be creative expressions of sympathy, whether formal or informal. Personal preferences of theme or accessories can contribute to a more individualized tribute.

Vase

Vase arrangements are flowers that are normally arranged in plastic or ceramic containers. As stated earlier, these arrangements can take on a variety of forms. Designs that range from Western to European can be adapted to create beautiful sympathy tributes. *Figures 7.25 through 7.27 on pages 213 and 214* are examples of the abstract, landscape, and curvilinear design styles used as sympathy vase arrangements.

Papier-maché

Papier-maché containers are disposable, inexpensive containers typically used for sympathy arrangements. They can be purchased in either white or green. In order to increase the style and design potential of papier-maché containers, they should be camouflaged. Leaves, moss, or fabric can be effectively used to create a desired effect. The container should be sprayed with floral adhesive *(see Figure 7.28a on page 214)*, then covered with leaves, moss, or fabric. *(See Figure 7.28b on page 214.)* A ribbon or raffia accent bow can be added for an effective finish. *(See Figure 7.28c on page 214.)*

Baskets

Several baskets can be wired together to form foundations for complex designs. They can be used as separate designs or combined to give the appearance of a single arrangement. *(See Figure 7.29 on page 214.)* Baskets can be covered or left with natural textures. Baskets should always be lined to ensure proper water holding capacity.

Advanced Floral Design

Heirloom Containers

Heirloom containers usually hold sentimental value aside from possible monetary value. They are provided by the family or friends of the deceased, and special care should be taken to ensure the safe use of such containers. Lining the vases and carefully packing and displaying them are the responsibilities of the florists. Minimizing the risk of scratches, chips, and cracks shows respect for the property of the customer and prevents future problems and expenses which might result from carelessness. It is wise to be prepared with knowledge concerning the insurance coverage of the florist.

Creating a Setting

The complete setting of a funeral, whether at a church, mortuary, or grave site, must be kept in perspective. It is vitally important to designers as they coordinate personal creativity, wishes of the bereaved, and mortuary policies to establish a setting where comfort, warmth, and beauty can exist harmoniously.

The Funeral Environment

Designers should attempt to balance sympathy pieces to create a setting free from the distractions of incompatible individual designs. Knowing what the family has chosen for casket design, colors, and grave site can be quite helpful. This information can be useful when helping other family members or mourners make selections. This will assist designers in coordinating styles and colors for impact. Grouping similar arrangement styles, colors, or even potted plants can assist designers in establishing a warm and comforting entrance area. This may be where the guest book is placed or where the family greets funeral attendees.

To create a focal area for the service, group similar arrangements, wreaths, sprays, or plants on various levels surrounding the casket. Remember that the casket and its design are the main focus of most funerals. *(See Figure 7.30 on page 215.)*

Grave Site

The grave site can often be a cold and forbidding place where the family and friends pay their respects. For this reason, it may be especially important to coordinate with the cemetery and

Figure 7.27 Curvilinear Vase Arrangement

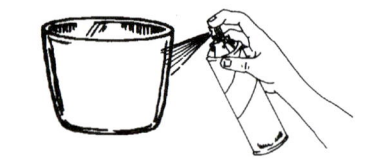

Figure 7.28a Designing with Papier-maché Containers

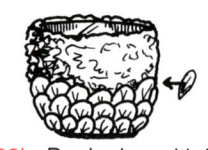

Figure 7.28b Designing with Papier-maché Containers

Figure 7.28c Designing with Papier-maché Containers

Figure 7.29 Designing with Baskets

Sympathy Design

Figure 7.30 Creating a Proper Funeral Environment

mortuary so that an environment of beauty can be created prior to the arrival of the family.

Florists may be able to service the funeral by either leaving immediately from the funeral with some of the more beautiful and showy designs, or better yet, by creating arrangements that will be used solely for the graveside service. Perhaps a garland of white roses, ranunculus, and asparagus fern could accompany a large white vase arrangement. White azalea plants could be banked to line the crypt and provide an air of sensitivity for the bereaved. *(See Figure 7.31.)*

Figure 7.31 Graveside Decorations

Because of the circumstances surrounding the loss of loved ones, florists should take care to develop sensitivity to the needs of the purchaser. Caution should be taken to avoid placing sympathy flowers into a formula presentation, thereby minimizing personal creative inspiration. There are no limits on empathy and compassion. Florists should always remember that the person being honored at the funeral is someone important to the people giving the tribute. Applying personal interest in a professional design cannot alleviate the loss felt by loved ones, but it can help create an environment from which nature's beauty can be used to soften the harsh realities of life and death.

Advanced Floral Design

Notes, Photographs, Sketches, etc.

Sympathy Design

Notes, Photographs, Sketches, etc.

Wedding Design

Chapter 8

Contemporary weddings have few rules and many options. Brides are older, have longer engagements, and strive for individuality. They are more selective of church location, reception, florist, caterer, photographer, baker, bridal gown and veil, bridesmaids' dresses, and, of course, flowers. Every bride wants her bouquet to be outstanding. She pays attention to details to ensure that her personal flowers are perfectly coordinated with her gown. She often selects classic flowers, such as roses, lilies of the valley, stephanotis, phalaenopsis orchids, delphinium, and lilacs, for her bouquet, which is often complemented by romantic ribbons, lace handkerchiefs, and pearl or iridescent beads.

The traditional styles of bouquets, such as the colonial, cascade, and crescent, continue to be favorite styles; however, the individualistic nature of contemporary brides has created a need for a more advanced style of design. New bouquet styles have emerged and many classic styles have been revived. There is a trend toward reviving wedding bouquet styles of the past. Specific periods have been studied by florists and updated. Popular bouquet design styles that have emerged include composite, Biedermeier, herbal and foliage, European contemporary, and hand-tied. The increased interest in these revived and new styles has created a need for expertise in advanced design.

When a bride selects an advanced bouquet style for her wedding, all of the floral decorations are affected. Bouquets and body flowers for the bridal party should be coordinated with a complementary advanced style. Ceremony and reception decorations should also reflect the style chosen. The florist must provide imaginative options to the bride from which the personalized wedding setting desired can be created.

This chapter identifies advanced design styles for wedding flowers of all kinds. Construction steps are provided for a variety of advanced bouquets, body flowers, and ceremony and reception decorations. Where appropriate, suggested flower types are provided to ensure that the desired look is achieved. This chapter is written for designers who have already mastered traditional bouquet construction techniques. For more information about wedding design basics, refer to Redbook Florist Services' textbook *Selling and Design Wedding Flowers*.

Bouquets

As in traditional bouquet design, advanced wedding bouquets may be constructed with wire and tape, in foam bouquet holders, or by binding the natural stems. Although there are a few specific styles that are considered advanced, most advanced bouquets are free-style designs with no formal definition but with obvious use of advanced design techniques. Stylized versions of even the most traditional bouquet styles, including colonials, cascades, and crescents, which incorporate specialty flowers and foliage, can be considered advanced designs. In this section, advanced bouquet styles requiring specific steps and flower placements are described. Advanced floral designers may modify these styles to reflect their own creative bouquet interpretations.

Composite Flowers

A composite flower is made by wiring or gluing individual petals together to form a large, composite flower. The glamellia is made from individual gladiolus florets, the duchess rose from individual rose petals, etc.

Composite flowers have great visual impact and are often used in bouquets for brides or bridesmaids. Although the construction requires patience and practice, the end result is worth the effort. This flower can be sold for a higher price, because its construction requires time and expertise.

Glamellia *(Figure 8.1)*

A glamellia is designed from one or more stems of gladiolus into a composite flower that resembles a camellia blossom. A large, single glamellia can be carried as a bouquet. Several sizes of glamellias can also be used in combination with other flowers and greenery to create a romantic look.

Notes

Wedding Design

Figure 8.1a Glamellia Step 1

Figure 8.1b Glamellia Step 2

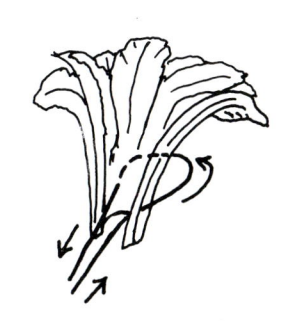

Figure 8.1c Glamellia Step 5

Materials Needed

- One gladiolus bud
- Number 28 gauge wire
- Sixteen to twenty gladiolus florets
- Number 20 gauge wire
- Cardboard
- Floral adhesive

Design Steps

1. Wire a gladiolus bud with two #28 gauge wires by using the cross pierce method. Pull the wires down and use one of the wires to bind the other three. *(Figure 8.1a)*

2. Remove the green ovary from the smallest gladiolus floret by pinching it off. To open the floret, cut from the base of the petals to the end of the floret between two petals. *(Figure 8.1b)* It is important to always cut opposite the needed petals. To use the dorsal petals, cut the lip area. To use the lip area, cut on the dorsal side.

3. Wrap the floret around the bud and pierce it with a #28 gauge wire until the wire extends 2 inches beyond the flower. Take the opposite end of the wire and circle the floret two times (make sure that the wrapping wire is above the extended wire); bring the wire down and bind the stem.

4. Cut the extended wire 1/4 inch from the flower. With the shears, bend this small wire over the encircled wires and insert it into the flower. This hook gives support and security to the circled wires.

5. Open the next floret as described in step 2. Pierce the floret with a #28 gauge wire on a diagonal line until the wire is halfway through the flower. Bring the top wire around to form a loop, and pierce the wire back through the floret. *(Figure 8.1c)*

6. Position the wired floret around the composite flower, and use the wires to bind it in place.

7. Continue adding florets in this manner until the flower is the desired size. This usually takes four or five florets.

8. To enlarge the glamellia to a dramatic size, cut a cardboard circle (approximately the size of a salad plate). The cardboard circle can be cut to any size to create the diameter of the bouquet desired. Cut a circle in the center of the cardboard 1/2 inch in diameter (the stem of the glamellia will go through this circle later). *(Figure 8.1d)*

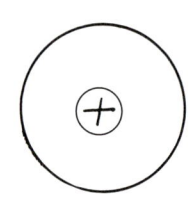

9. Cut open all remaining florets.

10. Using floral adhesive, add glue to the bottom 1 inch of the base of the florets. Also, glue the florets to the outer circle of the cardboard, making sure that the florets extend at least 1 1/2 inches beyond the edge of the cardboard and positioning them so they overlap slightly. *(Figures 8.1e and 8.1f)*

11. When the first circle is completed, glue a second, smaller circle inside the first, making sure the rings of flowers overlap.

12. Glue a third circle inside the second in the same manner.

13. Pierce three #20 gauge wires through the cardboard approximately 1/2 inch from the center opening. These wires will be used for support and stability.

14. Insert the stem of the pre-made glamellia into the center opening. Bind the stem and the #20 gauge wires together. Tape the stem with floral tape. *(Figure 8.1g)*

15. The stem can be extended with additional wire, then taped and leaves added to resemble a natural flower stem. For variation and an impressive look, a natural stem of curly willow or another woody stem, approximately 18 inches long, can be added. When

Figure 8.1d Glamellia Step 8

Figure 8.1e Glamellia Step 10

Figure 8.1f Glamellia Step 10

Figure 8.1g Glamellia Step 14

Wedding Design

this method is used, the wire stem is not extended and the natural stem is wired and taped to the flower stem.

Glamellia Bouquet *(Figure 8.2)*

The bouquet described here is a simple style incorporating three glamellias of varying sizes. The cascade created by the flowers and foliage give the bouquet size and movement. Hosta leaves and ivy strands complement the composite flowers and help soften the bouquet's lines.

Materials Needed

- Twenty-eight gladiolus florets
- Twelve hosta leaves that are 8 to 9 inches long
- Number 24 gauge wire
- Ivy cascades

Figure 8.2 Glamellia Bouquet

Design Steps

1. Design three glamellias of varying sizes: salad plate, saucer, and corsage size.

2. Wire each hosta leaf with a #24 gauge wire, using the stitch method, and tape.

3. The cascade is begun by taping the smallest leaf and smallest glamellia together. Add two more small leaves at different levels around the glamellia and tape.

4. Add the medium glamellia to the cascade and tape it into position a few inches above the first. Hosta leaves can be added around the glamellia for fullness.

5. Bend the stem downward just above the second glamellia.

6. Join this stem together with the stem of the largest glamellia and tape.

7. With a #24 gauge wire, wire the ivy cascades.

8. Add the cascades of ivy to the stem of the bouquet so that they trail down alongside the glamellia cascade.

9. Finish the bouquet by adding the remaining hosta leaves behind the large glamellia, making sure they extend no more than 1 1/2 to 2 inches beyond the flower.

10. Ribbon can be added, if desired.

Biedermeier Bouquet

The Biedermeier bouquet came about following the opulent period of the Napoleon empire. During the Biedermeier period, round forms emerged in home decoration, wreaths, flower arrangements, and bridal bouquets. The classic Biedermeier bouquet was designed in a round style with flowers tightly patterned into concentric rings of color and/or flower type. Variations of this style are still popular alternatives to the colonial bouquet.

Materials Needed

- Leatherleaf
- Twenty-five pink roses
- One-half bunch of purple statice
- One-half bunch of pink bouvardia
- One-half bunch of purple miniature carnations
- Galax leaves
- Pink and purple picot ribbon

Design Steps

1. Soak a foam bouquet holder in preservative solution.

2. Lightly green the bouquet holder with small pieces of leatherleaf.

Wedding Design

Notes

3. Cut the stems of three pink roses to lengths of 4 inches and insert them into the center circle of the bouquet holder, making sure that all flowers are very close together.

4. Form a circle of purple miniature carnations around the three roses. The flowers should be placed tightly next to each other.

5. Add a circle of pink bouvardia around the purple carnations.

6. Add a circle of pink roses around the bouvardia.

7. Finish the circle with a ring of galax leaves.

8. Cover the back of the bouquet by gluing a circle of galax leaves to the bouquet holder with floral adhesive.

9. Add multiple streamers of pink and purple picot ribbon by attaching ribbons to a wooden pick and inserting into the base of the bouquet holder.

Herb and Foliage Bouquet

Herbal and foliage bouquets are timeless; they have reappeared periodically through the years as favorite styles of bridal bouquets.

In medieval times, chaplets of roses were worn around the head, while Swiss brides wore orange blossoms and English brides wore rosemary. Herbs were carried in the bouquets for fragrance and to ward off evil spirits.

A modern look is given to herbal and foliage bouquets by using variegated greenery, greenery with patterns or distinctive shapes, and herbs with fragrance and color variations. They may be designed entirely with foliage or accented with a few specialty flowers in the focal area.

Materials Needed

- Fifty galax leaves
- Number 24 gauge wire
- Three nephthytis leaves

- Three marantha leaves
- Six variegated dracaena leaves
- Three stems of pittosporum
- Four stems of dusty miller
- Four stems of rosemary
- Sprengeri or ivy

Design Steps

1. Take two galax leaves, place one on top of the other, and roll. Use a #24 gauge wire to pierce through the center of the roll; pull down both wires, then bind one wire around the base of the roll and the other wire.

2. Starting with the smallest galax leaves, wrap the remaining unwired leaves in circles around the wired roll to create a galax rosette. Every time a leaf is added, extend it 1 inch higher than the previous leaf.

3. After the addition of every three or four leaves, pierce a #24 gauge wire through the rosette.

4. Using a #24 gauge wire, bind all of the wires together. Cut the stem approximately 6 inches long.

5. Wire the marantha, nephthytis, and dracaena leaves individually with #24 gauge wires, using the stitch method, and tape.

6. Using the hairpin method, wire the pittosporum, dusty miller, and rosemary and then tape.

7. Using the galax rosette as the center of the bouquet, add the marantha leaves in a diagonal line, then add the dracaena leaves in an opposite diagonal line.

8. The nephthytis leaves are added in the upper right area of the bouquet.

Notes

Wedding Design

9. The pittosporum clusters are placed behind the galax rosette.

10. In the lower quadrant of the bouquet, add the dusty miller and rosemary.

11. Add garlands of sprengeri or ivy for a cascading effect.

Hand-tied Bouquet *(Figure 8.3)*

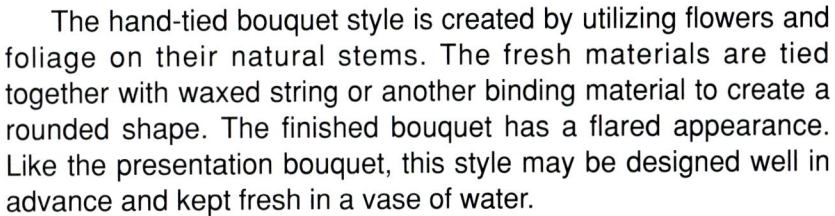

The hand-tied bouquet style is created by utilizing flowers and foliage on their natural stems. The fresh materials are tied together with waxed string or another binding material to create a rounded shape. The finished bouquet has a flared appearance. Like the presentation bouquet, this style may be designed well in advance and kept fresh in a vase of water.

Two common methods are used to create the hand-tied bouquet. Both require practice in order to achieve the desired shape and appearance.

Dutch Spiral Technique

1. Assemble a collection of mixed, long-stemmed flowers and foliage and remove the leaves from the lower half of the stems.

2. Begin by holding the flowers 6 to 8 inches down the stems in a crisscrossed manner.

3. Tie a piece of waxed string to the flowers and wrap it around the stems two or three times.

4. Add the next flowers around the first placements so that the stems follow the same direction. Bind them into place with the waxed string after the addition of every two or three stems. The stems should begin to create a spiral pattern with each flower positioned at an angle.

5. Add flowers and foliage, working from the center to the perimeter of the bouquet, until reaching the desired size.

6. Tie the ends of the waxed string tightly together.

Figure 8.3 Hand-tied Bouquet

7. Finish the design with a bow and ribbon wrapped around the binding point, if desired.

German Nesting Technique

1. Assemble a collection of mixed long-stemmed flowers and foliage and remove the leaves from the lower half of the stems.

2. Begin with a base foliage, such as leatherleaf. Form a circle with the fingers and thumb of one hand and insert three or four stems of the fern at angles into the circle, as if it were a vase.

3. Add flowers in the same manner, as if designing a vase arrangement.

4. Add foliage, as needed for support around the flowers. Moss may also be inserted deep into the bouquet to form a supporting nest, which helps separate and hold stems in the desired positions.

5. Continue adding flowers and foliage until the bouquet reaches the desired size.

6. Use waxed string to tie the flowers together where they are joined in the hand.

7. Finish the bouquet with ribbon, as desired.

European Contemporary Bouquet (Figure 8.4)

The European contemporary bouquet is a modern style with an upright thrust and an emphasis on strong lines and minimal flower placements. Unique botanical specimens are typically used at the focal area of the design. Exotic types of foliage often replace massed flowers at the perimeter. Open space and a less obvious geometric outline are key ingredients of this style. An emphasis on grouped materials with strong textural contrasts is also important. European contemporary bouquets may be designed with natural-stemmed flowers, wired and taped blossoms, or a foam bouquet holder. The dramatic, contemporary styling of this bouquet makes it best suited for use with sheath or mermaid style gowns.

Figure 8.4 European Contemporary Bouquet

Wedding Design

Notes

Materials Needed

- Four paphiopedilum orchids
- Number 24 gauge wire
- Marantha leaves
- Galax leaves
- Two stems of oncidium orchids
- Bear grass

Design Steps

1. Wire each paphiopedilum orchid with two #24 gauge wires and then tape.

2. Wire each oncidium orchid with a #24 gauge wire, using the hairpin method, and tape.

3. Wire five marantha leaves with a #24 gauge wire, using the stitch method, and tape.

4. Wire five galax leaves, using the stitch method, and tape.

5. Cut the bear grass to lengths of 9 inches. Use five pieces to form a loop. Bind the loop with a #24 gauge wire, using the wraparound method. Make a second bear grass loop in the same manner.

6. Cut several strands of bear grass to lengths of 16 inches and bind them together with a #24 gauge wire, using the wraparound method.

7. Begin assembly by holding the two oncidium orchids upright at a 45-degree angles.

8. Add galax leaves at the base of the orchids in a horizontal position.

9. On a diagonal plane, add three marantha leaves to the left of the orchids and two to the right of the orchids.

10. Add one paphiopedilum orchid at the base of the oncidium orchid stems and another orchid in a vertical position approximately 6 inches above the first.

11. Bend the third paphiopedilum orchid on a downward angle and position it below and slightly to the side of the first orchid.

12. Add the last orchid in a vertical line several inches below the third orchid to create a cascading line.

13. Add the two bear grass loops and the cascade of bear grass to the lower right section of the bouquet.

Flowers to Wear

The body flowers worn at weddings often go beyond the basics. These flowers are personalized to satisfy unique customers who have individual tastes and styles.

The flowers are designed to complement and accent the ensemble being worn and to express the personality of the wearer. To personalize the flowers, it is important to establish personal preferences, along with the color and style of dress.

Flowers can be custom designed to perch on the shoulder, attach to the waistline; attach to a sleeve; accent a neckline; wear on a wrist; or attach to a purse, shoe, hat, or anklet.

Shop image can be established by offering custom-designed body flowers that have been personalized and that display uniqueness of design. The key to advanced body flowers is technique, texture, unusual flowers, and an exciting finished product.

Composite Flowers

Composite flowers are constructed from petals or leaves that have been detached from the original flower, glued or wired, and assembled to form a new flower. Glamellias and duchess roses are examples of composite flowers that can be designed into a corsage.

Glamellia Corsage *(Figure 8.5)*

The initial steps in constructing a glamellia corsage are the same as those for constructing a glamellia bouquet. A

Figure 8.5 Glamellia Corsage

Wedding Design

Notes

small, single glamellia is assembled and then accented with foliage and additional gladiolus buds. If desired, other flowers, such as sweetheart roses, may be added to the corsage to increase its size and value.

Materials Needed

- Three gladiolus buds
- Five gladiolus florets
- Camellia leaves
- Wires (#28 gauge, #24 gauge, and #20 gauge)
- Floral tape

Design Steps

1. Follow steps 1 through 7 for constructing a glamellia on pages 221-222.

2. Use #28 gauge wire to pierce wire two additional gladiolus buds, then tape.

3. Make three separate loops from the dracaena leaves by taping the base of the loop. Next, pierce the tape with a #28 gauge wire and bend the wires down and continue taping.

4. Make two dracaena loops with tails and wire and tape in the same manner as described in step 3.

5. Wire the camellia leaves individually with a #28 gauge wire, using the stitch method.

6. Tape the two wired gladiolus buds together; leave at least 2 inches between the buds. Add two camellia leaves and one loop and tail of dracaena.

7. Add this cascade to the glamellia, then add the three loops of dracaena around the glamellia flower.

8. Add the remaining dracaena loop and tail by placing the stem next to the glamellia stem. Bend the

greenery over the thumb and down toward the floor, and then tape.

9. Add the remaining camellia leaves behind the glamellia.

10. A bow can be added, if desired.

Duchess Rose Corsage

A duchess rose is a composite flower similar to a glamellia. It is designed using an open rose and several additional rose petals to create the look of an oversized, old-fashioned rose. The duchess rose may be worn singly in the hair, on the shoulder, or at the waist. It may also be designed into a larger corsage as described here.

Materials Needed

- Two large open roses
- Wires (#28 gauge, #24 gauge, and #20 gauge)
- Eight camellia leaves
- Gardenia shield or cardboard
- Floral adhesive
- Five clusters of gypsophila

Design Steps

1. Pull all of the petals off of one rose.

2. Wire the other rose with two #24 gauge wires, using the cross pierce method, and tape.

3. Wire the eight camellia leaves, using the stitch method, with a #28 gauge wire on each leaf. Tape each leaf with floral tape.

4. Spread floral adhesive around the outer edge of the gardenia shield or cardboard circle. Lay a circle of rose petals around the gardenia shield; make sure that they extend over the edge of the cardboard.

Notes

Wedding Design

Notes

5. Continue gluing rows of rose petals until reaching the center of the circle. Each circle of petals should overlap the previous circle at least 1/2 inch.

6. Insert the stem of the wired rose through the hole in the center of the circle and pull it through.

7. Align two half-length #20 gauge wires along the stem of the flower and tape.

8. Add the clusters of un-wired gypsophila to the rose, and tape it into place. If additional control of the clusters is needed, wire the cluster with #28 gauge wire, using the wraparound method.

9. Add three of the wired camellia leaves to the rose and tape to secure. To keep the flower lightweight, cut the stems of the leaves below the binding point.

10. A cascade of two buds can be made by rolling two rose petals together. Tape the bottom 1/4 inch of the petals with floral tape (do not break off the tape). Pierce the tape with a one-half length of #24 gauge wire; pull the wires down and continue taping.

11. Form a cascade by putting the two buds together (leaving 2 inches between the buds) and adding three leaves. Tape them together.

12. Add this cascade to the rose and tape the stems together.

13. To complete the design, add the remaining two leaves at the base of the flower.

14. A bow can be added, if desired.

Gerbera Cascade Corsage

This corsage is a simple design featuring only one flower; however, it has a dramatic appearance created by a cascade which flows over the shoulder. A variety of flowers can be used to achieve different looks to complement the color and style of the wedding attire.

Materials Needed

- One gerbera
- Eight pittosporum leaves

Design Steps

1. Remove twelve to fourteen petals from the underside of a gerbera blossom so that the face of the flower and remaining petals remain intact.

2. Cut the stem of the gerbera to a length of 1 1/2 inches, and wire with #24 gauge wire, using the pierce method, and then tape.

3. Make five individual "flowers" with the gerbera petals by taping the lower portions of two or three petals together. Pierce the tape with a one-half length #26 gauge wire; pull the wires down and continue taping.

4. Wire and tape the pittosporum leaves, using #28 gauge wire.

5. Make two cascades; place two flowers in one and three flowers in the other. As each cascade is being constructed, add the leaves alternately and tape after each blossom is added.

6. Add the first cascade with three flowers above and to the right of the gerbera. Tape the stem together. Bend this cascade to create a sweeping arch to cascade over the shoulder.

7. Add the second cascade with two flowers beneath the gerbera flower, and bend the cascade over the thumb so that it cascades toward the floor.

8. Add the remaining leaves around the central gerbera and tape.

Boutonnieres

Boutonnieres are flowers worn on the lapels of men's coats. Originally, a single flower was worn in the buttonhole of the coat.

Notes

Wedding Design

Notes

However, in contemporary society, men wear multi-flower, custom-designed boutonnieres with style and uniqueness. They are worn on the sleeve, hat, or even on the shoulder.

A number of boutonnieres are used for weddings. These include boutonnieres for the groom, groomsmen, ushers, ring bearer, fathers, grandfathers, and minister. Traditionally, the groom's boutonniere is made of the same type of flowers that are carried in the bridal bouquet. The groomsmen's boutonnieres are often made of the same type of flowers that are carried by the bridesmaids. Other boutonnieres may either be coordinated with the other flowers in the bridal party or they may be designed for uniqueness.

Berry Boutonniere with Cording

Ordinary boutonnieres can become sophisticated when they are made with unusual materials. Berries, pods, and mosses add an appealing textural look to boutonnieres. Sometimes interesting materials with unique colors and textures can be combined to create boutonnieres without any flowers. Following is an example of such a design.

Materials Needed

- Pepper berries
- Ligustrum berries
- Pittosporum leaves
- Number 28 gauge wire
- Cording

Design Steps

1. Wire small clusters of berries together, using the wraparound method, and tape.

2. Wire three pittosporum leaves with a one-half length #28 gauge wire, using the stitch method.

3. Form a small loop of cording and bind it with a one-half length #28 gauge wire, using the wraparound method.

Notes

4. Group three additional loops together and bind them with a single #28 gauge wire.

5. Group the berry clusters together and tape them just below the berries.

6. Add the three pittosporum leaves around the berry cluster.

7. Add the single cord loop to the top of the boutonniere above the berries.

8. Add the multi-looped cording to the bottom of the boutonniere and tape at a single binding point.

9. Cut the individual stems in a tapered fashion to finish the boutonniere.

Contemporary Boutonniere

Contemporary boutonnieres are very showy and stylized. This style requires unusual forms, textures, and grasses or greenery with strong lines. The boutonniere described below has great visual impact.

Materials Needed

- Drumstick allium
- Wires (#28 gauge and #24 gauge)
- Pepper berries
- Bear grass
- Ivy leaves

Design Steps

1. Cut the stem of one drumstick allium to 1/2 inch in length. Wire the stem with a #24 gauge wire, using the wraparound method.

2. Wire three clusters of pepper berries with a one-half length #28 gauge wire, using the wraparound method, and then tape.

Wedding Design

Notes

3. Wire three 2-inch loops of bear grass individually with one-half length #28 gauge wires, using the wraparound method, and tape.

4. Wire three to five tips of the bear grass 8 inches long (face the grass together so that it goes in the same direction) and bind with a #28 gauge wire and tape.

5. Wire three small ivy leaves with #28 gauge wire, using the stitch method.

6. Begin assembly by adding the three clusters of berries below the wired allium.

7. Position the loops of bear grass behind the flower and the long bear grass in the upper right area of the boutonniere so that it flows over the shoulder.

8. Encircle the boutonniere with the three ivy leaves to provide a light backing.

Hair Flowers

Hair flowers for weddings may be worn by the bride, bridesmaids, flower girls, mothers, or even the guests. They can be worn in place of, or as a complement to, a corsage or other body flowers. Hair decorations may be as simple as a single flower or as complicated as a cascading spray conforming to the head. Examples of some of the various options for hair flowers are explained here.

Single Flower Hairpiece

Featuring a single showy flower, such as a rubrum lily, can have a very dramatic effect for any occasion. The flower alone is lovely; however, when it is accented with another specialty flower, such as a lilac, a great look is achieved.

Materials Needed

- Rubrum lily
- Wires (#28 gauge and #24 gauge)
- Lilac
- Ivy leaves

Design Steps

1. Cut a stem of lily to a length of 2 inches, and wire it with two #24 gauge wires by cross wiring through the base of the lily petals, and then tape.

2. Cut the stem of the lilac to a length of 1 inch, and wire with a #24 gauge wire, using the hairpin method, and then tape.

3. Add the lilac to the rubrum lily, and tape them together at the base of the lily. Tape just the width of the tape so that the stems can remain free.

4. Wire four to six ivy leaves with #28 gauge wires, using the stitch method.

5. Add the leaves around the lily to provide background, and cover the mechanics. Position the leaves so they will lay flat against the head.

6. Taper the stem ends and shape the design to form a crescent.

Phalaenopsis Orchid Hairpiece

A phalaenopsis orchid makes a sophisticated headpiece that can be worn just as a flower adornment or can be added to veiling. It has a very tailored look and is flattering to the face.

Materials Needed

- Phalaenopsis orchid
- Wire (#28 gauge and #26 gauge)
- Seven stephanotis
- Small ivy strands

Design Steps

1. Wire a phalaenopsis orchid with a #26 gauge wire and then tape.

Wedding Design

2. Make a cascade of three wired stephanotis, and tape it together.

3. Make a cascade with four wired stephanotis, taping each flower as it is placed into the cascade.

4. Wire two separate strands of ivy 3 inches in length with a one-half length #28 gauge wire. Tape each strand.

5. Add the four-flower stephanotis cascade to the top right portion of the orchid and tape.

6. Add the second stephanotis cascade to the bottom section of the orchid by placing the stems of the cascade and the flower together and bending the flowers over the thumb so that they cascade toward the floor, and then tape.

7. Add one ivy strand to each end of the orchid following the stephanotis strands.

8. Trim the stems short so they will be hidden beneath the flower.

Structured Headpieces

Although most brides select traditional veils, there are always a few who desire to have a more unique headpiece coordinated with their bridal gown. Florists can use their skills as designers to create structured headpieces custom designed for individual brides. The possibilities for floral wreaths, hats, crowns, and other pieces are endless. The following examples offer creative ideas for constructing one-of-a-kind floral headpieces.

Horsehair Hat with Flowers *(Figure 8.6)*

Hats of all kinds can be accented with flowers, but when the florist constructs the hat as well as the floral decorations, a more creative look can be achieved. This headpiece involves covering a basic hat frame with horsehair, as well as decorating it with flowers. Hat frames can be purchased at millinery or fabric stores in various sizes. Horsehair fabric can also be purchased at these stores.

Figure 8.6 Horsehair Hat with Flowers

Materials Needed

- Hat frame
- Horsehair fabric
- Nerine lilies
- Dendrobium orchids
- Number 28 gauge wire
- Pepper berries
- Coral vine
- Coordinating ribbon

Design Steps

1. Begin with a pre-made hat frame; sew the horsehair fabric around the edge to form a brim. Fold a 10 to 12-inch piece of horsehair into a double loop, and bind it in the center to form the bow. Sew the bow to the back of the hat.

2. Wire and tape all flowers and berries. Dendrobium orchid blossoms and buds should be wired individually with one-half lengths of #28 gauge wires.

3. Assemble the flowers to form a cascading corsage.

4. Attach this corsage to the center of the horsehair bow with pins, glue, or needle and thread.

Floral Skull Cap *(Figure 8.7)*

When a bride requests something unusual, an ideal suggestion is a floral skull cap. Made of plaster, this custom-made skull cap provides a base on which to superimpose a mass of individual flowers for a bold look. Skull caps can be made quickly and easily, and they can command very good prices when created by innovative floral designers. The skull cap must be custom designed to conform to the shape of the bride's head. Plan to prepare the plaster cap several days in advance and store it until ready to decorate on the wedding day.

Wedding Design

Figure 8.7a Floral Skull Cap Step 2

Figure 8.7b Floral Skull Cap Step 3

Figure 8.7c Floral Skull Cap Step 4

Figure 8.7d Floral Skull Cap Step 5

Figure 8.7e Floral Skull Cap Step 8

Materials Needed

- Two or three rolls of quick-setting plaster bandages
- Plastic wrap or plastic bag
- Thirty gladiolus florets
- Floral adhesive

Design Steps

1. Have the bride pin up her hair as close to the scalp as possible or use a stocking cap.

2. Cover the bride's head with plastic, making sure that the plastic extends just over the hair line, but not over the face. *(Figure 8.7a)*

3. Tape the plastic very tightly just over the brow line and around the neck. *(Figure 8.7b)*

4. Cut 8-inch strips of the plaster bandages, and submerge them one at a time in cold water. Start applying bandages at the brow line and neck line, and continue adding the wet strips until the crown of the head is covered. *(Figure 8.7c)*

5. Add additional strips over the entire area to strengthen the cap. *(Figure 8.7d)*

6. Leave the cap on the head until the plaster hardens (this usually takes 10 minutes).

7. With a pencil, draw a line across the forehead and around the ears.

8. Trim off the excess plaster and let the cap dry overnight. *(Figure 8.7e)*

9. Apply floral adhesive to the outer edge of the hat. Open the gladiolus florets and make a circle around the edge of the entire cap. The first row must extend at least 1 inch over the edge of the cap and should be slightly overlapped all the way around.

10. Continue adding rows of florets until the hat is covered.

11. Veiling and flowers can be added to the back of the hat with glue, if desired. **(Figure 8.7f)**

Cascading Veil Flowers

Flowers that complement the wedding ensemble can be added to a veil selected by a bride. The flowers can range from simple and elegant to bold and showy. Above all, the flowers should reflect the personality of the bride and should enhance the statement she wishes to make.

Figure 8.7f Floral Skull Cap Step 11

Materials Needed

- Stephanotis
- Wire (#28 gauge and #24 gauge)
- White roses
- Pearl sprays

Design Steps

1. Wire the roses with #24 gauge wire, using the pierce method, and then tape.

2. Wire the stephanotis with #28 gauge wire, and then tape.

3. Extend the pearl sprays with a #28 gauge wire, using the wraparound method, and then tape.

4. Begin the cascade with a long pearl spray, approximately 8 inches long. Tape the stephanotis blossoms in a zigzag pattern, adding the cascading pearl sprays intermittently and taping after each flower.

5. After the third stephanotis has been added, start adding the roses along with the stephanotis until the cascade has reached a length of at least 14 inches. This will establish the binding point.

6. While holding the stems of the cascade, bend the remaining pearl sprays and flowers over the thumb to form the lower part of the cascade. Bind all of the

Wedding Design

Notes

stems together (cut out some of the stems so that the headpiece will not be heavy).

7. Fill in the center portion with the remaining flowers for a finished look, and bind with tape.

8. Cut the stems off to 1 1/2 inches, and bend them against the flowers.

9. Attach the headpiece onto the veil with safety pins, or needle and thread, so that the flowers arch across the crown of the head.

Ceremony Decorations

Floral decorations for wedding ceremonies may be simple or elaborate, bright or subdued, traditional or contemporary. The formality of the ceremony, the size and style of the ceremony location, and the bride's desired wedding mood all influence the type of decorations to be created. Regardless of what the bride chooses for her ceremonial decor, florists must be careful to create floral decorations that will enhance, not detract from, the ceremony.

A variety of different decorations may be used for wedding ceremonies. Although it is important to decorate the area where the bride and groom exchange vows, the site of the ceremony has a more unified appearance when the entryway and seating areas are also decorated. Florists should encourage decoration of the entire ceremonial site, beginning with the entryway, continuing into the vestibule or guest book area, down the aisle, surrounding the seating area, and finishing with a strong impact at the altar area.

Advanced styles of ceremonial decorations are often most appropriate at large, lavish weddings. However, they may also be suitable for small, simple affairs. The bouquet style and flower choices of the bride and the desired wedding atmosphere typically dictate the appropriateness of advanced floral designs as ceremony decorations.

Altar Decorations

The altar is the focal area of the church, and the flowers used to decorate this area should complement and respect the architecture of the church. Individual clergy also impose restrictions that often influence the choice of decorations. Some churches have very strict rules, and it is important to know these rules before selling an idea to a customer.

Symmetrical or vertical arrangements work best in the typically symmetrical surroundings of churches. The flowers selected should have distinct shapes and forms in order to be visible from long distances. Lilies are a good choice because of their size and long-lasting qualities. Color is also a major concern, because churches often have low light. For this reason, flowers with advancing colors should be used for good visibility.

Since altar space is limited, due to the candles and other church articles placed on it, the height and width of an altar arrangement should be predetermined before the wedding. This will prevent confrontations with clergy.

To decorate the altar more elaborately, florists must use creative ideas. For example, long foliage garlands extending from the altar arrangements over the surface of the altar table and cascading down to the floor make a strong impact. Flowers, such as gardenias, may be glued into the garlands to add fragrance and impact. On the floor of the altar, a European garden might be designed in a raquette, using parallel systems of flowers and greenery. *Figure 8.8* shows an elaborately-decorated altar which is fitting to the architecture of the pictured church.

When selecting the containers for the altar, classical urns work best for upright arrangements, and they fit into the formal church background. The primary consideration for all containers is their suitability to where they will be placed and their size in relation to the scale of the church. The best colors for containers are green, earth colors, and stone. White containers are so dominant that they often separate the flowers from the container and prevent unity in the design. However, white containers will work well if the arrangement is all white. Most white plastic containers can be effectively spray painted. If the plastic container does not "take" paint, then the container can be rubbed with sandpaper to create a surface to which paint will cling.

Figure 8.8 Decorated Church Altar

Pedestals

Pedestals are ideal for use in churches because of their scale. They are useful for holding large arrangements for placement on each side of the altar. The height of pedestals provides arrangements with the lift they need to be seen by the congregation. *(See Figure 8.9.)*

Pedestals can be decorated with flowing garlands of greenery and flowers to add an Old World charm. Pedestals are often made

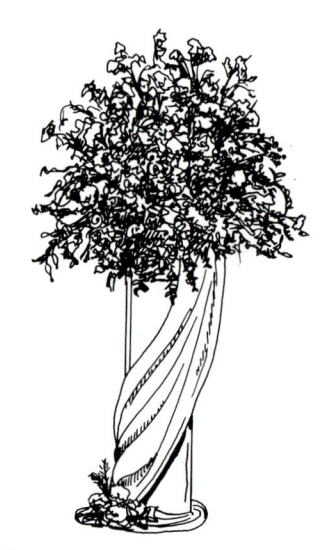

Figure 8.9 Decorated Pedestals

Wedding Design

of wrought iron, wood, or foam board. Many churches have memorial pedestals donated to them by members of the church. These pedestals are usually permanent and strong in construction. Pedestals for elaborate decorations can be made by sawing two circles of wood 12 inches in diameter and nailing the two circles to a 2-inch dowel that is 5 feet tall. The column is completed by gluing foam board or rippled cardboard to the circles to form a circular column. Fabric can also be used to drape these columns.

Pedestals can also be constructed from PVC pipe by attaching a fitting on a square wooden base with screws (this fitting will accept a 4-inch PVC pipe). A round dish can then be attached to the top of the PVC pipe and floral foam secured inside the dish with waterproof tape. A tall, symmetrical design can then be constructed in the designer dish. The PVC pipe can be painted or covered with fabric or garlands of greens and flowers.

Tree-like Altar Arrangements *(Figure 8.10)*

Tall, tree-like arrangements are excellent for providing impact on altars. These trees can be made in several different ways. The following method is recommended because of its ease and practicality.

1. Select a large vase with a base that will support a large amount of floral material.

2. Fill the vase with saturated floral foam, making sure that the foam extends at least 3 inches above the lip of the container.

3. Cover the foam with a layer of chicken wire (just enough to cover the surface and fold over).

4. Secure the chicken wire over the foam with waterproof tape.

5. Design a large symmetrical arrangement in the container.

6. Add European extenders or funnels attached to hyacinth sticks to the top of the design. (The funnels and the sticks should be painted matte green to help them blend in.)

Figure 8.10 Tree-like Altar Arrangements

7. Add floral foam to the extenders and design additional flowers and foliage within them to increase the height of the design.

Chuppah

Traditional Jewish weddings are held under a canopy, or chuppah, which symbolizes the couple's home. The significance of the chuppah is that it strengthens the idea of the presence of God in the heavens above our heads.

The chuppah has four poles and is covered with fabric, such as satin, velvet, tulle, or taffeta. The chuppah can also be embellished with greenery and flowers. Always check with the rabbi to ensure that the chuppah to be used and the decorations planned are in keeping with local traditions and preference.

Many temples have their own chuppahs, and they should not be decorated without consulting the rabbi. Many temples wish to keep the decorations simple to respect the architecture of the church. Florists should be very careful not to scar or damage the wood of the temple's chuppah. Any garlands or flowers used to decorate the chuppah should be attached with professionalism.

Sometimes it is requested that the chuppah be made with the groom's tallis. The tallis is a special prayer shawl worn by men. It is given to a boy at his bar mitzvah (age 13) and worn in the temple and whenever the man is called to prayer. To use these in a wedding, florists should take four bamboo poles and attach them to the four corners of the shawl. The poles are held by four close friends or relatives during the actual wedding ceremony. **(See Figure 8.11.)**

Chuppahs can be constructed by using pre-made frames; lattice; PVC pipe; or natural materials, such as twigs, vines, or wooden poles. Florists must consider the practicality of transporting these structures. A simple chuppah, which is easily assembled, can be made very elaborate by adding floral decorations.

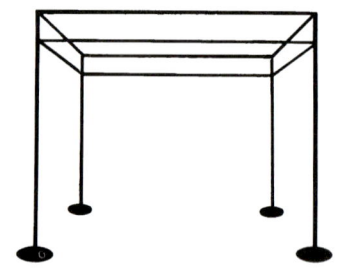

Figure 8.11 Basic Chuppah

Lattice Chuppah

The lattice chuppah can be constructed or purchased pre-made. This type of chuppah is popular because it is easily assembled, transported, and stored. The basic decorations are usually greens; however, an elaborate decoration will have clusters of flowers placed every 2 feet (these are made in IGLU®

Wedding Design

Notes

Holders and are attached to the lattice) on the top surface and on the poles. The top of the chuppah is flat, making an excellent area to place a large, upright flower arrangement. For a dramatic look, lilies, gerberas, orchids, and carnations can be used in this decoration; however, any type of flower can be used if the budget permits.

Brass Chuppah

A brass chuppah frame is especially appropriate when using fabric. The fabric can be festooned on each of the four posts and gathered to add fullness and rhythm. Any fabric can be used; however, satin and velvet are the favorites. Tulle has also become very popular because of its romantic look. Flowers are added to the chuppah by designing them in IGLU® Holders and attaching them to the poles at the top of the chuppah.

PVC Chuppah *(Figure 8.12)*

PVC pipe is very popular for use in constructing chuppahs. The pipe can be purchased from hardware stores and can be used repeatedly. Florists should make sure that the fittings used are correct and adequate so that the mechanics are secure.

Materials Needed

- Four 3-inch by 7-feet PVC pipes
- Heavy plastic
- Duct tape
- Plaster of Paris
- Papier-maché containers
- Four *U*-bolts
- Number 22 gauge wire
- Fabric
- Large safety pins

Design Steps

1. Wrap the bottom 10 inches of each PVC pipe with heavy plastic, and tape it with duct tape around the top of the plastic. *(Figure 8.12a)*

2. Mix the plaster of Paris and fill the papier-maché pots, one at a time, to 3 inches below the top edge.

3. Insert the plastic-covered end of the PVC pipe into the wet plaster. *(Figure 8.12b)* As it dries, cut the duct tape to release the plastic away from the pole. Periodically, twist the pole. This will allow the pole to be removed for easy delivery and storage.

4. While the plaster is still wet, insert a *U*-bolt into the planter so that it forms a handle that rises 4 inches above the plaster surface and is sunken securely into the plaster. Make sure that a wall of at least 1 inch of plaster surrounds the handle. *(Figure 8.12c)*

5. Twist the PVC pipe again, and continue twisting periodically until the plaster is dry.

6. When dry, remove the PVC pipe from the container, and trim the plastic to the top of the container.

7. Drill two small holes at the top of each PVC pole. Pass a #22 gauge wire through the hole to reinforce the stability of the fabric which will be secured at the top.

8. Put the papier-maché pot in a container with straight sides, and glue a strip of Velcro around the base.

9. Measure and calculate the amount of fabric needed to wrap around the base of the container, including a few inches to overlap. Glue Velcro to the back side of the fabric along the bottom edge and attach it to the container.

10. Pull the fabric up to the top of the pole, and secure it with two large safety pins in an *X* fashion.

11. Measure the fabric to drape between the two poles.

Figure 8.12a PVC Chuppah Step 1

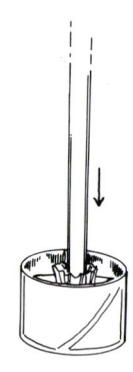

Figure 8.12b PVC Chuppah Step 3

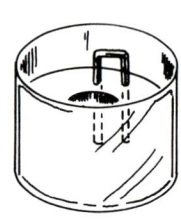

Figure 8.12c PVC Chuppah Step 4

Wedding Design

12. Gather the outer edges, and pin them to the poles.

13. Adjust the top edge so that the fabric is taut across the top. Secure the pins and fabric with the wire at the top of the pole.

14. Repeat the fabric treatment on all four poles and the sides of the chuppah.

15. Light nylon chiffon or tulle can be used to create a ceiling for the chuppah. The edges of the ceiling fabric are also pinned to the PVC pipe. The enclosed ceiling treatment is considered to be a part of the Hebrew bridal tradition.

16. Pew clip cages can be tucked into the PVC pipe to hold fresh flowers or greenery. Be sure that the weight of each arrangement is balanced so that the poles are secure. **(Figure 8.12d)**

Figure 8.12d PVC Chuppah Step 16

Window Decorations

The windows in a church are ideal for featuring candles, flowers, or greenery. The ledges are narrow and usually no more than 3 feet long. Many churches have stained glass windows, and the colors in these windows should be respected when decorating the area.

Placing two *L*-shaped arrangements in the corners of a window and trailing long cascades of sprengeri over the window ledge creates an Old World look. To add height and excitement to this grouping of flowers, flowering quince branches or flowering plum branches can be used.

If the church permits, candles can be added to the flower arrangements. The candlelight adds a romantic glow to the church and a strong vertical thrust to the arrangements.

Choir Stalls

All decorations placed in this area must not interfere with the service or the people seated in the area.

The railing can be decorated for great visual impact. The entire railing can take on the appearance of a Southern garden by placing floral cages on the railing and inserting boughs of greenery into the foam, allowing the greenery to cascade to the floor. The cage can be covered with a variety of greens. Flowing foliage, such as Southern smilax, plumosus fern, bear grass, sprengeri, and ivy, are the best choices for this dynamic look. Flowers can also be added to this "waterfall" look, if desired.

Individual garlands of greenery or flowers are also very effective on railings. Make sure that each arrangement is secured with materials that do not mar the wood on the railing (raffia or chenille). These individual arrangements can also be used as decorations at the reception. **(See Figure 8.13.)**

English Style Decorations

The English style is best described as opulent, large, bold, and abundant. Swags, garlands, trees, and hedges of flowers are all very much at home in an old English church steeped with tradition.

The extensive garlands, which are usually hand tied, have been popular through the ages since the days of the ancient Greeks and Romans. These English garlands are made from fresh flowers, dried materials, and even fruits.

Figure 8.13 Choir Stalls

Hand-tied Garland *(Figure 8.14)*

A hand-tied garland of greens or flowers is timeless. Mastering the art of hand-tying requires patience and practice. Flowers of any type can be used; however, it is important to consider mass, filler, and form when making selections. A great amount of filler materials is used; therefore, flowers with fullness should be selected.

Figure 8.14 Hand-tied Garland

Materials Needed

- Greenery, such as plumosus, sprengeri, commodore fern, or cedar

- Flowers - mass, filler, and form

- Number 24 gauge spool of wire or waxed thread

Design Steps

1. Gather all materials in one central area.

2. Groom the materials by removing all foliage on the lower half of the stems.

Wedding Design

Notes

3. Place like flowers in groupings.

4. Begin with three pieces of fern. Lay one piece flat on the table and add the next two pieces by crossing their stems diagonally at the base of the lowest leaf on the first piece of fern.

5. Bind the three pieces of fern together at the crossing point. (Do not break or cut the binding wire, because a continuous wire will be needed to construct the garland.)

6. Add the first flower 6 inches from the top of the first fern; add two more flowers in front of the second and third pieces of greenery. Bind the stems at the crossing point with the spool wire.

7. Add greenery to the left and to the right of the design, and add flowers in front of each fern. Add filler material between the flowers and bind. Make sure that the flowers are extended high enough to give depth to the design. Some heavy flowers might require wiring to maintain control.

8. Continue adding greens, mass, and form flowers and then filler flowers, and bind approximately every 6 inches. When the desired length is reached, tie off by pulling the wire around the stem and forming a knot. Repeat this several times for security.

9. A second garland is designed in the same manner (approximately 14 inches long).

10. The two garlands should be joined together and tied with wire.

11. To cover the joining point, additional flowers are glued into this area, or a bow can be added to the joining point instead.

Hedges of Flowers

Hedges of flowers are one of the most popular decorations for weddings held in large churches. The hedge effect is visually powerful, but basically easy to construct.

The height of the hedge is determined by the placement and the budget. Once the height is determined, inexpensive containers that are rectangular in shape and very low in height should be selected and filled with saturated floral foam. Arrangements of the selected flowers (open garden style roses are an English favorite) are made in each container. The multiple arrangements are then placed on the floor side by side to form a hedge. As many as three hundred of these individual arrangements are often used to line aisles, altar railings, window ledges, and other areas. This is an easy method of making a great impact on the viewers, and one of the best advantages is that a great many varieties of flowers can be used to achieve this look.

Topiaries

Topiaries became popular in the 1600s when the German gardeners began pruning green plants in their gardens into unusual forms. The English people, who were avid gardeners, immediately adopted this new creative style for their gardens. It was only natural that floral designers would take this form and use it in decorating. One of the great advantages of using topiary forms in churches is that the ball at the top, which actually holds the arrangement, is lifted so high that it can be seen from great distances.

Topiary Construction *(Figure 8.15)*

1. Use plaster of Paris to anchor a 3- to 5-foot PVC pipe or tree limb (2 inches in diameter) into a 2-gallon bucket.

2. Soak an Oasis® Corso™, turn it upside down, and wrap the open flaps over the top of the pipe or limb. Press the foam slightly into the post. *(Figure 8.15a)*

3. Use waxed string or wire to secure the flaps tightly around the post.

4. Green the foam in a globular form proportioned to the length of the post.

5. Add flowers to conform to the round shape. *(Figure 8.15b)*

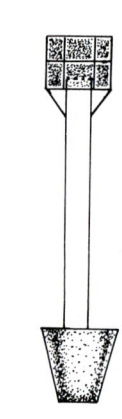

Figure 8.15a Topiary Step 2

Figure 8.15b Topiary Step 5

Wedding Design

Figure 8.15c Topiary Step 6

6. Branches may be used to create a more dynamic and stylized shape. *(Figure 8.15c)*

7. If desired, a piece of floral foam may be added to the base container and an accent design created in it.

Aisle Decorations

Aisles or pew ends can be decorated with flowers, greenery topiaries, tulle, taffeta bows, aisle candelabras, or garlands of flowers. The important thing to remember is never to obstruct the progress of the clergy, congregation, or wedding party by placing arrangements in the aisle.

The use of fabric has always been a unique method of adding drama, impact, and a romantic look to a church, hall, temple, garden, or home.

The fabrics most frequently used are satin, taffeta, printed fabrics, and tulle. These fabrics can be made into bows. The bows can cascade to the floor, be festooned from pew to pew or on altar railings, gathered on aisle candelabras, or used at the back aisle opening to prevent the entrance of anyone other than the wedding party. *(See Figure 8.16.)*

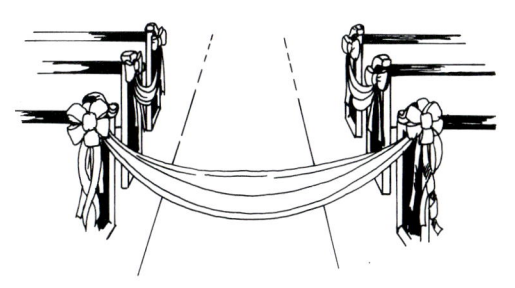

Taffeta Pew Bows *(Figure 8.17)*

Pew bows designed with #9 or #40 satin ribbon are commonly used in weddings. For brides that like the look of pew bows but desire something more unique, large taffeta bows can be used. The construction of these bows is rather simple, and they offer the added advantage of being reusable.

Figure 8.16 Aisle Decorations

Materials Needed

- Taffeta fabric
- Glue gun or needle and thread
- Fabric sheers
- Number 18 gauge wires

Design Steps

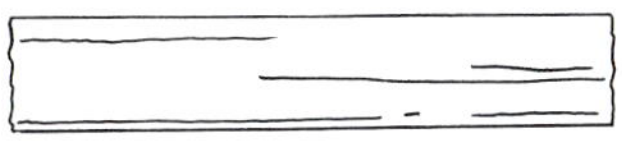

1. Cut a piece of taffeta to a length of 36 inches and a width of 16 inches. *(Figure 8.17a)*

Figure 8.17a Taffeta Pew Bows Step 1

2. Lay the fabric lengthwise and fold the sides of the fabric to the center. **(Figure 8.17b)**

3. Cut a piece of taffeta 7 inches wide by 12 inches long.

4. Fold this piece around the first folded fabric to form a bow. Sew or glue the ends of this piece together. **(Figure 8.17c)**

5. Cut two streamers that are floor length, and glue them to the back of the bow. **(Figure 8.17d)**

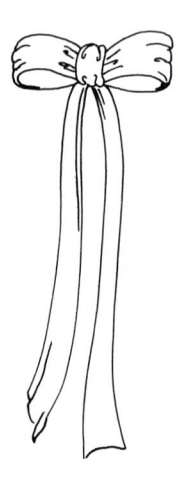

6. The bow can be secured to the pew by wrapping two #18 gauge wires together (lengthwise). This will create a wire that is 32 inches long. Bend it in half (like a hairpin), and bind the ends of the wires. Secure the bottom 4 inches to the back center of the taffeta bow with hot glue.

7. Bend the loop over the pew to hold the bow in place.

8. For additional impact, secure an IGLU® to the wire immediately above the bow. Make sure the foam has been saturated with water. Add variegated ivy garlands and Casablanca lilies.

Figure 8.17b Taffeta Pew Bows Step 2

Figure 8.17c Taffeta Pew Bows Step 4

Figure 8.17d Taffeta Pew Bows Step 5

Fabric Festoons

Fabric can be festooned down a church aisle for an elaborate church decoration. Any soft fabric, such as tulle, chiffon, or satin, can be used very effectively.

The mechanics of festooning the fabric vary from church to church because of the difference in the styles of the pews. The best method is to use pew clips that fit over the pew ends whenever possible. When using this technique, the fabric is attached to the first pew clip on the first pew by using a chenille stem. The fabric is then festooned to the third pew, and every third pew until the fabric flows down the aisle and reaches the back pew. Greenery or puffs of fabric can then be added to the foam in the pew clip.

Reception Decorations

The wedding reception offers a multitude of ways to decorate with flowers. A formal wedding ceremony decorated extensively

Wedding Design

Notes

with flowers should naturally be followed by a reception that is lavishly decorated. The many activities associated with a reception, including eating, dancing, picture taking, gift giving, and tossing a garter and bouquet, can all be enhanced with special floral touches. The focal point of all this activity is typically the wedding cake. This particular item should be given the special attention it deserves by accenting it, and the table it rests upon, with the appropriate floral treatments. The bride's table is another key area that requires an exaggerated use of flowers. Table and room decorations are also important elements. Many of these designs can be styled as variations of specialty party arrangements. Small details, such as carriage flowers or an entry archway, often create the greatest impact. With so many possibilities for decorations, florists must be careful to coordinate each detail. Unity in combining the freshest flowers with original design ideas will make the desired impression on the bride and all her guests.

Themes

The bride and groom strive to make their wedding memorable and meaningful, and for these reasons, they plan events that are beautifully articulated. Many couples select themes for their wedding ceremony and/or reception. Often a site will suggest a theme, such as a seaside home as the site for a nautical wedding, with sailor dresses, flags, and a getaway boat. A farm wedding could inspire a picnic theme, with Laura Ashley prints, wheat stacks, and a buggy ride. The most important goal when using a theme for a wedding is to carry it out in all of the details. The flowers, room decorations, accessories, table linens, tents, food, and wedding cake, as well as the wedding color scheme and attire, must all be coordinated to create a unified effect.

Fabric

Fabric is an excellent decorating tool, which can be used to create or unify a theme. Fabrics used at receptions should be carefully selected to enhance the statement the bride is striving to make. Whatever fabric theme is selected, fabric accents or decorations should start at the entrance and be used on tables, napkins, archways, pedestals, and any other appropriate location. For example, if an English country theme has been selected, Laura Ashley prints (botanical prints) can be used to cover pedestals holding beautiful English garden style arrangements, with garlands of greenery cascading to the floor. Each table might

Advanced Floral Design

then be covered with a cloth of Laura Ashley prints with napkins to match. The napkin rings could be covered with the same print and finished with a sprig of greenery and an open rose, and the chair backs and seats could also be covered with custom design prints.

Fabric can also be used to cover walls and objects that are not attractive. In some situations, a staple gun can be used to attach fabric directly to a surface. In other cases, fabric-covered foam board may be utilized. This is an excellent method of converting a lodge or church hall into a wonderful room with warmth and ambiance.

Entrance Decorations

The entrance to a church, club, home, or tent can be changed from a very plain opening to a fantasy. This treatment will depend on the theme and the budget. Fabric can be used simply or lavishly to create a stunning entrance. *(See Figure 8.18.)* Props can be grouped and decorated for a marvelous look.

PVC Pipe Archway

An archway can also be created to frame an entrance area. The following arch built out of PVC pipe is simple to construct and transport.

Figure 8.18 Entrance Decorations

Materials Needed

- Twelve-foot length of 1-inch PVC pipe

- Two squares of wood that measure 12 inches X 12 inches X 2 inches

- Two 1-inch PVC pipe fittings

Design Steps

1. Screw a 1-inch PVC pipe fitting into the center of each block of wood.

2. Place the wood blocks on each side of the entrance, and insert each end of the 12-foot PVC pipe into the fittings. The 1-inch PVC pipe is pliable and will bend to form an arch.

Wedding Design

3. The arch can then be covered with greenery, flowers, tulle, or fabric. Lights can also be attached, if desired; however, the decorations must be kept lightweight to maintain balance.

4. Cover the squares of wood with fabric, flowers, or potted plants.

Cake Decorations

The cutting of the wedding cake by the bride and the groom is one of the highlights of the reception. The wedding cake can be traced to ancient Rome, where a wheat cake or biscuit was broken during the wedding ceremony and eaten by the bride and groom. However, the traditional wedding cake did not appear in the United States until after the Civil War. This cake replace the fruitcake that had previously been introduced by the British. The fruitcake then became the groom's cake.

Wedding cakes have become the focal point of receptions. They are designed in tiers; waterfalls; and in the shape of wedding rings, bells, hearts, circles, or squares. The round cake is a perennial favorite, however. The top layer on a round cake is usually 6 to 8 inches in diameter and each tier is approximately 2 inches larger than the one above it. Square cakes usually have a top that is 9 inches in diameter.

The top of a cake can be decorated in a variety of ways. The traditional bride and groom have always been favorites; however, fresh flowers have become a popular choice for not only the top of the cake, but for each tier and the base, as well.

The elaborate decorations can be traced to Victorian times when confectioners vied to create elaborate decorations for society and royal weddings. One example of this elaborate work was the cake decorated for Queen Victoria's favorite daughter, Princess Louise. The cake's lower tier had baskets of flowers and fruits; the second tier was festooned with roses, shamrocks, and thistles; and the third level had cornucopias and monogrammed shields. The entire cake was crowned with a vase of fresh flowers and silk banners edged with silver fringe.

Designing cake flowers on an advanced level requires imagination, good technique, and cooperation with the baker or caterer. Garlands, cascades, miniature nosegays, and individual flowers remain favorites for decorating cakes. Cake pillar may also be decorated for a more lavish look. Cascades of ivy or fresh flowers can be glued directly onto the pillars. *(See Figure 8.19a.)*

Figure 8.19a Cake Decorations

If a florist will be setting up the cake decorations, flowers may be used between the layers by simply laying the materials on the plastic separator plate, acrylic disc, mirrored plate, or paper doily. Begin with delicate greenery, and cover the surface with individual flowers, such as star gazer lilies, making sure that the flowers overlap for a unified look.

If the baker or caterer will be setting up the decorations, the flowers should be wired and taped and designed into nosegays, cascades, or garlands. The small corsage-like arrangements should be finished with short stems that have been folded flat so that the flowers will lie flat on the separator plates or cake layers. *(See Figure 8.21b.)* Flowers can also be glued onto broad-leaved types of foliage, such as salal, instead of wiring and taping.

A garland of greenery with flowers glued into it can surround the base of the cake, and a hand-tied garland of gypsophila with white roses glued into it is a beautiful adornment to the cake base as well. A simpler base decoration, which is also eye-catching, can be made by stapling broad leaves in a zigzag manner onto a piece of #9 ribbon which has been measured to equal the circumference of the cake. Flowers should then be glued onto the foliage to cover the staples. This decoration can then be easily positioned around the cake by the baker, caterer, or florist.

Figure 8.19b Cake Decorations

Head Table Decorations

People seated at the head table want to see their guests, so it is important to keep all decorations at heights of 14 inches or lower. The theme will greatly influence the decorations used for this important table. A series of low arrangements, placed end to end, creates a "hedge of flowers," or the arrangements can be placed every 3 feet and connected with 3-foot garlands of greenery.

The draping of the head table with festoons of tulle gives an opulent look to this focal area. The connecting areas of the tulle can be embellished with flower cascades that can be added by pinning into the fabric and adding showers of ribbon cascading to the floor. *(See Figure 8.20.)*

Ribbon also can be braided to form a swag for the head table. Use ribbon lengths two times the length of the table for braiding. This should be enough ribbon to swag the table and allow for shrinkage during the braiding process.

Bows of satin, tulle, or velvet are lovely additions to the head table. The streamers on the bows can be embellished with flowers by gluing flowers onto the streamers. Creative designs can be

Figure 8.20 Head Table Decoration

Wedding Design

fashioned out of flower petals and glued to the bows or even the tablecloth, to create a very special look.

A head table that is draped with taffeta can become spectacular by overlaying the taffeta with netting and gluing designs onto the netting with petals of flowers and fronds of greenery. An arrangement using the same theme as the flowers can be placed on the table for a completed look.

Car and Carriage Decorations

Decorating the bridal car or carriage adds excitement and contributes to the festivity of the occasion. When the car is decorated with flowers and ribbons, it makes the exit of the bride and groom more charming. The family car is usually selected; however, a limousine, hot air balloon, or English taxi would be quite effective.

Flowers can be placed on the hood, in front of the radiator, on the bumper, on the fenders, or on the back of the car. There are many areas on a carriage that can be decorated. The sides are ideal, however, because they are highly visible and decorations can be easily attached to them. Flowers for the horses and the carriage driver can add the perfect finishing touches.

Floral foam cages are often used to design sprays of flowers for the car or carriage. Cages with suction cup bases work particularly well. The holes in each end of the cages are useful for securing designs into place. Fishing line works well for attaching the cages to bumpers, windshield wipers, rear-view mirrors, or any other stationary parts of the car. Wire or ribbons can also be used for this purpose.

Horizontal arrangements work best for cars, because they can be kept low, thus ensuring good visibility. Garlands of flowers and greenery across the hood or over the windows are particularly effective. *(See Figures 8.21a and 8.21b.)* For a finishing touch, a sign for the rear of the car can be made with flowers spelling out the words "Just Married."

Figure 8.212a Auto Decorations

Figure 8.21b Auto Decorations

The designing of wedding flowers is often considered the most difficult of all types of floral design. Mastery of advanced wedding design styles and techniques is, thus, rewarding, as well as challenging. It can also be very profitable, because brides who request advanced style decorations frequently have large wedding budgets and are willing to pay the price for the look they desire.

Advanced Floral Design

Advanced styles for wedding design are numerous. Bouquets and body flowers can take on an advanced look with the use of specialty flowers masterfully combined. Ceremony decorations, including fanciful altar and aisle treatments, can set the mood for the entire wedding. Reception decorations coordinated with an innovative theme make the day memorable for all in attendance. The successful design of only one or two lavish weddings of this kind can lead to an ever-increasing list of client referrals. Thus, the time spent learning the skills involved in advanced wedding design is well worth the end results: satisfied customers, repeat business, and a positive reputation as a wedding florist.

Notes

Wedding Design

Notes, Photographs, Sketches, etc.

Advanced Floral Design

Notes, Photographs, Sketches, etc.

Wedding Design

Notes, Photographs, Sketches, etc.

Uniqueness in Design

Chapter 9

Uniqueness in design is the hallmark of a creative mind. Experimenting with various ideas and alternate media can inspire new approaches to design and provide opportunities for growth. There is nothing mystical about the imagination; it is within all of us. However, it is sometimes hampered by convention. The liberation of the creative spirit can result in the visual realization of a concept and its expression through flowers.

Sometimes customers resist innovation, but florists can still find applications for innovative work. Flower shows, trade exhibitions, visual displays, and professional competitions can be the incentive for stretching creativity. The intent of this chapter is to instill in designers the belief that they are never finished learning. The ideas presented do not include illustrations so that individual florists will not be overtly influenced. Instead, it is hoped that each reader will delve into his own sources of inspiration to bring new and innovative design styles to life.

Developing Creativity

The development of creativity is an ongoing process. It is often the result of the intense power of observation coupled with the ability to retain, retrieve, and visually reproduce a mental image. That which is consciously known expands when combined with a desire to explore the unknown. Sorting through the many ideas that require consideration and elimination allows the emergence of a unique perspective. Technical skills with which flowers are handled, processed, and manipulated are the foundation for growth beyond preconceptions. Creativity starts with a heightened awareness and a curious mind. These traits can be developed by seeking inspiration and analyzing trends. Ongoing experimentation with abstract concepts, tangible designs, and alternate media can result in enriched artistic creativity.

Advanced Floral Design

Sources of Creative Inspiration

Creative ideas rarely come to designers out of thin air. They are almost always a result of influences and experiences which occur throughout life. When attempting to develop greater creativity, designers may seek inspiration from a variety of sources. Art and nature are two of the most likely sources of inspiration. Both are closely associated with floral design. Therefore, it is natural to study them in order to become more creative as a designer.

Art

Art can be a wonderful source of floral design inspiration. Classical art may be used as an influence in creating traditional designs, and modern art may serve as inspiration for creating contemporary and free-form designs. Different types of art should be observed in order to gather ideas for using colors, textures, lines, and forms. Painting, sculpture, architecture, and even dance and music are all art forms from which design inspiration might be obtained. Even landscape and garden design can provide creative ideas for using flowers and foliage in arrangements (as evidenced by the popularity of the vegetative and landscape design styles). Following are suggested ways of using art as a design inspiration.

- *Interpret a design style.* Look at a painting of flowers and use the imagination to change the elements of the design. Flower substitutions and color changes are easy to implement. The resultant floral arrangement will reflect the look of the period if the flowers used were actually available during the time that the original painting was done. When the flowers used in an arrangement are not typical of the period, but the design shape and form are, the style of the arrangement is said to be interpretive of the period.

- *Use art within a design.* Sculpture is the most popular medium for this. The sculpture should dictate the arrangement of the elements of the floral design. For example, a contemporary sculpture which shows dynamic movement will require flower placement which does not contradict the lines that the eye will naturally follow when viewing the total composition.

Notes

Uniqueness in Design

Notes

- *Interpret the lines of sculpture.* Find a piece of sculpture which has a strong sense of line, perhaps a reclining nude or an abstract form. Decide which are the major lines in the sculpture. (A quick sketch will provide a pattern which can be used to establish the main lines of the floral design.) Use flowers which will visually create the same lines. It might be necessary to remove foliage to accent the drama of a line created by a stem. After primary floral lines are in place, look at secondary lines in the sculpture. Then, select and place secondary flowers. This type of design is especially challenging because the mechanics and container must be very inconspicuous. Ralph Null, a member of the American Institute of Floral Designers (AIFD) and one of the foremost designers and educators in the country, made a strong statement when he presented an arrangement at a recent AIFD symposium which dramatized the sculptural essence of line and space. It had a single gladiolus placed to the far left of a long, low container. At the opposite end of the container, he used a vertical cluster of gladioli foliage. The space between was filled with horizontal, thin, white birch logs and moss. "Music, pause, music" was the description he gave of the strong lines separated by an open area. Applied to sculpture, the description is vertical, horizontal, vertical. Deliberate manipulation of the elements controlled the total effect. This arrangement successfully presented a striking sculptural interpretation.

- *Analyze paintings for actual patterns of lines.* Consider the effect on the observer. For example, when deep space is used in a painting, attempt to determine how that characteristic can be used in floral design. Perhaps the most important quality of deep space is the way that it makes the viewer feel. He is drawn into a place far beyond his physical environment. This concept is expressed in designs when they have a path which winds through the base of the arrangement with no obvious end. It seems as if the path could go beyond the boundary of the design.

- *Consider the emotions expressed within a painting or sculpture.* Experiment with flowers, and strive to capture those emotions. A piece of art which depicts a mother holding a child can convey a sense of tenderness. It is similar to when two flowers are placed in a design so that the taller one is bending downward and the shorter one is facing it with an upstretched head. A strong sense of tenderness and intimacy is evoked. Learn to control the elements which contribute to the feelings of an expressive floral composition.

Nature

Exploration of nature is one of the most rewarding and beneficial sources of creative inspiration. Physical and mental rejuvenation is possible by spending a little time with nature. Walking in the woods or gazing at the sea can bring happy memories to mind. The smell of dry leaves or the mist of the ocean can help dispel anxiety and allow the subconscious to weave a sensation of well being. Time spent relaxing can purge negativism and open the mind to creative exploration. Learn to delight in the gifts of nature in order to gain creativity. Following are suggested ways of using nature as a design inspiration.

Water

Water can be soothing to see and hear. It can also be an expression of the power of nature. People relate to water on many levels. Not unlike experimental design, some prefer to sit appreciatively at the edge while others dive in. Of course, there is also the mixed pleasure of walking in the rain. A creative block can often be dislodged with time spent near water. The effect of water can be expressed in a design, or water can actually be incorporated into a design. Either way, design inspired by water can be rewarding.

Look at a waterfall in the sunlight. The sparkle of the surface, the color seen at various points, and the contrast of texture between wet rocks and slippery moss are elements which can easily be expressed in a design. A direct interpretation of this is the waterfall arrangement. It uses glistening accents on the surface, layers of various materials to convey the depth and color of the water, and contrasting plant materials and accessories to highlight texture. This type of interpretation can be applied to the diverse and personal impressions of water.

Botanical Elements

Appreciation of the various stages of the life cycle of a plant lends itself to application within a floral design. For example, the

Notes

Uniqueness in Design

Notes

exposed root system of a massive tree in a flood area is impressive. The juxtaposition of the magnitude of the tree and the vulnerability of the root system presents a strong contrast. A correlating botanical design could show the seeds, roots, seedlings, stems, leaves, branches, flowers, fruits, and the decline of a plant. A single arrangement could show five or six of the stages of flower or plant development.

Geological Elements

The diversity and scale of the earth's geology provides an unending source of design inspiration. For example, look at the buttes (hills rising abruptly with flat tops) found in the Southwestern United States. They are climactic in their rise from the desert floor. The colors of a sunset displayed across them provide an inspirational palette for floral designers. The shapes can be scaled down and recreated with foam board as a free-standing backdrop for a Southwestern motif.

Caverns have a sense of mystery about them. In design, the forms of stalagmites and stalactites will add unexpected drama. They can be made of aerosol insulation and painted. Slag glass chunks can be used in the same design to suggest the mineral deposits hidden beneath the surface. In a small arrangement, celastic can be used to build the effect of a cavern without tremendous time expenditure.

Mountains

The beauty of mountains is quite compelling. They can be interpreted through the use of many diverse materials. While large stones suggest the solidity of the mountains, a material as delicate as glass can serve the same purpose. An arrangement of woodsy plant material, flowers, moss, and lichen can suggest mountains in the distance when plexiglass or glass is cut to shape and inserted into the back of the design. The effect will vary with the type of material from which the mountains are made.

Recognizing Trends

The need for change is a constant in the American business community. To meet the demands made upon designers, knowledge of the events shaping the attitudes of consumers is vital. Florists must not only be able to recognize trends, they must also be able to build on those trends and to begin new trends. The First Lady is often a trend setter. Her life in a fishbowl is reflected by the media which details her every preference.

In the 1950s, Mamie Eisenhower began a trend by using pink bathroom fixtures. That was the first time that fixtures in any color other than white had ever been used in the White House. This created a market for accessory items in complementary colors. Because bathroom fixtures last a long time, the impact of this trend was felt for several years.

Jackie Kennedy loved fresh flowers in the White House. As a result, baby's breath became popular because it was something which she liked to have included in designs.

Fashion is an industry which is in a continual state of flux. It is important that florists consider the colors, patterns, and spirit of popular fashions. The trends which appeal to the same client base that patronizes the floral shop should be observed.

Home furnishings always relate directly to the type of floral products which are in demand. When massive, heavy furniture is being used in homes, floral arrangements which creatively accent the furniture are likely to be very popular. Florists should explore new ways of meeting the evolving demands of local customers. Receptivity to creative interpretation is heightened when customers can envision it within their own homes.

Innovation

Awareness of new products and media can spur the flow of innovative design ideas. Through floral wholesalers and trade and design shows, florists can learn about the products which lend themselves to new design applications. Trade magazines feature creative examples of the ways in which designs may incorporate alternate media. Ideas may be stimulated by attending craft shows and borrowing concepts. Exhibiting artists frequently use materials which can be adapted for use in arrangements and visual displays.

The investment of time spent experimenting with new media is worthwhile when it evokes innovative ideas and unconventional applications. An innovative mind will observe things as they are and then superimpose a new perspective. It is much easier to stay with that which is proven; however, it can also be terminally boring. At what point is "different" synonymous with "weird?" The distinction is related to the ability of the viewer to understand the intention of the designer. More importantly, it is the ability of a designer to share his creative vision and to communicate that which goes beyond the expected, while still making his perspective relate to the customer. The challenge can assist florists in reaching an even higher level of innovation. The satisfaction of developing a distinctive approach to either

Notes

Uniqueness in Design

Notes

business or design can bring ample compensation for the effort extended.

Style Influences

The myriad of influences on designers can serve as catalysts for unique presentations. Design perspective can spring from personal preferences, mentor relationships, other designers industry professionals, symposiums, trade programs, and publications. Collectively, these forces can create a new spirit of creativity within the most seasoned professional.

Creative design can be the result of a designer's desire to express his innermost sensitivity. By looking within, remembering, and dreaming, it is possible to visualize the things in life which provide aesthetic pleasure. Individual experiences and preferences can be translated into a resource for design ideas. For example, a love of fantasy, travel, simplicity, or outrageousness can be the basis of a unique design style. Personality is inextricably linked to the dynamics of distinctive design. The essence of emotions can be tangibly expressed with flowers; they provide a palette for the expressionism of the florist.

Another substantial influence on florists is the actual or intellectual presence of a mentor. Ideally, he should teach, inspire, and set free the imagination of his students. To create clones is the antithesis of the endeavor. A mentor can establish a point of reference from which to measure future growth. The respect with which he is regarded can serve to inspire the attainment of even the most difficult goals. After all, the experience of learning is as important as the finished work.

Flower arrangements exhibited at design shows provide the opportunity to view an alternative approach to design. Progressive florists will examine the designs to see what ideas will serve the needs of local clients. By analyzing flower arrangements, florists can draw out that which is adaptable to his/her own needs.

The appeal of unique qualities can be tailored to meet and surpass the expectations of customers. When looking at a design, imagine the arrangement as it would be if it were scaled up or down, or think about the impact of a different color harmony. Take ideas and make them work through personal interpretations.

The professional perspective of style influences is often presented in magazines and lectures. This type of education is invaluable in developing a unique style. Creative expression coupled with professionalism can magnify the opportunities for success.

Experimentation

The quest to develop a unique look can be broached by experimenting with new concepts, attitudes, media, and design styles. When thinking of how a particular concept could be interpreted, write down the ideas that come to mind. Then stretch the imagination past the comfortable, predictable ideas, and attempt to go beyond the obvious. "As we mature, most of us grow more and more enslaved to the stock conceptions with which we have once become familiar, and less and less capable of assimilating impressions in any but the old ways." (James, 58) It takes courage, creative confidence, and a strong belief in that which is possible to abandon the predictable endeavor and search for a new intensity of a shared vision.

Seek new ways to express creativity. A good starting point would be to experiment with contrived containers. They are containers which can be enhanced by customized alterations or by changing from the normal way of using them. A vase can be turned over or sideways to create a new perspective. A simple example is to start with a maché container. Glue water vials to the outside. Cover with moss, and tie twigs to the moss. Insert flowers between the twigs. The finished product is not like anything customers are likely to see elsewhere. As a result, the shop's image is more distinctive. Other media can be used to alter containers. Textured paint, faux finishes, or contrasting accessories can be used to produce distinctive special effects on props and containers.

As a florist evolves past basic skills and matures into a seasoned professional, it is obvious that this growth is directly correlated with receptivity to new concepts. Approximately every two years, a designer's style will change. Designers should strive to create a highly personalized style, but should not stop incorporating new ideas. If a floral shop focuses on traditional design, these interpretations need to be fabulous. It is suggested that distinctive containers and out of the ordinary accents or color harmonies be used. Designers should create a specialized niche and be the best within it. Experimentation with new ideas and media can be the razor's edge of fear and excitement when put into actual use. Of course, there is a chance that new ideas will be rejected. However, they do not have a chance of being accepted if the customer is not even aware that they are available. Creative challenge can be compelling, and involved designers will find it an experience that is both fascinating and motivating.

Notes

Uniqueness in Design

Notes

Alternate Media

Alternate media are the nontraditional materials which can be incorporated into floral designs, visual displays, or the construction of props. Alternate media combine with flowers to expand the creative realm of designers and to allow an uncommon level of design excitement to emerge.

Creating a unique statement is possible if an arrangement is begun with the components of a basic design and some of them are embellished. Personalized focus and perspective can be implemented to control the design elements. Designers might wrap purple suede around a container and add accents of orange and olive green for a striking effect. Alternatively, viewers may be invited to get a closer look with the use of texture. Contrast the smooth, waxy surface of a Gothic candle, nestled in an oversized banksia by placing velvety clump moss at the base of the candle and gold-leafed galax leaves clustered beneath the banksia. The design can be finished by placing an irregular mass of crushed automobile window glass around the base. The tactile quality of such a design creates a design element which is subtle, yet fascinating.

Alternate media can be found in a junkyard or at a variety of businesses, including hardware, art supply, paint, home decorating, plumbing, plastics, and fabric stores. New materials are constantly inundating the various markets. New applications are always emerging for standard products. Following is a reference list of materials which fall beyond the conventional floral resources. Individualistic designers can use the materials as tools for imaginative floral interpretation. This list can be expanded and personalized for in-shop use. An ongoing commitment to experiment with new media will provide aesthetic stimulation for the design staff, diverse alternatives for customers, and new market opportunities for increased profitability.

Alternate Media for Advanced Designs

- Aerosol Insulation - Lightweight and fast drying. It expands after it is sprayed and provides texture. Twisted newspaper can be covered to make stone-like formations. (Read cleanup directions carefully.) Available in hardware stores.

- Celastic - Canvas-like material available from display houses, which becomes limp and moldable when immersed in acetone but dries stiff and weather resistant. Excellent for props.

- Copper - Available in sheets, flexible tubing, pipes, and wires. It is used in designs and as props.

- Envirotex - Two-part plastic resin which is used for glass-like surface on wood, foam board, stone, etc. Waterproofs and permanently bonds surfaces together.

- Feathers - Varies color and textures in designs. Hackles are small felt pads which are covered with feathers and can be used to cover containers or as an accent.

- Fleckstone - Faux stone finish in an aerosol can. Effectively used on shaped floral foam and other surfaces. It is recommended that the accompanying sealer be used.

- Foam Board - Usually 3/16 inches thick, paper-laminated styrofoam. Used for back drops, props, and containers.

- Fur/Suede - Scraps are available from manufacturers of coats and accessories. Has a wonderful texture for covering containers with an ethnic touch.

- Glass - Tempered glass is found in the back or side windows of cars and is available at junkyards. When smashed, it can be used with envirotex to build props or in arrangements for a sparkling texture. For best results, windows should be cleaned and covered with a sheet before smashing.

- Grout - Intended for use between ceramic tile or artificial interior brick face. Serves as a lava-like texture when spread thinly over shaped styrofoam.

- Light Boxes - Usually a wood box which contains a single light bulb. Used to dramatize a translucent or transparent vase.

- Metal Leaf - Paper thin sheets of precious or

Notes

Uniqueness in Design

Notes

inexpensive versions of gold, silver, and multi-colored metallics. Used to finish the surface of containers, branches, foliage, etc.

- Plexiglass - Available in sheets, tubes, or rods. It can be shaped with gentle, even heat and can be cut with a power saw. Hollow rods are excellent for creating height in design.

- Protoplast - Thermoplastic is sold in sheets which are 1/16 inch to 3/16 inch thick. Becomes limp and moldable when dipped in hot water (140 degrees Fahrenheit). Moldable even after it is set, which takes 2 to 3 minutes. Can be used to look like sculptured fabric.

- PVC - Plastic pipe intended for use in plumbing. Not available everywhere due to building codes. Can be used as framework for structures or as a prop. Easy to cut with a power saw and can be painted or covered with fabric, moss, pods, etc.

- Screening - Plastic or metal that can be structural or a component of design.

- Textiles - Double knit polyester that is wrinkle resistant and excellent for continued use in visual display. Nylon and chiffon works well for aisle treatments and chuppahs. Lamé catches even minimal light and can look lush and elegant. These fabrics are used for draping, covering containers, creating props, making rental tablecloths, etc.

- Wood - It can be used to create frames for wall pieces or as structural support for props and display units.

Designing with Alternate Media

Following are suggestions for using alternate media within floral arrangements. Florists should work with these ideas to develop innovative, new applications for alternate media.

- Foam board - Use it to disguise a simple design dish. Cut it into a triangle with a base that measures 2 to 3 feet and score it vertically every 2 inches. Bend it along the score lines; wrap the lowest corner of the triangle around the edge of the dish; curve the board behind it to make a sweeping, descending line. Glue the board to the dish (after the foam is in the dish) and it will totally conceal the container and allow a dramatic vertical design to ascend.

- Metal leaf - Spray a branch or dry pod with paint the same color as the metal leaf. Use floral spray glue to secure the metal leaf to the branch or dry pod. The coat of paint will go into any irregular surface areas which may be difficult to reach with the metal leaf.

- Textiles - Tulle can be used to totally or partially enclose a design to create a soft, romantic look.

- Fur/Suede - Both synthetic and natural are available. Ideal for adding texture which is natural looking and primitive as an accent around the edge of a basket.

- Grout - Use 2-inch styrofoam to support a piece of driftwood and attach an IGLU® Holder behind the wood for the arrangement. Bevel the top edge of any exposed styrofoam in an irregular pattern. Cover it with grout to make the drift look as if it is emerging from a natural stone formation.

- Feathers - Use within waterfall arrangements, bridal work, and especially in fall designs to add texture, line, and drama.

Visual Display with Alternate Media

Maximum impact for merchandising designs which incorporate alternate media is achieved by repeating the theme and materials in a dramatic visual display. Grab the customer's attention with the display and have a small-scale arrangement selection available for immediate purchase or special order prototypes.

For example, a window display in celebration of Earth Day could be charmingly interpreted with flowers and trees in a garden setting. Earth Day is an acknowledgement of man's common need to protect and nurture the earth. To expand beyond the typical interpretation, consider installing an educational and visually stimulating window display. If the project is too complex in its entirety, incorporate some elements into a different interpretation of the same concept.

Notes

Uniqueness in Design

Notes

To begin the Earth Day window display installation, make a platform to elevate the garden's ground level. It should start at the top one-third of the window. The bottom two-thirds of the window can allow the viewer to peer into a cross section of the underside of the earth. This project would involve the use of some special media and would make a dramatic statement. The top level should feature grass, flowers, and the lower section of the tree trunks. To build the underside, use crumpled, brown craft paper for the back of the cave. Make an artificial root system directly below the tree by hanging an inverted manzanita branch. Use nonsalable plants or weeds to make the exposed root systems under the rest of the plant material. Stalactites and stalagmites can be quickly made form twisted newspaper which has been coated with aerosol insulation. A subterranean pool or stream can be constructed with an outline of bricks which is lined with heavy black plastic. Lay the plastic over the bricks, then tuck it under them and fill with water. Disguise the edges with appropriate natural materials. Include a sign with a message which says, "Say 'thanks' to the earth, plant a flower today." Remember, as with obvious ideas, the surface of the earth is just a starting point from which to look beyond.

Even when working with the diversity of alternate media, designers can experience creative blocks. However, they can be dislodged when dreams, fantasies and optimistic attitudes are brought into the forefront of a designer's consciousness. A narrow-minded perspective can develop and dominate a designer's attitude. Designers should attempt to let go of preconceptions and look at the alternatives. The professional's scope is greatly enhanced with the exploration of alternate media. For floral designers, the everyday, ongoing process of life can be viewed as an opportunity to expand and change. Flowers and new materials can be used in combination for the translation of spatial experience and to evoke the essence of beauty. The emerging design can capture the imagination, evoke an emotion, or even embrace a dream.

Advanced Floral Design

Notes, Photographs, Sketches, etc.

Glossary

Alternate Media - Materials which are not generally available through floral wholesale suppliers or materials which can be used in designs in nontraditional ways.

Baroque - A pearl of irregular shape.

Biedermeier Bouquet - A classic round form in which brilliantly-colored flowers are placed in concentri circles.

Boutonnieres - Flowers worn by men on their lapels, shoulders, or sleeves.

Cachepot - Decorative container for a potted plant or flower arrangement. It is derived from the French *cacher*, meaning to hide or conceal.

Chaplet - Garland or wreath worn on the head.

Chuppah - A covering or canopy that is usually covered with fabric and supported by four poles. This canopy symbolizes the home and is used in traditional Jewish weddings. The significance of the chuppah is that it strengthens the idea of the presence of God in the heavens above our head.

Composite Flower - A flower made by removing the petals from a flower and wiring or gluing the individual petals together to form a new and larger flower.

Contrived Container - A container which is used in a nontraditional way or which is changed by a designer in the name of creativity.

Duchess Rose - A composite flower made from the petals of multiple roses to create a very large rose.

European Style Bouquet - A bouquet with segmented areas of plant material in groupings, lines, and multiple levels of the flowers. Textures, succulents, and foliage with strong characteristics of the Euro-style are frequently used.

Faience - A tin-enameled earthenware made of finely ground silicate glazed in blue, blue green, green, violet, chrome, and lemon yellow. The Egyptians and the Italians (at Faenza, Italy) produced faience.

Festooning - A swag of fabric that extends from one area to the next. Example: attaching fabric to a pew and draping the fabric in a swag, then attaching it to the next pew.

Gadrooning - Pattern of fluting or beading on decorative containers, such as metalware or glassware.

Galax Rose - A composite flower made from galax leaves.

Glamellia - A composite flower made from gladiolus florets.

Gothic Candle - A hand-dipped candle which is usually 2 to 3 inches in diameter and has a smooth, round top.

Hand-tied Garland - A garland that is made by binding flowers together with floral thread or paddle wire in a continuous pattern until the desired length of garland is reached.

Hedge of Flowers - A series of containers holding low arrangements of flowers, such as garden roses. The arrangements are placed side by side to form a hedge.

Horsehair Fabric - A fabric with a loose weave that has body which gives it a firm texture.

Ikebana - A style and philosophy of floral design dating from the fifteenth century in Japan. Ikebana is divided into four major styles: the classical rikka and seika and the naturalistic moribana and nageire.

Glossary

Plaster Skull Cap - A custom-designed skull cap made from a quick-setting plaster bandage.

PVC Pipe - A plastic pipe used in plumbing.

Rococo - Based on the French word *rocaille*; refers to the delicate rock-and-shell ornamentation typical in the eighteenth century.

Tazza - Low, shallow pedestal bowl.

Topiaries - A design featuring a round ball on top of a pole, rod, or branch which has been secured in a suitable container with an arrangement in it.

Tuzzie Muzzie - A tiny Victorian bouquet, often conveying a sentimental floral message.

Bibliography

"A History of Flower Arrangement." Teleflora Spirit. March 1971.

Abbey, R. 1986. Art and Geology. Utah: G.M. Smith Co.

Alberts, Dries. 1986. Floral Design & Art. Wormerveer, Holland: De Uitgeverij BV.

Benz, M. 1979. Flowers: Abstract Form II. Huston: San Jacinto Publishing Co.

Berrall, Julia S. 1953. A History of Flower Arrangement. London and New York: The Studio Publications, Inc., in association with Thomas Y. Crowell Company.

Dreams Come True. 1991. The John Henry Company.

Dutton, Joan Parry. 1962. The Flower World of Williamsburg. New York: Holt, Rinehart and Winston.

Erickson, Melissa Dodd. "A History of Western Floral Design." Flowers &. March 1990.

Gilliatt, Mary. 1986. English Country Style. Great Britain: Orbis Book Publishing Corp.

James, William. Professional Floral Design. Oklahoma City: American Floral Services. December 1989.

Lersch, Gregor. 1987. Straube flieBend, leicht und farbig. Gunzburg: Donau-Verlag.

Marcus, Margaret Fairbanks. 1952. Period Flower Arrangement. New York: M. Barrows & Company, Inc.

Bibliography

Miller, Judith and Martin. 1990. <u>International Country</u>. New York: Viking Studio Books.

Mitchell, Herb, editor-in-chief. "The History of Flower Arrangement." <u>Design with Flowers</u>. March/April 1989.

Morley, Jim. 1989. <u>The Professional Floral Design Manual</u>. Oklahoma City: American Floral Services.

Pfahl, Peter Blair. 1982. <u>American Style Flower Arranging</u>. Englewood Cliff: Prentice-Hall, Inc.

Porterfield, Frances. "Florists' Glossary of Terms." <u>Florists' Review: Sourcebook</u>. Vol. 81, 1988. pp. 24-28.

Reuschenbach, Michael. 1989. <u>Blattwerk</u>. Augsburger: Appel-Druck Donau-verlag GmbH.

Rulloda, Phillip. 1990. <u>Tropical and Contemporary Floral Design</u>. Phoenix: Carol Publishing Group.

Sato, Shozo. 1966. <u>The Art of Arranging Flowers - A Complete Guide to Japanese Ikebana</u>. New York: Harry N. Abrams, Inc.

Sparnon, Norman. 1982. <u>Creative Japanese Flower Arrangement</u>. Tokyo: Shufunotomo.

Stewart, Martha. 1987. <u>Weddings</u>. New York: Clarkson N. Potter, Inc.

Tober, Barbara. 1984. <u>The Bride - A Celebration</u>. New York: Harry N. Abrams, Inc.

Vance, Georgia S. 1972. <u>The Decorative Art of Dried Flower Arrangement</u>. New York: Doubleday and Company.

Webb, Iris, editor. 1979. <u>The Complete Guide to Flower and Foliage Arrangement</u>. New York: Doubleday and Company.

Wright, Bruce. "The Art of Ikebana." <u>Flowers &</u>. December 1984.

Webb, Iris. 1979. <u>The Complete Guide to Flower and Foliage Arrangement</u>. Garden City, New York: Doubleday and Company, Inc.

Index

A

Abstract casket cover *200-201*
    design of *201*
Abstract design *37*
Abstract experimental design *37*
Accent *37*
Achromatic *38*
Advanced design styles *157-190*
    Biedermeier *160-162*
    country bouquets *162-166*
    crescent *176-178*
    Flemish *158-160*
    free-form *184-185*
    hand-tied bouquet *185-187*
    Hogarth curve *174-176*
    ikebana *166-171*
    landscape *179-180*
    leafwork table *187*
    line-mass *174-179*
    linear *166-173*
    mass *158-166*
    natural *179-184*
    new convention *171-173*
    parallelism *171*
    Phoenix *176-179*
    topiary *188-189*
    vegetative *179-182*
    waterfall *182-184*
Aerosol insulation *273*
Airbrush *38*
Aisle decorations *253-254*
    fabric festoons *254*
    pew bows, taffeta *253-254*

Allium, techniques for using *127*
Alstroemeria *107-108*
    techniques for using *128*
Altar decorations *243-253*
    choir stalls *249-250*
    chuppah *246-249*
    flower hedges *251-252*
    topiaries *252-253*
    tree-like *245-246*
    window *249*
Alternate media *273-277*
    designing with *275-276*
    visual display with *276-277*
Amaryllis, techniques for using *128*
American country bouquet *162-166*
American floral design history *28-31*
    at a glance *30*
Analogous color harmony *38*
Anthurium *118-120*
Anti-transpirant *126*
Arch, PVC pipe *256-257*
Art *266-268*
Astilbe *110*
    techniques for using *128*
Asymmetrical arrangement *38*
Asymmetrical balance *39, 66*
Availability, fresh flower *88-89*
Axis *39*

B

Baby's breath, techniques for using *129*
Balance *39, 65-66*
    physical *39*
    visual, types of *39*

Index

Bamboo extenders *125*
Bamboo tripod *212-213*
Banding *39*
Bark container finish *153*
Baroque floral design *14-18*
Base line *39*
Basing *40*
Basket arrangements, sympathy *213*
Bending technique *38*
Bent easel *212*
Berry boutonniere *235-236*
Biedermeier arrangements *65, 160-162*
    design of *161-162*
Biedermeier bouquet *224-225*
Biedermeier style *40*
Binding point *40*
Binding technique *40*
Bird of paradise *118-120*
    techniques for using *128*
Body flowers
    See Flowers to wear
Boston fern *123*
Botanical design *40, 269*
Boutonnieres *234-237*
    berry *235-236*
    contemporary *236-237*
Bouquet *40*
Bouquets, wedding *220-230*
    Biedermeier *224-225*
    European contemporary *228-230*
    glamellia *223-224*
    hand-tied *227-228*
    herb and foliage *225-227*
Bouvardia *108-109*
    techniques for using *128*
Braided ribbon wreath *208*
Braiding technique *54*
Branch-covered easel *211-212*
Broken line *48*
Bud opening *100-101*
Budget *91*
Bullet *85*
Bullhead *65*
Bunching technique *40-41*
Bundling technique *41*
Buying habits
  customer *93*
  supplier *89*

C

Cake decorations *257-258*
Calla *109-110*
    techniques for using *128*
Candles, mechanics for *147*
Cap, floral skull *240-242*
Care and handling *93-133*
    basic flower needs *94-95*
    in design *124-133*
    flower deterioration *94, 96*
    special flower pointers *107-121*
    special foliage pointers *122-123*
    specialty flower techniques *100-107*
    specialty foliage techniques *121-122*
    steps *95-99*
        overview *97-99*
Cascading veil flowers *242-243*
Casket blanket *201-202*
    foliage, design of *201-202*
Casket covers
    See Casket designs
Casket designs *195-204*
    for children *203-204*
    mechanics for *195-196*
    styles of *196-203*
        abstract *200-201*
        blanket *201-202*
        landscape *199-200*
        new convention *197-198*
        scarf *202-203*
        vegetative *196-197*
        waterfall *198-199*
Casket scarf *202-203*
    design of *202-203*
Celastic *273-274*
Center of interest *67*
Ceremony decorations, wedding *243-254*
    aisle *253-254*
    altar *243-253*
    chuppah *246-249*
Chabana *12*
Chain of Life *94*
Chaplet *6*
Children's casket cover *203-204*
    design of *203-204*
Choir stall decorations *249-250*

Index

Chroma *41*
Chuppah *246-249*
    brass *247*
    lattice *246-247*
    PVC *247-249*
Clay, floral *141*
Closed form *41*
Clustering *41*
Collage *148*
Colonial period *28-31*
    at a glance *29*
Colonial Williamsburg arrangement *165*
Colonial Williamsburg period *28-31*
    at a glance *29*
Color *71-72*
    analogous *38*
    chroma *41*
    hue *46*
    secondary *55*
Columnar design frame *143*
Commercial floral design *41*
Composite easel spray *209*
Composite flowers *38, 220-224*
    to wear *230-233*
Composite foliage *38*
Composite grapevine wreath *207*
Composition *41*
Concinnity *42*
Conditioning *42*
Container coverings *151-153*
Contemporary boutonniere *236-237*
Contemporary design *42*
Continuous line *48*
Contour line *48*
Copper *274*
Cornflower, techniques for using *128*
Corsages *230-234*
    duchess rose *232-233*
    gerbera cascade *233-234*
    glamellia *230-232*
Corso™ Holder *138*
Country bouquets *162-166*
Creativity, development of *265-277*
    sources of inspiration *266-269*
Crescent arrangement *42, 44, 176-178*
    design of *177-178*
Cull *86*

Curvilinear line *48*
Cylinders, floral foam *140*

D

Dahlia *110*
    techniques for using *128*
Delaying flower development *101-103*
Delft *17*
della Robbia, Luca *10*
Delphinium *110*
Depth *42, 66-67*
Design, defined *42*
Design aids *125-127*
Design elements *71-73*
    See also Elements of design
Design media, alternate *273-277*
Design principles
    defined *54*
    See also Principle of design
Design Style, defined *42*
Design styles, advanced *157-190*
    See also Advanced design styles
Design techniques
    defined *42*
    for special flowers *127-130*
    specialty *137-153*
Design tips *124-125*
Designer block *139*
Detaching technique *38*
Detailing technique *42*
Diagonal line *48*
Dips, finishing *125-127*
Disbud *85*
Discounts, supplier *89-90*
Display
    with alternate media *276-277*
Distressed Neguro Nuri finish *151*
Domestically-grown flowers *87*
Dominance *67*
Duchess rose corsage *232-233*
Dutch Flemish floral design *14-18*
    at a glance *18*

E

Earth line *43*
Easel covers *211-212*

Index

Easel covers (continued)
    branch *211-212*
    fabric *212*
    moss *211*
Easel designs *208-213*
    cross *210-211*
    hearts *210*
    pillows *210*
    sprays *208-209*
Egyptian floral design *6-7*
    at a glance *7*
Elements of design *71-73*
    color *71-72*
    defined *43*
    form *72*
    line *72*
    texture *72-73*
English church decorations *250*
English country bouquet *162-166*
English floral design *21-28*
    early English tradition *22-23*
        at a glance *24*
    Victorian era *23-28*
        at a glance *29*
Entrance decorations *256-257*
    PVC pipe archway *256-257*
Envirotex *274*
Equilateral triangle arrangement *43*
Ethylene reduction treatment *86*
European baroque floral design *14-18*
European contemporary bouquet *228-230*
European Designer Collection *137-139*
European extenders *125*
European funeral wreath *205*
Experimentation, design *272*
Extenders, flower *125*
Extensions, mass design *142-143*

F

Fabric, decorating with *255-256*
    festoons *254*
Fabric-covered easel *212*
Faux finishes *151-153*
Faux marble finish *152*
Feathering technique *43*
Feathers *274*
    designing with *276*

Fibonnaci principle *43, 70-71*
Field-grown crops *88*
Field-grown flowers
    care and handling of *110*
Filler flower *44*
Filler Stix *140*
Finishes, container *151-153*
Finishing dips *125-127*
Finishing sprays *125-127*
Five-fingered vase *28*
Fleckstone *274*
Flemish arrangements *158-160*
    design of *159-160*
Flemish floral design *14-18, 43*
    at a glance *18*
Floating line *48*
Flob *43*
Floracage® Grande Holder *138*
Floracage® Holder *138*
Floral blossom container finish *153*
Floral clay *141*
Floral object *43*
Flower classifications *44*
Flower deterioration *94, 96*
    causes of *96*
Flower life
    long-lasting *131*
    short-lived *131-132*
Flower meanings, Victorian *26*
Flowering branches
    techniques for using *128*
Flowers to wear *230-243*
    boutonnieres *234-237*
    corsages *230-234*
    hair flowers *237-239*
    headpieces, structured *239-243*
Foam board *274*
    designing with *275-276*
Foam, floral *137-142*
    contouring *140-141*
    pre-caged *137-139*
    securing *141-142*
    specialty-cut *139-140*
Form flower *44*
Focal area *44, 67*
Foliage
    bouquet *225-227*

Index

Foliage *(continued)*
    classifications *44*
    cuttings *122*
    glosses, waxes and sprays *121*
    pointers *122-123*
    soaking *121*
Forcing technique *44*
Form *44-45, 72*
Formal linear arrangement *49*
Framing *45*
Free-form arrangements *184-185*
Free-form design *45*
Free-form line *44*
French country bouquet *162-166*
French period of floral design *18-21*
French rococo *19-21*
    at a glance *21*
Frenching technique *43*
Funeral designs *195-215*
    See also Sympathy design
Funeral environment *214*
Funeral settings *214-215*
Fur *274*
    designing with *276*

G

Gadrooning *10*
Galax *123*
    rosette *226*
Garden flowers
    care and handling of *110*
    preparing *106-107*
Gardenias *111*
    techniques for using *129*
Garland, hand-tied *250-251*
Gelatin sealer *126*
Georgian sealer *126*
Georgian period *22*
Gerbera *111-112*
    cascade corsage *233-234*
    techniques for using *129*
Gilding *152*
Ginger *118-120*
    techniques for using *129*
Glamellia *38, 220-223*
    bouquet *223-224*
    corsage *230-232*

Glass *274*
Glass container mechanics *146-147*
Gloriosa lily, techniques for using *129*
Glory lily, techniques for using *129*
Gloss, foliage *121*
Glue dip *126*
Gluing technique *45*
Golden Mean *46, 69-71*
Graded plane *46*
Grapevine wreath, composite *207*
Grave site decorations *214-215*
Greco-Roman period *8-9*
    at a glance *9*
Greek floral design *8-9*
Greenhouse-grown crops *87*
Grouping *46*
Grout *274*
    designing with *276*
Grower *79*
Gypsophila, techniques for using *129*

H

Hair flowers *237-239*
    phalaenopsis orchid *238-239*
    single *237-238*
Hana-mai style *46*
Hand-tied bouquet *46, 185-187, 227-228*
    design of *185-187*
    Dutch spiral technique *227-228*
    German nesting technique *228*
Hand-tied garland *250-251*
Hanging line *48*
Harmony *46, 69*
Hat, horsehair *239-240*
Head table decorations *258-259*
Headpieces, structured *239-243*
    cascading veil flowers *242-243*
    floral skull cap *240-242*
    horsehair hat *239-240*
Heart, funeral *210*
Hedge, floral *251-252*
Heirloom containers, use of *214*
Heliconia *118-120*
Herb and foliage bouquet *225-227*
Hikae *13, 167*
    proportions for *167-168*

Index

History of floral design *5-32*
    American *28-31*
    Dutch Flemish *14-18*
    Egyptian influence *6-7*
    English influence *21-28*
    European baroque *14-18*
    French period *18-21*
    Greek and Roman era *8-9*
History of floral design *(continued)*
    Italian Renaissance *9-11*
    Japanese influence *12-14*
    Victorian era *23-28*
Hogarth, William *16, 174*
Hogarth curve *45*
    design *174-176*
Hogarth line *49*
Horizontal line *49*
Horsehair hat *239-240*
Horsetail cross *210-211*
Hue *46*
Hyacinth, techniques for using *129*

I

IGLU® Grande Holder *139*
IGLU® Holder *138-139*
Ikebana *46-47, 166-171*
    moribana *168-170*
    nageire *170-171*
Ikenobo School *47*
Implied line *49*
Importer *79*
Innovation *270-271*
Inspiration, sources of *266-269*
Insulation, aerosol *273*
Intermediate line *49*
Internationally-grown flowers *87*
Interpretive design *47*
Interpretive linear arrangement *49-50*
Interweaving *52*
Inventory control *92*
Iris *112-113*
    techniques for using *129*
Isosceles triangle *45*
Italian Renaissance floral design *9-11*
    at a glance *11*
Ivy *123*

J

Japanese floral design *12-14*
    at a glance *14*
Japanese ikebana *12-14*

K

Kenzan *12*
    use of *144-145*
Kinetic motion *51*
Kubari *145-146*

L

Lacing technique *47*
Landscape arrangement *47-48, 179-180*
Landscape casket cover *199-200*
    design of *200*
Lasso taping method *141-142*
Layering *48, 65*
Leafwork *48, 65, 152-153*
    table *187*
Light boxes *274*
Lilac, techniques for using *129*
Lilies *113-114*
    techniques for using *130*
Line *48-49, 72*
Line of beauty *49, 174*
Line flower *44*
Line-mass designs *174-179*
    crescent *176-178*
    Hogarth curve *174-176*
    Phoenix *178-179*
Linear arrangement *49-50*
Linear designs *166-172*
    ikebana *166-171*
    new convention *171-173*
    parallelism *171*
Lines of confusion *50*
Lines of parallelism *50*
Long-lasting flowers *131*
Loving cup *31*

M

Madonna lily *9*
Maidenhair fern *123*

Index

Marigold *110*
    techniques for using *130*
Market, flower *78-79*
Mass designs *158-166*
    Biedermeier *160-162*
    country bouquets *162-166*
    Flemish *158-160*
Mass flower *44*
Massaging technique *38*
Mechanics *137-153*
    defined *50*
Media, alternate *273-277*
Mentoring *271*
Metal leaf *274-275*
    designing with *276*
Micro Brick *140*
Mille de Coleurs arrangement *50*
Mille de Fleurs arrangement *50*
Ming fern *122*
Mini Deco™ Holder *140*
Minimalism *50*
Mirroring *51*
Modified styrofoam wreath *207-208*
Moribana *12, 51, 167*
    design of *168-170*
Moss container finish *153*
Moss-covered easel *211*
Motion *51*
Mound arrangement *51*

N

Nageire *12, 52, 167*
    design of *170-171*
Natural designs *179-184*
    landscape *179-180*
    vegetative *179-182*
    waterfall *182-184*
Natural picking *54*
Naturalistic design *52*
Nature *268-269*
Negative space *52, 68*
Neguro Nuri finish, distressed *151*
New convention arrangement *52, 171-173*
    design of *172-173*
New convention casket cover *197-198*
    design of *198*

New wave design *52*
Novelty arrangement *53*

O

Ohara School *47*
Ono-no-Imoko *12*
Open balance *39, 66*
Open form *45*
Orchids *114-115*
Oval form *45*

P

Papier-maché *133*
    container covers *213*
Parallel flower placement *53*
Parallel lines *64-65*
Parallel systems arrangement *53*
Parallelism *50, 53, 171*
Partitioning
    of containers *145*
Pavé *53*
Pedestals *344-345*
Period design
    See History of floral design
Pew bows, taffeta *253-254*
Phoenix arrangement *543, 178-179*
    design of *179*
Photographic container finish *152*
Physical balance *39*
Picking *54*
Pillow, funeral *210*
Pillowing *54*
Place-It™ Grande Holder *138*
Place-It™ Holder *138*
Plating *54*
Plexiglass *275*
Plumosa *122*
Poinsettia, techniques for using *130*
Points of interest *67*
    See also Focal area
Point to point connection *54*
Polarity *54*
Positive space *54, 68*
Pre-caged floral foam *138-139*

Index

Price, wholesale 84
    factors affecting 88-90
Primary line 49
Principles of design 63-71
    balance 65-66
    center of interest 67
    defined 54
    depth 66-67
    dominance 67-68
    focal area 67-68
    Golden Mean 69-71
    proportion 64
    radiation 64-65
    repetition 65
    rhythm 67
    space 68
    unity 68
Product availability 82
Product sources
    domestic 87
    field-grown 88
    greenhouse-grown 87
    international 87
Proportion 54, 64
Protoplast 275
Pruning 54-55
Purchasing 77-93
    factors to consider 84-93
        customer-related 90-93
        product-related 84-90
        shop-related 90-93
Pussy willow, techniques for using 130
PVC 275
    arch 256-257

R

Radial balance 39, 66
Radiating line 49
Radiation 64-65
RAQUETTES® 139
Realistic floral design 55
Reception decorations 254-259
    cake 257-258
    car and carriage 259

Reception decorations *(continued)*
    entrance 256-257
    fabric 255-256
    head table 258-259
Reflexing technique 38
Renaissance period 9-11
Repetition 65
Revival, flower 103-104
Rhythm 55, 67
Right triangle arrangement 55
Rikka style 12
Ring set holder 139
Roman floral design 8-9
Romantic age
    See Victorian era
Roses
    care and handling of 115-117
    revival of 103-104
Route supplier 79

S

Salt and pepper technique 55
Scale 55
Scalene triangle 45
Screening 275
Sculpture, use of 266-267
Sculpturing 55
Sealer, gelatin 126
Seasonality, fresh flower 88-89
Secondary colors 55
Sectioning 55
Seika Style 12
Sen-no-Rikyu 12
Sequencing 55-56, 65
Sewing 56
Shadowing 56, 65
Sheltering 56
Shin 13, 167
    proportions for 167-168
Shoka style 12
Short-lived flowers 131-132
Single flower hairpiece 237-238
Skull cap, floral 240-242
Soe 13, 167
    proportions for 167-168

Index

Sogetsu school of ikebana *47, 167-168*
    rules of *167-168*
Solid wreath ring *206-207*
Space *56, 68*
    negative *52*
    positive *54*
Spiral radiation *65*
Sponged container coating *152*
Spray, foliage *121*
Sprays, easel *208-209*
    composite *209*
Sprays, finishing *125-127*
Sprengeri *122*
Spring flowers, techniques for using *127*
Stabilizing large stems *142-143*
Stacking *56*
Stage of flower development *85-86*
Standing orders *89*
Static motion *51*
Stephanotis *117*
Stock rotation *92*
Storage *92*
    of floral arrangements *132-133*
Structured headpieces *239-243*
STS *86*
Style, defined *56*
Style influences *271*
Styrofoam wreath, modified *207-208*
Suede *274*
    designing with *276*
Super Cylinder *140*
Supplier
    buying habits *80-81*
    care and handling methods *81*
    product availability *82*
    product knowledge *82*
    quality *80-84*
Suppliers *78-84*
    selection of *79-84*
    services offered by *83*
    types of *78-79*
Support-seeking line *49*
Surrealistic design *56*
Suspended designs, mechanics for *148-149*
Sword fern *123*

Symbolic design *56*
Symmetrical arrangement *56-57*
Symmetrical balance *39, 66*
Sympathy design *195-215*
    arrangements *213-214*
    casket covers *195-204*
    easel designs *208-213*
    wreaths *204-208*
Synergy *57*

T

Taffeta pew bows *253-254*
Tai *13*
Tailoring *38-57*
Taping, lasso *141-142*
Target market *92-93*
Tazza *20*
Technique, defined *57*
Techniques, advanced design *37-59*
Techniques, special design *137-153*
Tension *57, 70*
Terminology, advanced design *37-59*
Terracing *57*
Textiles *275*
    designing with *276*
Texture *57, 72-73*
Themes, wedding *255*
Tinting *38*
Tokonoma *13-14*
Topiaries, mechanics for *149-150*
Topiary *22, 252-253*
    design of *188-189*
Tree fern *122*
Tree-like altar arrangements *245-246*
Trends
    influence of *269-271*
True form *58*
Triangular arrangement, classical *41*
Triple ring foliage wreath *205-206*
Tropicals *118-120*
Tufted arrangement *57*
Tulip *120-121*
    techniques for using *130*
Tying *57-58*

Index

U

Uniqueness in design *265-277*
    alternate media *273-277*
Uniqueness in design *(continued)*
    developing creativity *265-269*
    experimentation *272*
    recognizing trends *269-271*
    style influences *271*
Unity, *58, 68*

V

Vase arrangement, sympathy *213*
Vegetative arrangement *58, 179-182*
    design of *180-182*
Vegetative casket cover *196-197*
    design of *197*
Veil flowers *242-243*
Verdigris finish *151*
Vertical line *49*
Victorian era *23-28*
    at a glance *29*
    flower meanings *26*
Visual balance *39*
    types of *66*
Visual display
    with alternate media *276-277*
Void *58, 68*

W

Wall hanging, mechanics for *148-149*
Waterfall arrangement *58-59, 182, 184*
    design of *183, 184*
Waterfall casket cover *198-199*
    design of *199*
Wax, foliage *121*
Wedding design *219-260*
    bouquets *220-230*
    ceremony decorations *243-254*
    flowers to wear *230-243*
    reception decorations *254-259*
Wedding themes *255*
Western line design *59*
Wholesaler *78*

Window decorations, church *249*
Wood *275*
    tripod *212-213*
Wrapping technique *59*
Wreath rings *139*
Wreaths, funeral *204-208*
    braided ribbon *208*
    European *205*
    grapevine, composite *207*
    modified styrofoam *207-208*
    solid ring *206-207*
    triple ring foliage *205-206*

Z

Zinnia *110*
Zoning *59*

Hue - Full intensity of color

Tint - Hue lightened with white

Tone - Hue mixed with gray

Shade - Hue darkened with black

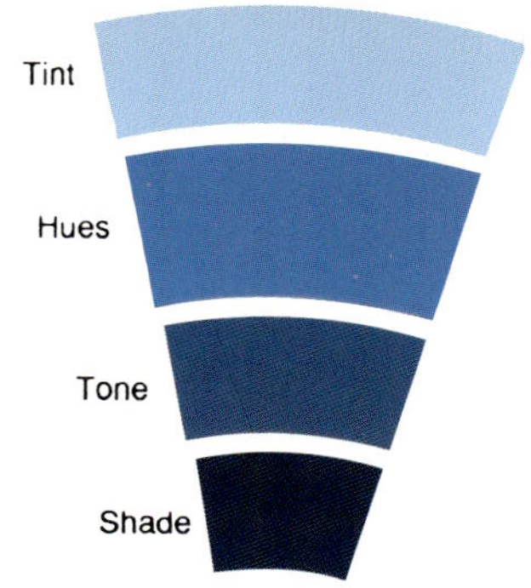

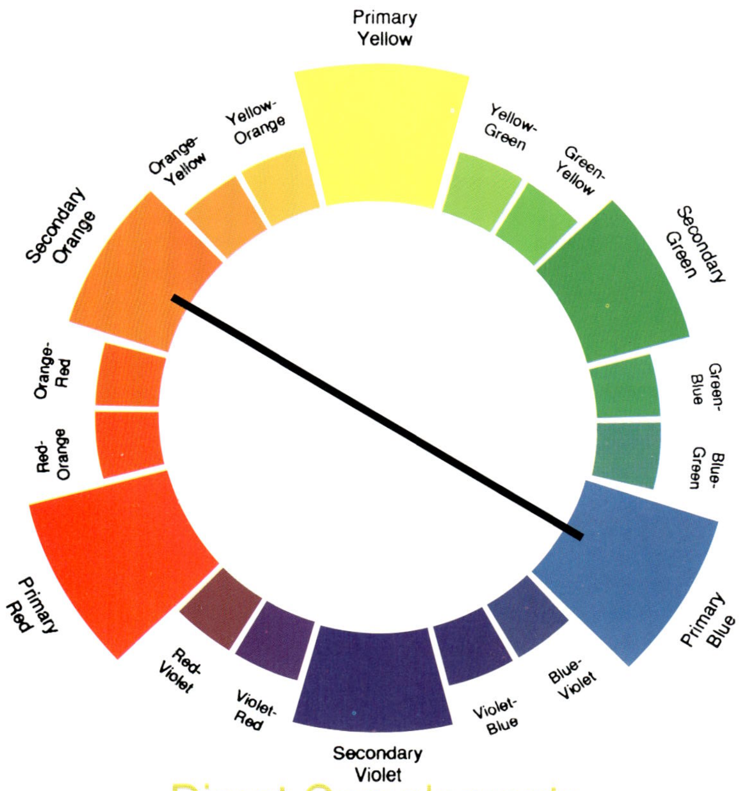

Direct Complements

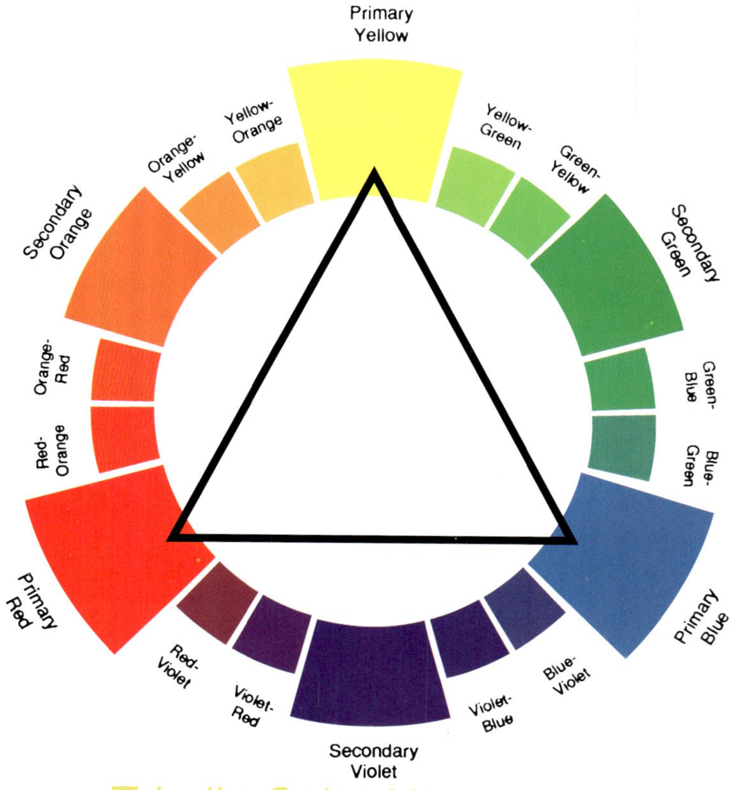

Triadic Color Harmony

Mono – Chromatic

© 1992 Redbook "Advanced Floral Design"
The Masters of Arrangement
REDBOOK Florist Services

The Color Wheel

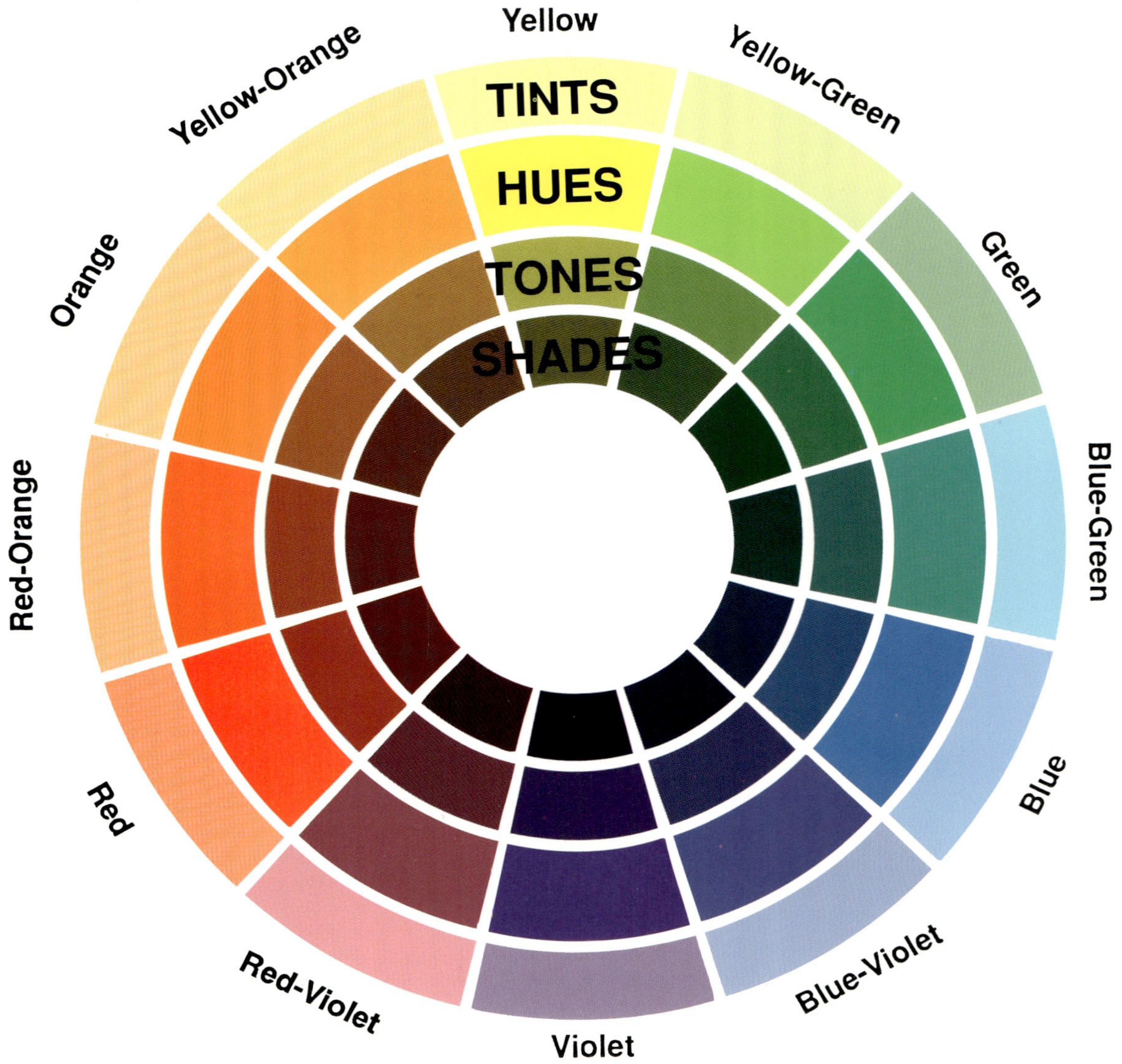

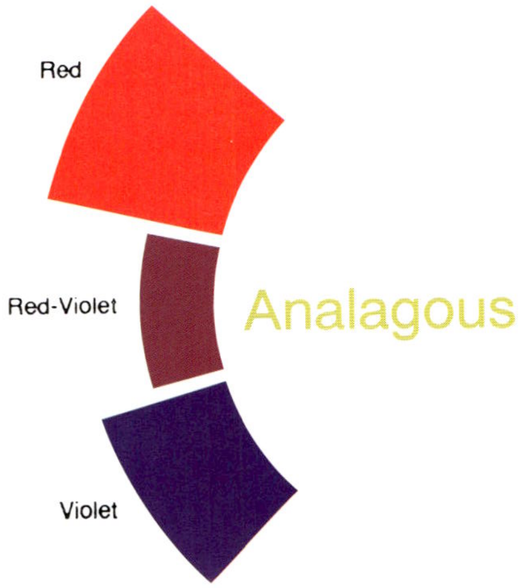